Taras Bul

By N____ Gogol

Introduction by John Cournos

Taras Bulba St. John's Eve The Cloak How the Two Ivans Quarrelled The Mysterious Portrait The Calash

INTRODUCTION

Russian literature, so full of enigmas, contains no greater creative mystery than Nikolai Vasil'evich Gogol (1809-1852), who has done for the Russian novel and Russian prose what Pushkin has done for Russian poetry. Before these two men came Russian literature can hardly have been said to exist. It was pompous and effete with pseudo-classicism; foreign influences were strong; in the speech of the upper circles there was an over-fondness for German, French, and English words. Between them the two friends, by force of their great genius, cleared away the debris which made for sterility and erected in their stead a new structure out of living Russian words. The spoken word, born of the people, gave soul and wing to literature; only by coming to earth, the native earth, was it enabled to soar. Coming up from Little Russia, the Ukraine, with Cossack blood in his veins, Gogol injected his own healthy virus into an effete body, blew his own virile spirit, the spirit of his race, into its nostrils, and gave the Russian novel its direction to this very day.

More than that. The nomad and romantic in him, troubled and restless with Ukrainian myth, legend, and song, impressed upon Russian literature, faced with the realities of modern life, a spirit titanic and in clash with its material, and produced in the mastery of this every-day material, commonly called sordid, a phantasmagoria intense with beauty. A clue to all Russian realism may be found in a Russian critic's observation about Gogol: "Seldom has nature created a man so romantic in bent, yet so masterly in portraying all that is unromantic in life." But this statement does not cover the whole ground, for it is easy to see in almost all of Gogol's work his "free Cossack soul" trying to break through the shell of sordid to-day like some ancient demon, essentially Dionysian. So that his works, true though they are to our life, are at once a reproach, a protest, and a challenge, ever calling for joy, ancient joy, that is no more with us. And they have all the joy and sadness of the Ukrainian songs he loved so much. Ukrainian was to Gogol "the language of the soul," and it was in Ukrainian songs rather than in old chronicles, of which he was not a little contemptuous, that he read the history of his people. Time and again, in his essays and in his letters to friends, he expresses his boundless joy in these songs: "O songs, you are my joy and my life! How I love you. What are the bloodless chronicles I pore over beside those clear, live chronicles! I cannot live without songs; they . . . reveal everything more and more clearly, oh, how clearly, gone-by life and gone-by men. . . . The songs of Little Russia are her everything, her poetry, her history, and her ancestral grave. He who has not penetrated them deeply knows nothing of the past of this blooming region of Russia."

Indeed, so great was his enthusiasm for his own land that after collecting material for many years, the year 1833 finds him at work on a history of "poor Ukraine," a work planned to take up six volumes; and writing to a friend at this time he promises to say much in it that has not been said before him. Furthermore, he intended to follow this work with a universal history in eight volumes with a view to establishing, as far as may be gathered, Little Russia and the world in proper relation, connecting the two; a quixotic task, surely. A poet, passionate, religious, loving the heroic, we find him constantly impatient and fuming at the lifeless chronicles, which leave him cold as he seeks in vain for what he cannot find. "Nowhere," he writes in 1834, "can I find anything of the time which ought to be richer than any other in events. Here was a people whose whole existence was passed in activity, and which, even if nature had made it inactive, was compelled to go forward to great affairs and deeds because of its neighbours, its geographic situation, the constant danger to its existence. . . . If the Crimeans and the Turks had had a literature I am convinced that no history of an independent nation in Europe would prove so interesting as that of the Cossacks." Again he complains of the "withered chronicles"; it is only the wealth of his country's song that encourages him to go on with its history.

Too much a visionary and a poet to be an impartial historian, it is hardly astonishing to note the judgment he passes on his own work, during that same year, 1834: "My history of Little Russia's past is an extraordinarily made thing, and it could not be otherwise." The deeper he goes into Little Russia's past the more fanatically he dreams of Little Russia's future. St. Petersburg wearies him, Moscow awakens no emotion in him, he yearns for Kieff, the mother of Russian cities, which in his vision he sees becoming "the Russian Athens." Russian history gives him no pleasure, and he separates it definitely from Ukrainian history. He is "ready to cast everything aside rather than read Russian history," he writes to Pushkin. During his seven-year stay in St. Petersburg (1829-36) Gogol zealously gathered historical material and, in the words of Professor Kotlyarevsky, "lived in the dream of becoming the Thucydides of Little Russia." How completely he disassociated Ukrainia from Northern Russia may be judged by the conspectus of his lectures written in 1832. He says in it, speaking of the conquest of Southern Russia in the fourteenth century by Prince

Guedimin at the head of his Lithuanian host, still dressed in the skins of wild beasts, still worshipping the ancient fire and practising pagan rites: "Then Southern Russia, under the mighty protection of Lithuanian princes, completely separated itself from the North. Every bond between them was broken; two kingdoms were established under a single name--Russia--one under the Tatar yoke, the other under the same rule with Lithuanians. But actually they had no relation with one another; different laws, different customs, different aims, different bonds, and different activities gave them wholly different characters."

This same Prince Guedimin freed Kieff from the Tatar yoke. This city had been laid waste by the golden hordes of Ghengis Khan and hidden for a very long time from the Slavonic chronicler as behind an impenetrable curtain. A shrewd man, Guedimin appointed a Slavonic prince to rule over the city and permitted the inhabitants to practise their own faith, Greek Christianity. Prior to the Mongol invasion, which brought conflagration and ruin, and subjected Russia to a two-century bondage, cutting her off from Europe, a state of chaos existed and the separate tribes fought with one another constantly and for the most petty reasons. Mutual depredations were possible owing to the absence of mountain ranges; there were no natural barriers against sudden attack. The openness of the steppe made the people war-like. But this very openness made it possible later for Guedimin's pagan hosts, fresh from the fir forests of what is now White Russia, to make a clean sweep of the whole country between Lithuania and Poland, and thus give the scattered princedoms a much-needed cohesion. In this way Ukrainia was formed. Except for some forests, infested with bears, the country was one vast plain, marked by an occasional hillock. Whole herds of wild horses and deer stampeded the country, overgrown with tall grass, while flocks of wild goats wandered among the rocks of the Dnieper. Apart from the Dnieper, and in some measure the Desna, emptying into it, there were no navigable rivers and so there was little opportunity for a commercial people. Several tributaries cut across, but made no real boundary line. Whether you looked to the north towards Russia, to the east towards the Tatars, to the south towards the Crimean Tatars, to the west towards Poland, everywhere the country bordered on a field, everywhere on a plain, which left it open to the invader from every side. Had there been here, suggests Gogol in his introduction to his never-written history of Little Russia, if upon one side only, a real frontier of mountain or sea, the people who settled here might have formed a definite political body. Without this natural protection it became a land subject to constant attack and despoliation. "There where three hostile nations came in contact it was manured with bones, wetted with blood. A single Tatar invasion destroyed the whole labour of the soil-tiller; the meadows and the cornfields were trodden down by horses or destroyed by flame, the lightly-built habitations reduced to the ground, the inhabitants scattered or driven off into captivity together with cattle. It was a land of terror, and for this reason there could develop in it only a warlike people, strong in its unity and desperate, a people whose whole existence was bound to be trained and confined to war."

This constant menace, this perpetual pressure of foes on all sides, acted at last like a fierce hammer shaping and hardening resistance against itself. The fugitive from Poland, the fugitive from the Tatar and the Turk, homeless, with nothing to lose, their lives ever exposed to danger, forsook their peaceful occupations and became transformed into a warlike people, known as the Cossacks, whose appearance towards the end of the thirteenth century or at the beginning of the fourteenth was a remarkable event which possibly alone (suggests Gogol) prevented any further inroads by the two Mohammedan nations into Europe. The appearance of the Cossacks was coincident with the appearance in Europe of brotherhoods and knighthood-orders, and this new race, in spite of its living the life of marauders, in spite of turnings its foes' tactics upon its foes, was not free of the religious spirit of its time; if it warred for its existence it warred not less for its faith, which was Greek. Indeed, as the nation grew stronger and became conscious of its strength, the struggle began to partake something of the nature of a religious war, not alone defensive but aggressive also, against the unbeliever. While any man was free to join the brotherhood it was obligatory to believe in the Greek faith. It was this religious unity, blazed into activity by the presence across the borders of unbelieving nations, that alone indicated the germ of a political body in this gathering of men, who otherwise lived the audacious lives of a band of highway robbers. "There was, however," says Gogol, "none of the austerity of the Catholic knight in them; they bound themselves to no vows or fasts; they put no self-restraint upon themselves or mortified their flesh, but were indomitable like the rocks of the Dnieper among which they lived, and in their furious feasts and revels they forgot the whole world. That same intimate brotherhood, maintained in robber communities, bound them together. They had everything in common--wine, food, dwelling. A perpetual fear, a perpetual danger, inspired them with a contempt towards life. The Cossack worried more about a good measure of wine than about his fate. One has to see this denizen of the frontier in his half-Tatar, half-Polish costume--which so sharply outlined the spirit of the borderland--galloping in Asiatic fashion on his horse, now lost in thick grass, now leaping with the speed of a tiger from ambush, or emerging suddenly from the river or swamp, all clinging with mud, and appearing an image of terror to the Tatar. . . ."

Little by little the community grew and with its growing it began to assume a general character. The beginning of the sixteenth century found whole villages settled with families, enjoying the protection of the Cossacks, who exacted certain obligations, chiefly military, so that these settlements bore a military character. The sword and the plough were friends which fraternised at every settler's. On the other hand, Gogol tells us, the gay bachelors began to make depredations across the border to sweep down on Tatars' wives and their daughters and to marry them. "Owing to this co-mingling, their facial features, so different from one another's, received a common impress, tending towards the Asiatic. And so there came into being a nation in faith and place belonging to Europe; on the other hand, in ways of life, customs, and dress quite Asiatic. It was a nation in which the world's two extremes came in contact; European caution and Asiatic indifference, niavete and cunning, an intense activity and the greatest laziness and indulgence, an aspiration to development and perfection, and again a desire to appear indifferent to perfection."

All of Ukraine took on its colour from the Cossack, and if I have drawn largely on Gogol's own account of the origins of this race, it was because it seemed to me that Gogol's emphasis on the heroic rather than on the historical--Gogol is generally discounted as an historian--would give the reader a proper approach to the mood in which he created "Taras Bulba," the finest epic in Russian literature. Gogol never wrote either his history of Little Russia or his universal history. Apart from several brief studies, not always reliable, the net result of his many years' application to his scholarly projects was this brief epic in prose, Homeric in mood. The sense of intense living, "living dangerously"--to use a phrase of Nietzsche's, the recognition of courage as the greatest of all virtues--the God in man, inspired Gogol, living in an age which tended toward grey tedium, with admiration for his more fortunate forefathers, who lived in "a poetic time, when everything was won with the sword, when every one in his turn strove to be an active being and not a spectator." Into this short work he poured all his love of the heroic, all his romanticism, all his poetry, all his joy. Its abundance of life bears one along like a fast-flowing river. And it is not without humour, a calm, detached humour, which, as the critic Bolinsky puts it, is not there merely "because Gogol has a tendency to see the comic in everything, but because it is true to life."

Yet "Taras Bulba" was in a sense an accident, just as many other works of great men are accidents. It often requires a happy combination of circumstances to produce a masterpiece. I have already told in my introduction to "Dead Souls"[1] how Gogol created his great realistic masterpiece, which was to influence Russian literature for generations to come, under the influence of models so remote in time or place as "Don Quixote" or "Pickwick Papers"; and how this combination of influences joined to his own genius produced a work quite new and original in effect and only remotely reminiscent of the models which have inspired it. And just as "Dead Souls" might never have been written if "Don Quixote" had not existed, so there is every reason to believe that "Taras Bulba" could not have been written without the "Odyssey." Once more ancient fire gave life to new beauty. And yet at the time Gogol could not have had more than a smattering of the "Odyssey." The magnificent translation made by his friend Zhukovsky had not yet appeared and Gogol, in spite of his ambition to become a historian, was not equipped as a scholar. But it is evident from his dithyrambic letter on the appearance of Zhukovsky's version, forming one of the famous series of letters known as "Correspondence with Friends," that he was better acquainted with the spirit of Homer than any mere scholar could be. That letter, unfortunately unknown to the English reader, would make every lover of the classics in this day of their disparagement dance with joy. He describes the "Odyssey" as the forgotten source of all that is beautiful and harmonious in life, and he greets its appearance in Russian dress at a time when life is sordid and discordant as a thing inevitable, "cooling" in effect upon a too hectic world. He sees in its perfect grace, its calm and almost childlike simplicity, a power for individual and general good. "It combines all the fascination of a fairy tale and all the simple truth of human adventure, holding out the same allurement to every being, whether he is a noble, a commoner, a merchant, a literate or illiterate person, a private soldier, a lackey, children of both sexes, beginning at an age when a child begins to love a fairy tale--all might read it or listen to it, without tedium." Every one will draw from it what he most needs. Not less than upon these he sees its wholesome effect on the creative writer, its refreshing influence on the critic. But most of all he dwells on its heroic qualities, inseparable to him from what is religious in the "Odyssey"; and, says Gogol, this book contains the idea that a human being, "wherever he might be, whatever pursuit he might follow, is threatened by many woes, that he must need wrestle with them--for that very purpose was life given to him--that never for a single instant must he despair, just as Odysseus did not despair, who in every hard and oppressive moment turned to his own heart, unaware that with this inner scrutiny of himself he had already said that hidden prayer uttered in a moment of distress by every man having no understanding whatever of God." Then he goes on to compare the ancient harmony, perfect down to every detail of dress, to the slightest action, with our slovenliness and confusion and pettiness, a sad result--considering our knowledge of past experience, our possession of superior weapons, our religion given to make us holy and superior beings. And in conclusion he asks: Is not the "Odyssey" in every sense a deep reproach to our nineteenth century?

[1] Everyman's Library, No. 726.

An understanding of Gogol's point of view gives the key to "Taras Bulba." For in this panoramic canvas of the Setch, the military brotherhood of the Cossacks, living under open skies, picturesquely and heroically, he has drawn a picture of his romantic ideal, which if far from perfect at any rate seemed to him preferable to the grey tedium of a city peopled with government officials. Gogol has written in "Taras Bulba" his own reproach to the nineteenth century. It is sad and joyous like one of those Ukrainian songs which have helped to inspire him to write it. And then, as he cut himself off more and more from the world of the past, life became a sadder and still sadder thing to him; modern life, with all its gigantic pettiness, closed in around him, he began to write of petty officials and of petty scoundrels, "commonplace heroes" he called them. But nothing is ever lost in this world. Gogol's romanticism, shut in within himself, finding no outlet, became a flame. It was a flame of pity. He was like a man walking in hell, pitying. And that was the miracle, the transfiguration. Out of that flame of pity the Russian novel was born.

JOHN COURNOS

Evenings on the Farm near the Dikanka, 1829-31; Mirgorod, 1831-33; Taras Bulba, 1834; Arabesques (includes tales, The Portrait and A Madman's Diary), 1831-35; The Cloak, 1835; The Revizor (The Inspector-General), 1836; Dead Souls, 1842; Correspondence with Friends, 1847; Letters, 1847, 1895, 4 vols. 1902.

ENGLISH TRANSLATIONS: Cossack Tales (The Night of Christmas Eve, Tarass Boolba), trans. by G. Tolstoy, 1860; St. John's Eve and Other Stories, trans. by Isabel F. Hapgood, New York, Crowell, 1886; Taras Bulba: Also St. John's Eve and Other Stories, London, Vizetelly, 1887; Taras Bulba, trans. by B. C. Baskerville, London, Scott, 1907; The Inspector: a Comedy, Calcutta, 1890; The Inspector-General, trans. by A. A. Sykes, London, Scott, 1892; Revizor, trans. for the Yale Dramatic

Association by Max S. Mandell, New Haven, Conn., 1908; Home Life in Russia (adaptation of Dead Souls), London, Hurst, 1854; Tchitchikoff's Journey's; or Dead Souls, trans. by Isabel F. Hapgood, New York, Crowell, 1886; Dead Souls, London, Vizetelly, 1887; Dead Souls, London, Maxwell 1887; Dead Souls, London, Fisher Unwin, 1915; Dead Souls, London, Everyman's Library (Intro. by John Cournos), 1915; Meditations on the Divine Liturgy, trans. by L. Alexeieff, London, A. R. Mowbray and Co., 1913.

LIVES, etc.: (Russian) Kotlyarevsky (N. A.), 1903; Shenrok (V. I.), Materials for a Biography, 1892; (French) Leger (L.), Nicholas Gogol, 1914.

TARAS BULBA

CHAPTER I

"Turn round, my boy! How ridiculous you look! What sort of a priest's cassock have you got on? Does everybody at the academy dress like that?"

With such words did old Bulba greet his two sons, who had been absent for their education at the Royal Seminary of Kief, and had now returned home to their father.

His sons had but just dismounted from their horses. They were a couple of stout lads who still looked bashful, as became youths recently released from the seminary. Their firm healthy faces were covered with the first down of manhood, down which had, as yet, never known a razor. They were greatly discomfited by such a reception from their father, and stood motionless with eyes fixed upon the ground.

"Stand still, stand still! let me have a good look at you," he continued, turning them around. "How long your gaberdines are! What gaberdines! There never were such gaberdines in the world before. Just run, one of you! I want to see whether you will not get entangled in the skirts, and fall down."

"Don't laugh, don't laugh, father!" said the eldest lad at length.

"How touchy we are! Why shouldn't I laugh?"

"Because, although you are my father, if you laugh, by heavens, I will strike you!"

"What kind of son are you? what, strike your father!" exclaimed Taras Bulba, retreating several paces in amazement.

"Yes, even my father. I don't stop to consider persons when an insult is in question."

"So you want to fight me? with your fist, eh?"

"Any way."

"Well, let it be fisticuffs," said Taras Bulba, turning up his sleeves. "I'll see what sort of a man you are with your fists."

And father and son, in lieu of a pleasant greeting after long separation, began to deal each other heavy blows on ribs, back, and chest, now retreating and looking at each other, now attacking afresh.

"Look, good people! the old man has gone man! he has lost his senses completely!" screamed their pale, ugly, kindly mother, who was standing on the threshold, and had not yet succeeded in embracing her darling children. "The children have come home, we have not seen them for over a year; and now he has taken some strange freak--he's pommelling them."

"Yes, he fights well," said Bulba, pausing; "well, by heavens!" he continued, rather as if excusing himself, "although he has never tried his hand at it before, he will make a good Cossack! Now, welcome, son! embrace me," and father and son began to kiss each other. "Good lad! see that you hit every one as you pommelled me; don't let any one escape. Nevertheless your clothes are ridiculous all the same. What rope is this hanging there?--And you, you lout, why are you standing there with your hands hanging beside you?" he added, turning to the youngest. "Why don't you fight me? you son of a dog!"

"What an idea!" said the mother, who had managed in the meantime to embrace her youngest. "Who ever heard of children fighting their own father? That's enough for the present; the child is young, he has had a long journey, he is tired." The child was over twenty, and about six feet high. "He ought to rest, and eat something; and you set him to fighting!"

"You are a gabbler!" said Bulba. "Don't listen to your mother, my lad; she is a woman, and knows nothing. What sort of petting do you need? A clear field and a good horse, that's the kind of petting for you! And do you see this sword? that's your mother! All the rest people stuff your heads with is rubbish; the academy, books, primers, philosophy, and all that, I spit upon it all!" Here Bulba added a word which is not used in print. "But I'll tell you what is best: I'll take you to Zaporozhe[1] this very week. That's where there's science for you! There's your school; there alone will you gain sense."

[1] The Cossack country beyond (za) the falls (porozhe) of the Dnieper.

"And are they only to remain home a week?" said the worn old mother sadly and with tears in her eyes. "The poor boys will have no chance of looking around, no chance of getting acquainted with the home where they were born; there will be no chance for me to get a look at them."

"Enough, you've howled quite enough, old woman! A Cossack is not born to run around after women. You would like to hide them both under your petticoat, and sit upon them as a hen sits on eggs. Go, go, and let us have everything there is on the table in a trice. We don't want any dumplings, honey-cakes, poppy-cakes, or any other such messes: give us a whole sheep, a goat, mead forty years old, and as much corn-brandy as possible, not with raisins and all sorts of stuff, but plain scorching corn-brandy, which foams and hisses like mad."

Bulba led his sons into the principal room of the hut; and two pretty servant girls wearing coin necklaces, who were arranging the apartment, ran out quickly. They were either frightened at the arrival of the young men, who did not care to be familiar with anyone; or else they merely wanted to keep up their feminine custom of screaming and rushing away headlong at the sight of a man, and then screening their blushes for some time with their sleeves. The hut was furnished according to the fashion of that period--a fashion concerning which hints linger only in the songs and lyrics, no longer sung, alas! in the Ukraine as of yore by blind old men, to the soft tinkling of the native guitar, to the people thronging round them-- according to the taste of that warlike and troublous time, of leagues and battles prevailing in the Ukraine after the union. Everything was cleanly smeared with coloured clay. On the walls hung sabres, hunting-whips, nets for birds, fishing-nets, guns, elaborately carved powder-horns, gilded bits for horses, and tether-ropes with silver plates. The small window had round dull panes, through which it was impossible to see except by opening the one moveable one. Around the windows and doors red bands were painted. On shelves in one corner stood jugs, bottles, and flasks of green and blue glass, carved silver cups, and gilded drinking vessels of various makes--Venetian, Turkish, Tscherkessian, which had reached Bulba's cabin by various roads, at third and fourth hand, a thing common enough in those bold days. There were birch-wood benches all around the room, a huge table under the holy pictures in one corner, and a huge stove covered with particoloured patterns in relief, with spaces between it and the wall. All this was quite familiar to the two young men, who were wont to come home every year during the dog-days, since they had no horses, and it was not customary to allow students to ride afield on horseback. The only distinctive things permitted them were long locks of hair on the temples, which every Cossack who bore weapons was entitled to pull. It was only at the end of their course of study that Bulba had sent them a couple of young stallions from his stud.

Bulba, on the occasion of his sons' arrival, ordered all the sotniks or captains of hundreds, and all the officers of the band who were of any consequence, to be summoned; and when two of them arrived with his old comrade, the Osaul or sub-chief, Dmitro Tovkatch, he immediately presented the lads, saying, "See what fine young fellows they are! I shall send them to the Setch[2] shortly." The guests congratulated Bulba and the young men, telling them they would do well and that there was no better knowledge for a young man than a knowledge of that same Zaporozhian Setch.

[2] The village or, rather, permanent camp of the Zaporozhian Cossacks.

"Come, brothers, seat yourselves, each where he likes best, at the table; come, my sons. First of all, let's take some corn-brandy," said Bulba. "God bless you! Welcome, lads; you, Ostap, and you, Andrii. God grant that you may always be successful in war, that you may beat the Musselmans and the Turks and the Tatars; and that when the Poles undertake any expedition against our faith, you may beat the Poles. Come, clink your glasses. How now? Is the brandy good? What's corn-brandy in Latin? The Latins were stupid: they did not know there was such a thing in the world as corn-brandy. What was the name of the man who wrote Latin verses? I don't know much about reading and writing, so I don't quite know. Wasn't it Horace?"

"What a dad!" thought the elder son Ostap. "The old dog knows everything, but he always pretends the contrary."

"I don't believe the archimandrite allowed you so much as a smell of corn-brandy," continued Taras. "Confess, my boys, they thrashed you well with fresh birch-twigs on your backs and all over your Cossack bodies; and perhaps, when you grew too sharp, they beat you with whips. And not on Saturday only, I fancy, but on Wednesday and Thursday."

"What is past, father, need not be recalled; it is done with."

"Let them try it know," said Andrii. "Let anybody just touch me, let any Tatar risk it now, and he'll soon learn what a Cossack's sword is like!"

"Good, my son, by heavens, good! And when it comes to that, I'll go with you; by heavens, I'll go too! What should I wait here for? To become a buckwheat-reaper and housekeeper, to look after the sheep and swine, and loaf around with my wife? Away with such nonsense! I am a Cossack; I'll have none of it! What's left but war? I'll go with you to Zaporozhe to carouse; I'll go, by heavens!" And old Bulba, growing warm by degrees and finally quite angry, rose from the table, and, assuming a dignified attitude, stamped his foot. "We will go to-morrow! Wherefore delay? What enemy can we besiege here? What is this hut to us? What do we want with all these things? What are pots and pans to us?" So saying, he began to knock over the pots and flasks, and to throw them about.

The poor old woman, well used to such freaks on the part of her husband, looked sadly on from her seat on the wall-bench. She did not dare say a word; but when she heard the decision which was so terrible for her, she could not refrain from tears. As she looked at her children, from whom so speedy a separation was threatened, it is impossible to describe the full force of her speechless grief, which seemed to quiver in her eyes and on her lips convulsively pressed together.

Bulba was terribly headstrong. He was one of those characters which could only exist in that fierce fifteenth century, and in that half-nomadic corner of Europe, when the whole of Southern Russia, deserted by its princes, was laid waste and burned to the quick by pitiless troops of Mongolian robbers; when men deprived of house and home grew brave there; when, amid conflagrations, threatening neighbours, and eternal terrors, they settled down, and growing accustomed to looking these things straight in the face, trained themselves not to know that there was such a thing as fear in the world; when the old, peacable Slav spirit was fired with warlike flame, and the Cossack state was instituted--a free, wild outbreak of Russian nature--and when all the river-banks, fords, and like suitable places were peopled by Cossacks, whose number no man knew. Their bold comrades had a right to reply to the Sultan when he asked how many they were, "Who knows? We are scattered all over the steppes; wherever there is a hillock, there is a Cossack."

It was, in fact, a most remarkable exhibition of Russian strength, forced by dire necessity from the bosom of the people. In place of the original provinces with their petty towns, in place of the warring and bartering petty princes ruling in their cities, there arose great colonies, kurens[3], and districts, bound together by one common danger and hatred against the heathen robbers. The story is well known how their incessant warfare and restless existence saved Europe from the merciless hordes which threatened to overwhelm her. The Polish kings, who now found themselves sovereigns, in place of the provincial princes, over these extensive tracts of territory, fully understood, despite the weakness and remoteness of their own rule, the value of the Cossacks, and the advantages of the warlike, untrammelled life led by them. They encouraged them and flattered this disposition of mind. Under their distant rule, the hetmans or chiefs, chosen from among the Cossacks themselves, redistributed the territory into military districts. It was not a standing army, no one saw it; but in case of war and general uprising, it required a week, and no more, for every man to appear on horseback, fully armed, receiving only one ducat from the king; and in two weeks such a force had assembled as no recruiting officers would ever have been able to collect. When the expedition was ended, the army dispersed among the fields and meadows and the fords of the Dnieper; each man fished, wrought at his trade, brewed his beer, and was once more a free Cossack. Their foreign contemporaries rightly marvelled at their wonderful qualities. There was no handicraft which the Cossack was not expert at: he could distil brandy, build a waggon, make powder, and do blacksmith's and gunsmith's work, in addition to committing wild excesses, drinking and carousing as only a Russian can--all this he was equal to. Besides the registered Cossacks, who considered themselves bound to appear in arms in time of war, it was possible to collect at any time, in case of dire need, a whole army of volunteers. All that was required was for the Osaul or sub-chief to traverse the market-places and squares of the villages and hamlets, and shout at the top of his voice, as he stood in his waggon, "Hey, you distillers and beer-brewers! you have brewed enough beer, and lolled on your stoves, and stuffed your fat carcasses with flour, long enough! Rise, win glory and warlike honours! You ploughmen, you reapers of buckwheat, you tenders of sheep, you danglers after women, enough of following the plough, and soiling your yellow shoes in the earth, and courting women, and wasting your warlike strength! The hour has come to win glory for the Cossacks!" These words were like sparks falling on dry wood. The husbandman broke his plough; the brewers and distillers threw away their casks and destroyed their barrels; the mechanics and merchants sent their trade and their shop to the devil, broke pots and everything else in their homes, and mounted their horses. In short, the Russian character here received a profound development, and manifested a powerful outwards expression.

[3] Cossack villages. In the Setch, a large wooden barrack.

Taras was one of the band of old-fashioned leaders; he was born for warlike emotions, and was distinguished for his uprightness of character. At that epoch the influence of Poland had already begun to make itself felt upon the Russian nobility. Many had adopted Polish customs, and began to display luxury in splendid staffs of servants, hawks, huntsmen, dinners, and palaces. This was not to Taras's taste. He liked the simple life of the Cossacks, and quarrelled with those of his comrades who were inclined to the Warsaw party, calling them serfs of the Polish nobles. Ever on the alert, he regarded himself as the legal protector of the orthodox faith. He entered despotically into any village where there was a general complaint of oppression by the revenue farmers and of the addition of fresh taxes on necessaries. He and his Cossacks executed justice, and made it a rule that in three cases it was absolutely necessary to resort to the sword. Namely, when the commissioners did not respect the superior officers and stood before them covered; when any one made light of the faith and did not observe the customs of his ancestors; and, finally, when the enemy were Mussulmans or Turks, against whom he considered it permissible, in every case, to draw the sword for the glory of Christianity.

Now he rejoiced beforehand at the thought of how he would present himself with his two sons at the Setch, and say, "See what fine young fellows I have brought you!" how he would introduce them to all his old comrades, steeled in warfare; how he would observe their first exploits in the sciences of war and of drinking, which was also regarded as one of the principal warlike qualities. At first he had intended to send them forth alone; but at the sight of their freshness, stature, and manly personal beauty his martial spirit flamed up and he resolved to go with them himself the very next day, although there was no necessity for this except his obstinate self-will. He began at once to hurry about and give orders; selected horses and trappings for his sons, looked through the stables and storehouses, and chose servants to accompany them on the morrow. He delegated his power to Osaul Tovkatch, and gave with it a strict command to appear with his whole force at the Setch the very instant he should receive a message from him. Although he was jolly, and the effects of his drinking bout still lingered in his brain, he forgot nothing. He even gave orders that the horses should be watered, their cribs filled, and that they should be fed with the finest corn; and then he retired, fatigued with all his labours.

"Now, children, we must sleep, but to-morrow we shall do what God wills. Don't prepare us a bed: we need no bed; we will sleep in the courtyard."

Night had but just stole over the heavens, but Bulba always went to bed early. He lay down on a rug and covered himself with a sheepskin pelisse, for the night air was quite sharp and he liked to lie warm when he was at home. He was soon snoring, and the whole household speedily followed his example. All snored and groaned as they lay in different corners. The watchman went to sleep the first of all, he had drunk so much in honour of the young masters' home-coming.

The mother alone did not sleep. She bent over the pillow of her beloved sons, as they lay side by side; she smoothed with a comb their carelessly tangled locks, and moistened them with her tears. She gazed at them with her whole soul, with every sense; she was wholly merged in the gaze, and yet she could not gaze enough. She had fed them at her own breast, she had tended them and brought them up; and now to see them only for an instant! "My sons, my darling sons! what will become of you! what fate awaits you?" she said, and tears stood in the wrinkles which disfigured her once beautiful face. In truth, she was to be pitied, as was every woman of that period. She had lived only for a moment of love, only during the first ardour of passion, only during the first flush of youth; and then her grim betrayer had deserted her for the sword, for his comrades and his carouses. She saw her husband two or three days in a year, and then, for several years, heard nothing of him. And when she did see him, when they did live together, what a life was hers! She endured insult, even blows; she felt caresses bestowed only in pity; she was a misplaced object in that community of unmarried warriors, upon which wandering Zaporozhe cast a colouring of its own. Her pleasureless youth flitted by; her ripe cheeks and bosom withered away unkissed and became covered with premature wrinkles. Love, feeling, everything that is tender and passionate in a woman, was converted in her into maternal love. She hovered around her children with anxiety, passion, tears, like the gull of the steppes. They were taking her sons, her darling sons, from her--taking them from her, so that she should never see them again! Who knew? Perhaps a Tatar would cut off their heads in the very first skirmish, and she would never know where their deserted bodies might lie, torn by birds of prey; and yet for each single drop of their blood she would have given all hers. Sobbing, she gazed into their eyes, and thought, "Perhaps Bulba, when he wakes, will put off their departure for a day or two; perhaps it occurred to him to go so soon because he had been drinking."

The moon from the summit of the heavens had long since lit up the whole courtyard filled with sleepers, the thick clump of willows, and the tall steppe-grass, which hid the palisade surrounding the court. She still sat at her sons' pillow, never removing her eyes from them for a moment, nor thinking of sleep. Already the horses, divining the approach of dawn, had ceased eating and lain down upon the grass; the topmost leaves of the willows began to rustle softly, and little by little the rippling rustle descended to their bases. She sat there until daylight, unwearied, and wishing in her heart that the night might prolong itself indefinitely. From the steppes came the ringing neigh of the horses, and red streaks shone brightly in the sky. Bulba suddenly awoke, and sprang to his feet. He remembered quite well what he had ordered the night before. "Now, my men, you've slept enough! 'tis time, 'tis time! Water the horses! And where is the old woman?" He generally called his wife so. "Be quick, old woman, get us something to eat; the way is long."

The poor old woman, deprived of her last hope, slipped sadly into the hut.

Whilst she, with tears, prepared what was needed for breakfast, Bulba gave his orders, went to the stable, and selected his best trappings for his children with his own hand.

The scholars were suddenly transformed. Red morocco boots with silver heels took the place of their dirty old ones; trousers wide as the Black Sea, with countless folds and plaits, were kept up by golden girdles from which hung long slender thongs, with tassles and other tinkling things, for pipes. Their jackets of scarlet cloth were girt by flowered sashes into which were thrust engraved Turkish pistols; their swords clanked at their heels. Their faces, already a little sunburnt, seemed to have grown handsomer and whiter; their slight black moustaches now cast a more distinct shadow on this pallor and set off their healthy youthful complexions. They looked very handsome in their black sheepskin caps, with cloth-of-gold crowns.

When their poor mother saw them, she could not utter a word, and tears stood in her eyes.

"Now, my lads, all is ready; no delay!" said Bulba at last. "But we must first all sit down together, in accordance with Christian custom before a journey."

All sat down, not excepting the servants, who had been standing respectfully at the door.

"Now, mother, bless your children," said Bulba. "Pray God that they may fight bravely, always defend their warlike honour, always defend the faith of Christ; and, if not, that they may die, so that their breath may not be longer in the world."

"Come to your mother, children; a mother's prayer protects on land and sea."

The mother, weak as mothers are, embraced them, drew out two small holy pictures, and hung them, sobbing, around their necks. "May God's mother--keep you! Children, do not forget your mother--send some little word of yourselves--" She could say no more.

"Now, children, let us go," said Bulba.

At the door stood the horses, ready saddled. Bulba sprang upon his "Devil," which bounded wildly, on feeling on his back a load of over thirty stone, for Taras was extremely stout and heavy.

When the mother saw that her sons were also mounted, she rushed towards the younger, whose features expressed somewhat more gentleness than those of his brother. She grasped his stirrup, clung to his saddle, and with despair in her eyes, refused to loose her hold. Two stout Cossacks seized her carefully, and bore her back into the hut. But before the cavalcade had passed out of the courtyard, she rushed with the speed of a wild goat, disproportionate to her years, to the gate, stopped a horse with irresistible strength, and embraced one of her sons with mad, unconscious violence. Then they led her away again.

The young Cossacks rode on sadly, repressing their tears out of fear of their father, who, on his side, was somewhat moved, although he strove not to show it. The morning was grey, the green sward bright, the birds twittered rather discordantly. They glanced back as they rode. Their paternal farm seemed to have sunk into the earth. All that was visible above the surface were the two chimneys of their modest hut and the tops of the trees up whose trunks they had been used to climb like squirrels. Before them still stretched the field by which they could recall the whole story of their lives, from the years when they rolled in its dewy grass down to the years when they awaited in it the dark-browed Cossack maiden, running timidly across it on quick young feet. There is the pole above the well, with the waggon wheel fastened to its top, rising solitary against the sky; already the level which they have traversed appears a hill in the distance, and now all has disappeared. Farewell, childhood, games, all, all, farewell!

CHAPTER II

All three horsemen rode in silence. Old Taras's thoughts were far away: before him passed his youth, his years--the swift-flying years, over which the Cossack always weeps, wishing that his life might be all youth. He wondered whom of his former comrades he should meet at the Setch. He reckoned up how many had already died, how many were still alive. Tears formed slowly in his eyes, and his grey head bent sadly.

His sons were occupied with other thoughts. But we must speak further of his sons. They had been sent, when twelve years old, to the academy at Kief, because all leaders of that day considered it indispensable to give their children an education, although it was afterwards utterly forgotten. Like all who entered the academy, they were wild, having been brought up in unrestrained freedom; and whilst there they had acquired some polish, and pursued some common branches of knowledge which gave them a certain resemblance to each other.

The elder, Ostap, began his scholastic career by running away in the course of the first year. They brought him back, whipped him well, and set him down to his books. Four times did he bury his primer in the earth; and four times, after giving him a sound thrashing, did they buy him a new one. But he would no doubt have repeated this feat for the fifth time, had not his father given him a solemn assurance that he would keep him at monastic work for twenty years, and sworn in advance that he should never behold Zaporozhe all his life long, unless he learned all the sciences taught in the academy. It was odd that the man who said this was that very Taras Bulba who condemned all learning, and counselled his children, as we have seen, not to trouble themselves at all about it. From that moment, Ostap began to pore over his tiresome books with exemplary diligence, and quickly stood on a level with the best. The style of education in that age differed widely from the manner of life. The scholastic, grammatical, rhetorical, and logical subtle ties in vogue were decidedly out of consonance with the times, never having any connection with, and never being encountered in, actual life. Those who studied them, even the least scholastic, could not apply their knowledge to anything whatever. The learned men of those days were even more incapable than the rest, because farther removed from all experience. Moreover, the republican constitution of the academy, the fearful multitude of young, healthy, strong fellows, inspired the students with an activity quite outside the limits of their learning. Poor fare, or frequent punishments of fasting, with the numerous requirements arising in fresh, strong, healthy youth, combined to arouse in them that spirit of enterprise which was afterwards further developed among the Zaporozhians. The hungry student running about the streets of Kief forced every one to be on his guard. Dealers sitting in the bazaar covered their pies, their cakes, and their pumpkin-rolls with their hands, like eagles protecting their young, if they but caught sight of a passing student. The consul or monitor, who was bound by his duty to look after the comrades entrusted to his care, had such frightfully wide pockets to his trousers that he could stow away the whole contents of the gaping dealer's stall in them. These students constituted an entirely separate world, for they were not admitted to the higher circles, composed of Polish and Russian nobles. Even the Waiwode, Adam Kisel, in spite of the patronage he bestowed upon the academy, did not seek to introduce them into society, and ordered them to be kept more strictly in supervision. This command was quite superfluous, for neither the rector nor the monkish professors spared rod or whip; and the lictors sometimes, by their orders, lashed their consuls so severely that the latter rubbed their trousers for weeks afterwards. This was to many of them a trifle, only a little more stinging than good vodka with pepper: others at length grew tired of such constant blisters, and ran away to Zaporozhe if they could find the road and were not caught on the way. Ostap Bulba, although he began to study logic, and even theology, with much zeal, did not escape the merciless rod. Naturally, all this tended to harden his character, and give him that firmness which distinguishes the Cossacks. He always held himself aloof from his comrades.

He rarely led others into such hazardous enterprises as robbing a strange garden or orchard; but, on the other hand, he was always among the first to join the standard of an adventurous student. And never, under any circumstances, did he betray his comrades; neither imprisonment nor beatings could make him do so. He was unassailable by any temptations save those of war and revelry; at least, he scarcely ever dreamt of others. He was upright with his equals. He was kind-hearted, after the only fashion that kind-heartedness could exist in such a character and at such a time. He was touched to his very heart by his poor mother's tears; but this only vexed him, and caused him to hang his head in thought.

His younger brother, Andrii, had livelier and more fully developed feelings. He learned more willingly and without the effort with which strong and weighty characters generally have to make in order to apply themselves to study. He was more inventive-minded than his brother, and frequently appeared as the leader of dangerous expeditions; sometimes, thanks to the quickness of his mind, contriving to escape punishment when his brother Ostap, abandoning all efforts, stripped off his gaberdine and lay down upon the floor without a thought of begging for mercy. He too thirsted for action; but, at the same time, his soul was accessible to other sentiments. The need of love burned ardently within him. When he had passed his eighteenth year, woman began to present herself more frequently in his dreams; listening to philosophical discussions, he still beheld her, fresh, black-eyed, tender; before him constantly flitted her elastic bosom, her soft, bare arms; the very gown which clung about her youthful yet well-rounded limbs breathed into his visions a certain inexpressible sensuousness. He carefully concealed this impulse of his passionate young soul from his comrades, because in that age it was held shameful and dishonourable for a Cossack to think of love and a wife before he had tasted battle. On the whole, during the last year, he had acted more rarely as leader to the bands of students, but had roamed more frequently alone, in remote corners of Kief, among low-roofed houses, buried in cherry orchards, peeping alluringly at the street. Sometimes he betook himself to the more aristocratic streets, in the old Kief of to-day, where dwelt Little Russian and Polish nobles, and where houses were built in more fanciful style. Once, as he was gaping along, an old-fashioned carriage belonging to some Polish noble almost drove over him; and the heavily moustached coachman, who sat on the box, gave him a smart cut with his whip. The young student fired up; with thoughtless daring he seized the hind-wheel with his powerful hands and stopped the carriage. But the coachman, fearing a drubbing, lashed his horses; they sprang forward, and Andrii, succeeding happily in freeing his hands, was flung full length on the ground with his face flat in the mud. The most ringing and harmonious of laughs resounded above him. He raised his eyes and saw, standing at a window, a beauty such as he had never beheld in all his life, black-eyed, and with skin white as snow illumined by the dawning flush of the sun. She was laughing heartily, and her laugh enhanced her dazzling loveliness. Taken aback he gazed at her in confusion, abstractedly wiping the mud from his face, by which means it became still further smeared. Who could this beauty be? He sought to find out from the servants, who, in rich liveries, stood at the gate in a crowd surrounding a young guitar-player; but they only laughed when they saw his besmeared face and deigned him no reply. At length he learned that she was the daughter of the Waiwode of Koven, who had come thither for a time. The following night, with the daring characteristic of the student, he crept through the palings into the garden and climbed a tree which spread its branches upon the very roof of the house. From the tree he gained the roof, and made his way down the chimney straight into the bedroom of the beauty, who at that moment was seated before a lamp, engaged in removing the costly earrings from her ears. The beautiful Pole was so alarmed on suddenly beholding an unknown man that she could not utter a single word; but when she perceived that the student stood before her with downcast eyes, not daring to move a hand through timidity, when she recognised in him the one who had fallen in the street, laughter again overpowered her.

Moreover, there was nothing terrible about Andrii's features; he was very handsome. She laughed heartily, and amused herself over him for a long time. The lady was giddy, like all Poles; but her eyes--her wondrous clear, piercing eyes--shot one glance, a long glance. The student could not move hand or foot, but stood bound as in a sack, when the Waiwode's daughter approached him boldly, placed upon his head her glittering diadem, hung her earrings on his lips, and flung over him a transparent muslin chemisette with gold-embroidered garlands. She adorned him, and played a thousand foolish pranks, with the childish carelessness which distinguishes the giddy Poles, and which threw the poor student into still greater confusion.

He cut a ridiculous feature, gazing immovably, and with open mouth, into her dazzling eyes. A knock at the door startled her. She ordered him to hide himself under the bed, and, as soon as the disturber was gone, called her maid, a Tatar prisoner, and gave her orders to conduct him to the garden with caution, and thence show him through the fence. But our student this time did not pass the fence so successfully. The watchman awoke, and caught him firmly by the foot; and the servants, assembling, beat him in the street, until his swift legs rescued him. After that it became very dangerous to pass the house, for the Waiwode's domestics were numerous. He met her once again at church. She saw him, and smiled pleasantly, as at an old acquaintance. He saw her once more, by chance; but shortly afterwards the Waiwode departed, and, instead of the beautiful black-eyed Pole, some fat face or other gazed from the window. This was what Andrii was thinking about, as he hung his head and kept his eyes on his horse's mane.

In the meantime the steppe had long since received them all into its green embrace; and the high grass, closing round, concealed them, till only their black Cossack caps appeared above it.

"Eh, eh, why are you so quiet, lads?" said Bulba at length, waking from his own reverie. "You're like monks. Now, all thinking to the Evil One, once for all! Take your pipes in your teeth, and let us smoke, and spur on our horses so swiftly that no bird can overtake us."

And the Cossacks, bending low on their horses' necks, disappeared in the grass. Their black caps were no longer to be seen; a streak of trodden grass alone showed the trace of their swift flight.

The sun had long since looked forth from the clear heavens and inundated the steppe with his quickening, warming light. All that was dim and drowsy in the Cossacks' minds flew away in a twinkling: their hearts fluttered like birds.

The farther they penetrated the steppe, the more beautiful it became. Then all the South, all that region which now constitutes New Russia, even as far as the Black Sea, was a green, virgin wilderness. No plough had ever passed over the immeasurable waves of wild growth; horses alone, hidden in it as in a forest, trod it down. Nothing in nature could be finer. The whole surface resembled a golden-green ocean, upon which were sprinkled millions of different flowers. Through the tall, slender stems of the grass peeped light-blue, dark-blue, and lilac star-thistles; the yellow broom thrust up its pyramidal head; the parasol-shaped white flower of the false flax shimmered on high. A wheat-ear, brought God knows whence, was filling out to ripening. Amongst the roots of this luxuriant vegetation ran partridges with outstretched necks. The air was filled with the notes of a thousand different birds. On high hovered the hawks, their wings outspread, and their eyes fixed intently on the grass. The cries of a flock of wild ducks, ascending from one side, were echoed from God knows what distant lake. From the grass arose, with measured sweep, a gull, and skimmed wantonly through blue waves of air. And now she has vanished on high, and appears only as a black dot: now she has turned her wings, and shines in the sunlight. Oh, steppes, how beautiful you are!

Our travellers halted only a few minutes for dinner. Their escort of ten Cossacks sprang from their horses and undid the wooden casks of brandy, and the gourds which were used instead of drinking vessels. They ate only cakes of bread and dripping; they drank but one cup apiece to strengthen them, for Taras Bulba never permitted intoxication upon the road, and then continued their journey until evening.

In the evening the whole steppe changed its aspect. All its varied expanse was bathed in the last bright glow of the sun; and as it grew dark gradually, it could be seen how the shadow flitted across it and it became dark green. The mist rose more densely; each flower, each blade of grass, emitted a fragrance as of ambergris, and the whole steppe distilled perfume. Broad bands of rosy gold were streaked across the dark blue heaven, as with a gigantic brush; here and there gleamed, in white tufts, light and transparent clouds: and the freshest, most enchanting of gentle breezes barely stirred the tops of the grass-blades, like sea-waves, and caressed the cheek. The music which had resounded through the day had died away, and given place to another. The striped marmots crept out of their holes, stood erect on their hind legs, and filled the steppe with their whistle. The whirr of the grasshoppers had become more distinctly audible. Sometimes the cry of the swan was heard from some distant lake, ringing through the air like a silver trumpet. The travellers, halting in the midst of the plain, selected a spot for their night encampment, made a fire, and hung over it the kettle in which they cooked their oatmeal; the steam rising and floating aslant in the air. Having supped, the Cossacks lay down to sleep, after hobbling their horses and turning them out to graze. They lay down in their gaberdines. The stars of night gazed directly down upon them. They could hear the countless myriads of insects which filled the grass; their rasping, whistling, and chirping, softened by the fresh air, resounded clearly through the night, and lulled the drowsy ear. If one of them rose and stood for a time, the steppe presented itself to him strewn with the sparks of glow-worms. At times the night sky was illumined in spots by the glare of burning reeds along pools or river-bank; and dark flights of swans flying to the north were suddenly lit up by the silvery, rose-coloured gleam, till it seemed as though red kerchiefs were floating in the dark heavens.

 The travellers proceeded onward without any adventure. They came across no villages. It was ever the same boundless, waving, beautiful steppe. Only at intervals the summits of distant forests shone blue, on one hand, stretching along the banks of the Dnieper. Once only did Taras point out to his sons a small black speck far away amongst the grass, saying, "Look, children! yonder gallops a Tatar." The little head with its long moustaches fixed its narrow eyes upon them from afar, its nostrils snuffing the air like a greyhound's, and then disappeared like an antelope on its owner perceiving that the Cossacks were thirteen strong. "And now, children, don't try to overtake the Tatar! You would never catch him to all eternity; he has a horse swifter than my Devil." But Bulba took precautions, fearing hidden ambushes. They galloped along the course of a small stream, called the Tatarka, which falls into the Dnieper; rode into the water and swam with their horses some distance in order to conceal their trail. Then, scrambling out on the bank, they continued their road.

 Three days later they were not far from the goal of their journey. The air suddenly grew colder: they could feel the vicinity of the Dnieper. And there it gleamed afar, distinguishable on the horizon as a dark band. It sent forth cold waves, spreading nearer, nearer, and finally seeming to embrace half the entire surface of the earth. This was that section of its course where the river, hitherto confined by the rapids, finally makes its own away and, roaring like the sea, rushes on at will; where the islands, flung into its midst, have pressed it farther from their shores, and its waves have spread widely over the earth, encountering neither cliffs nor hills. The Cossacks, alighting from their horses, entered the ferry-boat, and after a three hours' sail reached the shores of the island of Khortitz, where at that time stood the Setch, which so often changed its situation.

A throng of people hastened to the shore with boats. The Cossacks arranged the horses' trappings. Taras assumed a stately air, pulled his belt tighter, and proudly stroked his moustache. His sons also inspected themselves from head to foot, with some apprehension and an undefined feeling of satisfaction; and all set out together for the suburb, which was half a verst from the Setch. On their arrival, they were deafened by the clang of fifty blacksmiths' hammers beating upon twenty-five anvils sunk in the earth. Stout tanners seated beneath awnings were scraping ox-hides with their strong hands; shop-keepers sat in their booths, with piles of flints, steels, and powder before them; Armenians spread out their rich handkerchiefs; Tatars turned their kabobs upon spits; a Jew, with his head thrust forward, was filtering some corn-brandy from a cask. But the first man they encountered was a Zaporozhetz[1] who was sleeping in the very middle of the road with legs and arms outstretched. Taras Bulba could not refrain from halting to admire him. "How splendidly developed he is; phew, what a magnificent figure!" he said, stopping his horse. It was, in fact, a striking picture. This Zaporozhetz had stretched himself out in the road like a lion; his scalp-lock, thrown proudly behind him, extended over upwards of a foot of ground; his trousers of rich red cloth were spotted with tar, to show his utter disdain for them. Having admired to his heart's content, Bulba passed on through the narrow street, crowded with mechanics exercising their trades, and with people of all nationalities who thronged this suburb of the Setch, resembling a fair, and fed and clothed the Setch itself, which knew only how to revel and burn powder.

[1] Sometimes written Zaporovian.

At length they left the suburb behind them, and perceived some scattered kurens[2], covered with turf, or in Tatar fashion with felt. Some were furnished with cannon. Nowhere were any fences visible, or any of those low-roofed houses with verandahs supported upon low wooden pillars, such as were seen in the suburb. A low wall and a ditch, totally unguarded, betokened a terrible degree of recklessness. Some sturdy Zaporozhtzi lying, pipe in mouth, in the very road, glanced indifferently at them, but never moved from their places. Taras threaded his way carefully among them, with his sons, saying, "Good-day, gentles."--"Good-day to you," answered the Zaporozhtzi. Scattered over the plain were picturesque groups. From their weatherbeaten faces, it was plain that all were steeled in battle, and had faced every sort of bad weather. And there it was, the Setch! There was the lair from whence all those men, proud and strong as lions, issued forth! There was the spot whence poured forth liberty and Cossacks all over the Ukraine.

[2] Enormous wooden sheds, each inhabited by a troop or kuren.

The travellers entered the great square where the council generally met. On a huge overturned cask sat a Zaporozhetz without his shirt; he was holding it in his hands, and slowly sewing up the holes in it. Again their way was stopped by a whole crowd of musicians, in the midst of whom a young Zaporozhetz was dancing, with head thrown back and arms outstretched. He kept shouting, "Play faster, musicians! Begrudge not, Thoma, brandy to these orthodox Christians!" And Thoma, with his blackened eye, went on measuring out without stint, to every one who presented himself, a huge jugful.

About the youthful Zaporozhetz four old men, moving their feet quite briskly, leaped like a whirlwind to one side, almost upon the musicians' heads, and, suddenly, retreating, squatted down and drummed the hard earth vigorously with their silver heels. The earth hummed dully all about, and afar the air resounded with national dance tunes beaten by the clanging heels of their boots.

But one shouted more loudly than all the rest, and flew after the others in the dance. His scalp-lock streamed in the wind, his muscular chest was bare, his warm, winter fur jacket was hanging by the sleeves, and the perspiration poured from him as from a pig. "Take off your jacket!" said Taras at length: "see how he steams!"--"I can't," shouted the Cossack. "Why?"--"I can't: I have such a disposition that whatever I take off, I drink up." And indeed, the young fellow had not had a cap for a long time, nor a belt to his caftan, nor an embroidered neckerchief: all had gone the proper road. The throng increased; more folk joined the dancer: and it was impossible to observe without emotion how all yielded to the impulse of the dance, the freest, the wildest, the world has ever seen, still called from its mighty originators, the Kosachka.

"Oh, if I had no horse to hold," exclaimed Taras, "I would join the dance myself."

Meanwhile there began to appear among the throng men who were respected for their prowess throughout all the Setch--old greyheads who had been leaders more than once. Taras soon found a number of familiar faces. Ostap and Andrii heard nothing but greetings. "Ah, it is you, Petcheritza! Good day, Kozolup!"--"Whence has God brought you, Taras?"--"How did you come here, Doloto? Health to you, Kirdyaga! Hail to you, Gustui! Did I ever think of seeing you, Remen?" And these heroes, gathered from all the roving population of Eastern Russia, kissed each other and began to ask questions. "But what has become of Kasyan? Where is Borodavka? and Koloper? and Pidsuitok?" And in reply, Taras Bulba learned that Borodavka had been hung at Tolopan, that Koloper had been flayed alive at Kizikirmen, that Pidsuitok's head had been salted and sent in a cask to Constantinople. Old Bulba hung his head and said thoughtfully, "They were good Cossacks."

CHAPTER III

Taras Bulba and his sons had been in the Setch about a week. Ostap and Andrii occupied themselves but little with the science of war. The Setch was not fond of wasting time in warlike exercises. The young generation learned these by experience alone, in the very heat of battles, which were therefore incessant. The Cossacks thought it a nuisance to fill up the intervals of this instruction with any kind of drill, except perhaps shooting at a mark, and on rare occasions with horse-racing and wild-beast hunts on the steppes and in the forests. All the rest of the time was devoted to revelry--a sign of the wide diffusion of moral liberty. The whole of the Setch presented an unusual scene: it was one unbroken revel; a ball noisily begun, which had no end. Some busied themselves with handicrafts; others kept little shops and traded; but the majority caroused from morning till night, if the wherewithal jingled in their pockets, and if the booty they had captured had not already passed into the hands of the shopkeepers and spirit-sellers. This universal revelry had something fascinating about it. It was not an assemblage of topers, who drank to drown sorrow, but simply a wild revelry of joy. Every one who came thither forgot everything, abandoned everything which had hitherto interested him. He, so to speak, spat upon his past and gave himself recklessly up to freedom and the good-fellowship of men of the same stamp as himself--idlers having neither relatives nor home nor family, nothing, in short, save the free sky and the eternal revel of their souls. This gave rise to that wild gaiety which could not have sprung from any other source. The tales and talk current among the assembled crowd, reposing lazily on the ground, were often so droll, and breathed such power of vivid narration, that it required all the nonchalance of a Zaporozhetz to retain his immovable expression, without even a twitch of the moustache--a feature which to this day distinguishes the Southern Russian from his northern brethren. It was drunken, noisy mirth; but there was no dark ale-house where a man drowns thought in stupefying intoxication: it was a dense throng of schoolboys.

The only difference as regarded the students was that, instead of sitting under the pointer and listening to the worn-out doctrines of a teacher, they practised racing with five thousand horses; instead of the field where they had played ball, they had the boundless borderlands, where at the sight of them the Tatar showed his keen face and the Turk frowned grimly from under his green turban. The difference was that, instead of being forced to the companionship of school, they themselves had deserted their fathers and mothers and fled from their homes; that here were those about whose neck a rope had already been wound, and who, instead of pale death, had seen life, and life in all its intensity; those who, from generous habits, could never keep a coin in their pockets; those who had thitherto regarded a ducat as wealth, and whose pockets, thanks to the Jew revenue-farmers, could have been turned wrong side out without any danger of anything falling from them. Here were students who could not endure the academic rod, and had not carried away a single letter from the schools; but with them were also some who knew about Horace, Cicero, and the Roman Republic. There were many leaders who afterwards distinguished themselves in the king's armies; and there were numerous clever partisans who cherished a magnanimous conviction that it was of no consequence where they fought, so long as they did fight, since it was a disgrace to an honourable man to live without fighting. There were many who had come to the Setch for the sake of being able to say afterwards that they had been there and were therefore hardened warriors. But who was not there? This strange republic was a necessary outgrowth of the epoch. Lovers of a warlike life, of golden beakers and rich brocades, of ducats and gold pieces, could always find employment there. The lovers of women alone could find naught, for no woman dared show herself even in the suburbs of the Setch.

It seemed exceedingly strange to Ostap and Andrii that, although a crowd of people had come to the Setch with them, not a soul inquired, "Whence come these men? who are they? and what are their names?" They had come thither as though returning to a home whence they had departed only an hour before. The new-comer merely presented himself to the Koschevoi, or head chief of the Setch, who generally said, "Welcome! Do you believe in Christ?"--"I do," replied the new-comer. "And do you believe in the Holy Trinity?"--"I do."--"And do you go to church?"--"I do." "Now cross yourself." The new-comer crossed himself. "Very good," replied the Koschevoi; "enter the kuren where you have most acquaintances." This concluded the ceremony. And all the Setch prayed in one church, and were willing to defend it to their last drop of blood, although they would not hearken to aught about fasting or abstinence. Jews, Armenians, and Tatars, inspired by strong avarice, took the liberty of living and trading in the suburbs; for the Zaporozhtzi never cared for bargaining, and paid whatever money their hand chanced to grasp in their pocket. Moreover, the lot of these gain-loving traders was pitiable in the extreme. They resembled people settled at the foot of Vesuvius; for when the Zaporozhtzi lacked money, these bold adventurers broke down their booths and took everything gratis. The Setch consisted of over sixty kurens, each of which greatly resembled a separate independent republic, but still more a school or seminary of children, always ready for anything. No one had any occupation; no one retained anything for himself; everything was in the hands of the hetman of the kuren, who, on that account, generally bore the title of "father." In his hands were deposited the money, clothes, all the provisions, oatmeal, grain, even the firewood. They gave him money to take care of. Quarrels amongst the inhabitants of the kuren were not unfrequent; and in such cases they proceeded at once to blows. The inhabitants of the kuren swarmed into the square, and smote each other with their fists, until one side had finally gained the upper hand, when the revelry began. Such was the Setch, which had such an attraction for young men.

Ostap and Andrii flung themselves into this sea of dissipation with all the ardour of youth, forgot in a trice their father's house, the seminary, and all which had hitherto exercised their minds, and gave themselves wholly up to their new life. Everything interested them--the jovial habits of the Setch, and its chaotic morals and laws, which even seemed to them too strict for such a free republic. If a Cossack stole the smallest trifle, it was considered a disgrace to the whole Cossack community. He was bound to the pillar of shame, and a club was laid beside him, with which each passer-by was bound to deal him a blow until in this manner he was beaten to death. He who did not pay his debts was chained to a cannon, until some one of his comrades should decide to ransom him by paying his debts for him. But what made the deepest impression on Andrii was the terrible punishment decreed for murder. A hole was dug in his presence, the murderer was lowered alive into it, and over him was placed a coffin containing the body of the man he had killed, after which the earth was thrown upon both. Long afterwards the fearful ceremony of this horrible execution haunted his mind, and the man who had been buried alive appeared to him with his terrible coffin.

Both the young Cossacks soon took a good standing among their fellows. They often sallied out upon the steppe with comrades from their kuren, and sometimes too with the whole kuren or with neighbouring kurens, to shoot the innumerable steppe-birds of every sort, deer, and goats. Or they went out upon the lakes, the river, and its tributaries allotted to each kuren, to throw their nets and draw out rich prey for the enjoyment of the whole kuren. Although unversed in any trade exercised by a Cossack, they were soon remarked among the other youths for their obstinate bravery and daring in everything. Skilfully and accurately they fired at the mark, and swam the Dnieper against the current--a deed for which the novice was triumphantly received into the circle of Cossacks.

But old Taras was planning a different sphere of activity for them. Such an idle life was not to his mind; he wanted active employment. He reflected incessantly how to stir up the Setch to some bold enterprise, wherein a man could revel as became a warrior. At length he went one day to the Koschevoi, and said plainly:--

"Well, Koschevoi, it is time for the Zaporozhtzi to set out."

"There is nowhere for them to go," replied the Koschevoi, removing his short pipe from his mouth and spitting to one side.

"What do you mean by nowhere? We can go to Turkey or Tatary."

"Impossible to go either to Turkey or Tatary," replied the Koschevoi, putting his pipe coolly into his mouth again.

"Why impossible?"

"It is so; we have promised the Sultan peace."

"But he is a Mussulman; and God and the Holy Scriptures command us to slay Mussulmans."

"We have no right. If we had not sworn by our faith, it might be done; but now it is impossible."

"How is it impossible? How can you say that we have no right? Here are my two sons, both young men. Neither has been to war; and you say that we have no right, and that there is no need for the Zaporozhtzi to set out on an expedition."

"Well, it is not fitting."

"Then it must be fitting that Cossack strength should be wasted in vain, that a man should disappear like a dog without having done a single good deed, that he should be of no use to his country or to Christianity! Why, then, do we live? What the deuce do we live for? just tell me that. You are a sensible man, you were not chosen as Koschevoi without reason: so just tell me what we live for?"

The Koschevoi made no reply to this question. He was an obstinate Cossack. He was silent for a while, and then said, "Anyway, there will not be war."

"There will not be war?" Taras asked again.

"No."

"Then it is no use thinking about it?"

"It is not to be thought of."

"Wait, you devil's limb!" said Taras to himself; "you shall learn to know me!" and he at once resolved to have his revenge on the Koschevoi.

Having made an agreement with several others, he gave them liquor; and the drunken Cossacks staggered into the square, where on a post hung the kettledrums which were generally beaten to assemble the people. Not finding the sticks, which were kept by the drummer, they seized a piece of wood and began to beat. The first to respond to the drum-beat was the drummer, a tall man with but one eye, but a frightfully sleepy one for all that.

"Who dares to beat the drum?" he shouted.

"Hold your tongue! take your sticks, and beat when you are ordered!" replied the drunken men.

The drummer at once took from his pocket the sticks which he had brought with him, well knowing the result of such proceedings. The drum rattled, and soon black swarms of Cossacks began to collect like bees in the square. All formed in a ring; and at length, after the third summons, the chiefs began to arrive--the Koschevoi with staff in hand, the symbol of his office; the judge with the army-seal; the secretary with his ink-bottle; and the osaul with his staff. The Koschevoi and the chiefs took off their caps and bowed on all sides to the Cossacks, who stood proudly with their arms akimbo.

"What means this assemblage? what do you wish, gentles?" said the Koschevoi. Shouts and exclamations interrupted his speech.

"Resign your staff! resign your staff this moment, you son of Satan! we will have you no longer!" shouted some of the Cossacks in the crowd. Some of the sober ones appeared to wish to oppose this, but both sober and drunken fell to blows. The shouting and uproar became universal.

The Koschevoi attempted to speak; but knowing that the self-willed multitude, if enraged, might beat him to death, as almost always happened in such cases, he bowed very low, laid down his staff, and hid himself in the crowd.

"Do you command us, gentles, to resign our insignia of office?" said the judge, the secretary, and the osaul, as they prepared to give up the ink-horn, army-seal, and staff, upon the spot.

"No, you are to remain!" was shouted from the crowd. "We only wanted to drive out the Koschevoi because he is a woman, and we want a man for Koschevoi."

"Whom do you now elect as Koschevoi?" asked the chiefs.

"We choose Kukubenko," shouted some.

"We won't have Kukubenko!" screamed another party: "he is too young; the milk has not dried off his lips yet."

"Let Schilo be hetman!" shouted some: "make Schilo our Koschevoi!"

"Away with your Schilo!" yelled the crowd; "what kind of a Cossack is he who is as thievish as a Tatar? To the devil in a sack with your drunken Schilo!"

"Borodaty! let us make Borodaty our Koschevoi!"

"We won't have Borodaty! To the evil one's mother with Borodaty!"

"Shout Kirdyanga!" whispered Taras Bulba to several.

"Kirdyanga, Kirdyanga!" shouted the crowd. "Borodaty, Borodaty! Kirdyanga, Kirdyanga! Schilo! Away with Schilo! Kirdyanga!"

All the candidates, on hearing their names mentioned, quitted the crowd, in order not to give any one a chance of supposing that they were personally assisting in their election.

"Kirdyanga, Kirdyanga!" echoed more strongly than the rest.

"Borodaty!"

They proceeded to decide the matter by a show of hands, and Kirdyanga won.

"Fetch Kirdyanga!" they shouted. Half a score of Cossacks immediately left the crowd--some of them hardly able to keep their feet, to such an extent had they drunk--and went directly to Kirdyanga to inform him of his election.

Kirdyanga, a very old but wise Cossack, had been sitting for some time in his kuren, as if he knew nothing of what was going on.

"What is it, gentles? What do you wish?" he inquired.

"Come, they have chosen you for Koschevoi."

"Have mercy, gentles!" said Kirdyanga. "How can I be worthy of such honour? Why should I be made Koschevoi? I have not sufficient capacity to fill such a post. Could no better person be found in all the army?"

"Come, I say!" shouted the Zaporozhtzi. Two of them seized him by the arms; and in spite of his planting his feet firmly they finally dragged him to the square, accompanying his progress with shouts, blows from behind with their fists, kicks, and exhortations. "Don't hold back, you son of Satan! Accept the honour, you dog, when it is given!" In this manner Kirdyanga was conducted into the ring of Cossacks.

"How now, gentles?" announced those who had brought him, "are you agreed that this Cossack shall be your Koschevoi?"

"We are all agreed!" shouted the throng, and the whole plain trembled for a long time afterwards from the shout.

One of the chiefs took the staff and brought it to the newly elected Koschevoi. Kirdyanga, in accordance with custom, immediately refused it. The chief offered it a second time; Kirdyanga again refused it, and then, at the third offer, accepted the staff. A cry of approbation rang out from the crowd, and again the whole plain resounded afar with the Cossacks' shout. Then there stepped out from among the people the four oldest of them all, white-bearded, white-haired Cossacks; though there were no very old men in the Setch, for none of the Zaporozhtzi ever died in their beds. Taking each a handful of earth, which recent rain had converted into mud, they laid it on Kirdyanga's head. The wet earth trickled down from his head on to his moustache and cheeks and smeared his whole face. But Kirdyanga stood immovable in his place, and thanked the Cossacks for the honour shown him.

Thus ended the noisy election, concerning which we cannot say whether it was as pleasing to the others as it was to Bulba; by means of it he had revenged himself on the former Koschevoi. Moreover, Kirdyanga was an old comrade, and had been with him on the same expeditions by sea and land, sharing the toils and hardships of war. The crowd immediately dispersed to celebrate the election, and such revelry ensued as Ostap and Andrii had not yet beheld. The taverns were attacked and mead, corn-brandy, and beer seized without payment, the owners being only too glad to escape with whole skins themselves. The whole night passed amid shouts, songs, and rejoicings; and the rising moon gazed long at troops of musicians traversing the streets with guitars, flutes, tambourines, and the church choir, who were kept in the Setch to sing in church and glorify the deeds of the Zaporozhtzi. At length drunkenness and fatigue began to overpower even these strong heads, and here and there a Cossack could be seen to fall to the ground, embracing a comrade in fraternal fashion; whilst maudlin, and even weeping, the latter rolled upon the earth with him. Here a whole group would lie down in a heap; there a man would choose the most comfortable position and stretch himself out on a log of wood. The last, and strongest, still uttered some incoherent speeches; finally even they, yielding to the power of intoxication, flung themselves down and all the Setch slept.

CHAPTER IV

But next day Taras Bulba had a conference with the new Koschevoi as to the method of exciting the Cossacks to some enterprise. The Koschevoi, a shrewd and sensible Cossack, who knew the Zaporozhtzi thoroughly, said at first, "Oaths cannot be violated by any means"; but after a pause added, "No matter, it can be done. We will not violate them, but let us devise something. Let the people assemble, not at my summons, but of their own accord. You know how to manage that; and I will hasten to the square with the chiefs, as though we know nothing about it."

Not an hour had elapsed after their conversation, when the drums again thundered. The drunken and senseless Cossacks assembled. A myriad Cossack caps were sprinkled over the square. A murmur arose, "Why? What? Why was the assembly beaten?" No one answered. At length, in one quarter and another, it began to be rumoured about, "Behold, the Cossack strength is being vainly wasted: there is no war! Behold, our leaders have become as marmots, every one; their eyes swim in fat! Plainly, there is no justice in the world!" The other Cossacks listened at first, and then began themselves to say, "In truth, there is no justice in the world!" Their leaders seemed surprised at these utterances. Finally the Koschevoi stepped forward: "Permit me, Cossacks, to address you."

"Do so!"

"Touching the matter in question, gentles, none know better than yourselves that many Zaporozhtzi have run in debt to the Jew ale-house keepers and to their brethren, so that now they have not an atom of credit. Again, touching the matter in question, there are many young fellows who have no idea of what war is like, although you know, gentles, that without war a young man cannot exist. How make a Zaporozhetz out of him if he has never killed a Mussulman?"

"He speaks well," thought Bulba.

"Think not, however, gentles, that I speak thus in order to break the truce; God forbid! I merely mention it. Besides, it is a shame to see what sort of church we have for our God. Not only has the church remained without exterior decoration during all the years which by God's mercy the Setch has stood, but up to this day even the holy pictures have no adornments. No one has even thought of making them a silver frame; they have only received what some Cossacks have left them in their wills; and these gifts were poor, since they had drunk up nearly all they had during their lifetime. I am making you this speech, therefore, not in order to stir up a war against the Mussulmans; we have promised the Sultan peace, and it would be a great sin in us to break this promise, for we swore it on our law."

"What is he mixing things up like that for?" said Bulba to himself.

"So you see, gentles, that war cannot be begun; honour does not permit it. But according to my poor opinion, we might, I think, send out a few young men in boats and let them plunder the coasts of Anatolia a little. What do you think, gentles?"

"Lead us, lead us all!" shouted the crowd on all sides. "We are ready to lay down our lives for our faith."

The Koschevoi was alarmed. He by no means wished to stir up all Zaporozhe; a breach of the truce appeared to him on this occasion unsuitable. "Permit me, gentles, to address you further."

"Enough!" yelled the Cossacks; "you can say nothing better."

"If it must be so, then let it be so. I am the slave of your will. We know, and from Scripture too, that the voice of the people is the voice of God. It is impossible to devise anything better than the whole nation has devised. But here lies the difficulty; you know, gentles, that the Sultan will not permit that which delights our young men to go unpunished. We should be prepared at such a time, and our forces should be fresh, and then we should fear no one. But during their absence the Tatars may assemble fresh forces; the dogs do not show themselves in sight and dare not come while the master is at home, but they can bite his heels from behind, and bite painfully too. And if I must tell you the truth, we have not boats enough, nor powder ready in sufficient quantity, for all to go. But I am ready, if you please; I am the slave of your will."

The cunning hetman was silent. The various groups began to discuss the matter, and the hetmans of the kurens to take counsel together; few were drunk fortunately, so they decided to listen to reason.

A number of men set out at once for the opposite shore of the Dnieper, to the treasury of the army, where in strictest secrecy, under water and among the reeds, lay concealed the army chest and a portion of the arms captured from the enemy. Others hastened to inspect the boats and prepare them for service. In a twinkling the whole shore was thronged with men. Carpenters appeared with axes in their hands. Old, weatherbeaten, broad-shouldered, strong-legged Zaporozhtzi, with black or silvered moustaches, rolled up their trousers, waded up to their knees in water, and dragged the boats on to the shore with stout ropes; others brought seasoned timber and all sorts of wood. The boats were freshly planked, turned bottom upwards, caulked and tarred, and then bound together side by side after Cossack fashion, with long strands of reeds, so that the swell of the waves might not sink them. Far along the shore they built fires and heated tar in copper cauldrons to smear the boats. The old and the experienced instructed the young. The blows and shouts of the workers rose all over the neighbourhood; the bank shook and moved about.

About this time a large ferry-boat began to near the shore. The mass of people standing in it began to wave their hands from a distance. They were Cossacks in torn, ragged gaberdines. Their disordered garments, for many had on nothing but their shirts, with a short pipe in their mouths, showed that they had either escaped from some disaster or had caroused to such an extent that they had drunk up all they had on their bodies. A short, broad-shouldered Cossack of about fifty stepped out from the midst of them and stood in front. He shouted and waved his hand more vigorously than any of the others; but his words could not be heard for the cries and hammering of the workmen.

"Whence come you!" asked the Koschevoi, as the boat touched the shore. All the workers paused in their labours, and, raising their axes and chisels, looked on expectantly.

"From a misfortune!" shouted the short Cossack.

"From what?"

"Permit me, noble Zaporozhtzi, to address you."

"Speak!"

"Or would you prefer to assemble a council?"

"Speak, we are all here."

The people all pressed together in one mass.

"Have you then heard nothing of what has been going on in the hetman's dominions?"

"What is it?" inquired one of the kuren hetmans.

"Eh! what! Evidently the Tatars have plastered up your ears so that you might hear nothing."

"Tell us then; what has been going on there?"

"That is going on the like of which no man born or christened ever yet has seen."

"Tell us what it is, you son of a dog!" shouted one of the crowd, apparently losing patience.

"Things have come to such a pass that our holy churches are no longer ours."

"How not ours?"

"They are pledged to the Jews. If the Jew is not first paid, there can be no mass."

"What are you saying?"

"And if the dog of a Jew does not make a sign with his unclean hand over the holy Easter-bread, it cannot be consecrated."

"He lies, brother gentles. It cannot be that an unclean Jew puts his mark upon the holy Easter-bread."

"Listen! I have not yet told all. Catholic priests are going about all over the Ukraine in carts. The harm lies not in the carts, but in the fact that not horses, but orthodox Christians[1], are harnessed to them. Listen! I have not yet told all. They say that the Jewesses are making themselves petticoats out of our popes' vestments. Such are the deeds that are taking place in the Ukraine, gentles! And you sit here revelling in Zaporozhe; and evidently the Tatars have so scared you that you have no eyes, no ears, no anything, and know nothing that is going on in the world."

[1] That is of the Greek Church. The Poles were Catholics.

"Stop, stop!" broke in the Koschevoi, who up to that moment had stood with his eyes fixed upon the earth like all Zaporozhtzi, who, on important occasions, never yielded to their first impulse, but kept silence, and meanwhile concentrated inwardly all the power of their indignation. "Stop! I also have a word to say. But what were you about? When your father the devil was raging thus, what were you doing yourselves? Had you no swords? How came you to permit such lawlessness?"

"Eh! how did we come to permit such lawlessness? You would have tried when there were fifty thousand of the Lyakhs[2] alone; yes, and it is a shame not to be concealed, when there are also dogs among us who have already accepted their faith."

[2] Lyakhs, an opprobrious name for the Poles.

"But your hetman and your leaders, what have they done?"

"God preserve any one from such deeds as our leaders performed!"

"How so?"

"Our hetman, roasted in a brazen ox, now lies in Warsaw; and the heads and hands of our leaders are being carried to all the fairs as a spectacle for the people. That is what our leaders did."

The whole throng became wildly excited. At first silence reigned all along the shore, like that which precedes a tempest; and then suddenly voices were raised and all the shore spoke:--

"What! The Jews hold the Christian churches in pledge! Roman Catholic priests have harnessed and beaten orthodox Christians! What! such torture has been permitted on Russian soil by the cursed unbelievers! And they have done such things to the leaders and the hetman? Nay, this shall not be, it shall not be." Such words came from all quarters. The Zaporozhtzi were moved, and knew their power. It was not the excitement of a giddy-minded folk. All who were thus agitated were strong, firm characters, not easily aroused, but, once aroused, preserving their inward heat long and obstinately. "Hang all the Jews!" rang through the crowd. "They shall not make petticoats for their Jewesses out of popes' vestments! They shall not place their signs upon the holy wafers! Drown all the heathens in the Dnieper!" These words uttered by some one in the throng flashed like lightning through all minds, and the crowd flung themselves upon the suburb with the intention of cutting the throats of all the Jews.

The poor sons of Israel, losing all presence of mind, and not being in any case courageous, hid themselves in empty brandy-casks, in ovens, and even crawled under the skirts of their Jewesses; but the Cossacks found them wherever they were.

"Gracious nobles!" shrieked one Jew, tall and thin as a stick, thrusting his sorry visage, distorted with terror, from among a group of his comrades, "gracious nobles! suffer us to say a word, only one word. We will reveal to you what you never yet have heard, a thing more important than I can say-- very important!"

"Well, say it," said Bulba, who always liked to hear what an accused man had to say.

"Gracious nobles," exclaimed the Jew, "such nobles were never seen, by heavens, never! Such good, kind, and brave men there never were in the world before!" His voice died away and quivered with fear. "How was it possible that we should think any evil of the Zaporozhtzi? Those men are not of us at all, those who have taken pledges in the Ukraine. By heavens, they are not of us! They are not Jews at all. The evil one alone knows what they are; they are only fit to be spit upon and cast aside. Behold, my brethren, say the same! Is it not true, Schloma? is it not true, Schmul?"

"By heavens, it is true!" replied Schloma and Schmul, from among the crowd, both pale as clay, in their ragged caps.

"We never yet," continued the tall Jew, "have had any secret intercourse with your enemies, and we will have nothing to do with Catholics; may the evil one fly away with them! We are like own brothers to the Zaporozhtzi."

"What! the Zaporozhtzi are brothers to you!" exclaimed some one in the crowd. "Don't wait! the cursed Jews! Into the Dnieper with them, gentles! Drown all the unbelievers!"

These words were the signal. They seized the Jews by the arms and began to hurl them into the waves. Pitiful cries resounded on all sides; but the stern Zaporozhtzi only laughed when they saw the Jewish legs, cased in shoes and stockings, struggling in the air. The poor orator who had called down destruction upon himself jumped out of the caftan, by which they had seized him, and in his scant parti-coloured under waistcoat clasped Bulba's legs, and cried, in piteous tones, "Great lord! gracious noble! I knew your brother, the late Doroscha. He was a warrior who was an ornament to all knighthood. I gave him eight hundred sequins when he was obliged to ransom himself from the Turks."

"You knew my brother?" asked Taras.

"By heavens, I knew him. He was a magnificent nobleman."

"And what is your name?"

"Yankel."

"Good," said Taras; and after reflecting, he turned to the Cossacks and spoke as follows: "There will always be plenty of time to hang the Jew, if it proves necessary; but for to-day give him to me."

So saying, Taras led him to his waggon, beside which stood his Cossacks. "Crawl under the waggon; lie down, and do not move. And you, brothers, do not surrender this Jew."

So saying, he returned to the square, for the whole crowd had long since collected there. All had at once abandoned the shore and the preparation of the boats; for a land-journey now awaited them, and not a sea-voyage, and they needed horses and waggons, not ships. All, both young and old, wanted to go on the expedition; and it was decided, on the advice of the chiefs, the hetmans of the kurens, and the Koschevoi, and with the approbation of the whole Zaporozhtzian army, to march straight to Poland, to avenge the injury and disgrace to their faith and to Cossack renown, to seize booty from the cities, to burn villages and grain, and spread their glory far over the steppe. All at once girded and armed themselves. The Koschevoi grew a whole foot taller. He was no longer the timid executor of the restless wishes of a free people, but their untrammelled master. He was a despot, who know only to command. All the independent and pleasure-loving warriors stood in an orderly line, with respectfully bowed heads, not venturing to raise their eyes, when the Koschevoi gave his orders. He gave these quietly, without shouting and without haste, but with pauses between, like an experienced man deeply learned in Cossack affairs, and carrying into execution, not for the first time, a wisely matured enterprise.

"Examine yourselves, look well to yourselves; examine all your equipments thoroughly," he said; "put your teams and your tar-boxes[3] in order; test your weapons. Take not many clothes with you: a shirt and a couple of pairs of trousers to each Cossack, and a pot of oatmeal and millet apiece--let no one take any more. There will be plenty of provisions, all that is needed, in the waggons. Let every Cossack have two horses. And two hundred yoke of oxen must be taken, for we shall require them at the fords and marshy places. Keep order, gentles, above all things. I know that there are some among you whom God has made so greedy that they would like to tear up silk and velvet for foot-cloths. Leave off such devilish habits; reject all garments as plunder, and take only weapons: though if valuables offer themselves, ducats or silver, they are useful in any case. I tell you this beforehand, gentles, if any one gets drunk on the expedition, he will have a short shrift: I will have him dragged by the neck like a dog behind the baggage waggons, no matter who he may be, even were he the most heroic Cossack in the whole army; he shall be shot on the spot like a dog, and flung out, without sepulture, to be torn by the birds of prey, for a drunkard on the march deserves no Christian burial. Young men, obey the old men in all things! If a ball grazes you, or a sword cuts your head or any other part, attach no importance to such trifles. Mix a charge of powder in a cup of brandy, quaff it heartily, and all will pass off--you will not even have any fever; and if the wound is large, put simple earth upon it, mixing it first with spittle in your palm, and that will dry it up. And now to work, to work, lads, and look well to all, and without haste."

[3] The Cossack waggons have their axles smeared with tar instead of grease.

So spoke the Koschevoi; and no sooner had he finished his speech than all the Cossacks at once set to work. All the Setch grew sober. Nowhere was a single drunken man to be found, it was as though there never had been such a thing among the Cossacks. Some attended to the tyres of the wheels, others changed the axles of the waggons; some carried sacks of provisions to them or leaded them with arms; others again drove up the horses and oxen. On all sides resounded the tramp of horses' hoofs, test-shots from the guns, the clank of swords, the lowing of oxen, the screech of rolling waggons, talking, sharp cries and urging-on of cattle. Soon the Cossack force spread far over all the plain; and he who might have undertaken to run from its van to its rear would have had a long course. In the little wooden church the priest was offering up prayers and sprinkling all worshippers with holy water. All kissed the cross. When the camp broke up and the army moved out of the Setch, all the Zaporozhtzi turned their heads back. "Farewell, our mother!" they said almost in one breath. "May God preserve thee from all misfortune!"

As he passed through the suburb, Taras Bulba saw that his Jew, Yankel, had already erected a sort of booth with an awning, and was selling flint, screwdrivers, powder, and all sorts of military stores needed on the road, even to rolls and bread. "What devils these Jews are!" thought Taras; and riding up to him, he said, "Fool, why are you sitting here? do you want to be shot like a crow?"

Yankel in reply approached nearer, and making a sign with both hands, as though wishing to impart some secret, said, "Let the noble lord but keep silence and say nothing to any one. Among the Cossack waggons is a waggon of mine. I am carrying all sorts of needful stores for the Cossacks, and on the journey I will furnish every sort of provisions at a lower price than any Jew ever sold at before. 'Tis so, by heavens! by heavens, 'tis so!"

Taras Bulba shrugged his shoulders in amazement at the Jewish nature, and went on to the camp.

CHAPTER V

All South-west Poland speedily became a prey to fear. Everywhere the rumour flew, "The Zaporozhtzi! The Zaporozhtzi have appeared!" All who could flee did so. All rose and scattered after the manner of that lawless, reckless age, when they built neither fortresses nor castles, but each man erected a temporary dwelling of straw wherever he happened to find himself. He thought, "It is useless to waste money and labour on an izba, when the roving Tatars will carry it off in any case." All was in an uproar: one exchanged his plough and oxen for a horse and gun, and joined an armed band; another, seeking concealment, drove off his cattle and carried off all the household stuff he could. Occasionally, on the road, some were encountered who met their visitors with arms in their hands; but the majority fled before their arrival. All knew that it was hard to deal with the raging and warlike throng known by the name of the Zaporozhian army; a body which, under its independent and disorderly exterior, concealed an organisation well calculated for times of battle. The horsemen rode steadily on without overburdening or heating their horses; the foot-soldiers marched only by night, resting during the day, and selecting for this purpose desert tracts, uninhabited spots, and forests, of which there were then plenty. Spies and scouts were sent ahead to study the time, place, and method of attack. And lo! the Zaporozhtzi suddenly appeared in those places where they were least expected: then all were put to the sword; the villages were burned; and the horses and cattle which were not driven off behind the army killed upon the spot. They seemed to be fiercely revelling, rather than carrying out a military expedition. Our hair would stand on end nowadays at the horrible traits of that fierce, half-civilised age, which the Zaporozhtzi everywhere exhibited: children killed, women's breasts cut open, the skin flayed from the legs up to the knees, and the victim then set at liberty. In short, the Cossacks paid their former debts in coin of full weight. The abbot of one monastery, on hearing of their approach, sent two monks to say that they were not behaving as they should; that there was an agreement between the Zaporozhtzi and the government; that they were breaking faith with the king, and violating all international rights. "Tell your bishop from me and from all the Zaporozhtzi," said the Koschevoi, "that he has nothing to fear: the Cossacks, so far, have only lighted and smoked their pipes." And the magnificent abbey was soon wrapped in the devouring flames, its tall Gothic windows showing grimly through the waves of fire as they parted. The fleeing mass of monks, women, and Jews thronged into those towns where any hope lay in the garrison and the civic forces. The aid sent in season by the government, but delayed on the way, consisted of a few troops which either were unable to enter the towns or, seized with fright, turned their backs at the very first encounter and fled on their swift horses. However, several of the royal commanders, who had conquered in former battles, resolved to unite their forces and confront the Zaporozhtzi.

And here, above all, did our young Cossacks, disgusted with pillage, greed, and a feeble foe, and burning with the desire to distinguish themselves in presence of their chiefs, seek to measure themselves in single combat with the warlike and boastful Lyakhs, prancing on their spirited horses, with the sleeves of their jackets thrown back and streaming in the wind. This game was inspiriting; they won at it many costly sets of horse-trappings and valuable weapons. In a month the scarcely fledged birds attained their full growth, were completely transformed, and became men; their features, in which hitherto a trace of youthful softness had been visible, grew strong and grim. But it was pleasant to old Taras to see his sons among the foremost. It seemed as though Ostap were designed by nature for the game of war and the difficult science of command. Never once losing his head or becoming confused under any circumstances, he could, with a cool audacity almost supernatural in a youth of two-and-twenty, in an instant gauge the danger and the whole scope of the matter, could at once devise a means of escaping, but of escaping only that he might the more surely conquer. His movements now began to be marked by the assurance which comes from experience, and in them could be detected the germ of the future leader. His person strengthened, and his bearing grew majestically leonine. "What a fine leader he will make one of these days!" said old Taras. "He will make a splendid leader, far surpassing even his father!"

Andrii gave himself up wholly to the enchanting music of blades and bullets. He knew not what it was to consider, or calculate, or to measure his own as against the enemy's strength. He gazed on battle with mad delight and intoxication: he found something festal in the moments when a man's brain burns, when all things wave and flutter before his eyes, when heads are stricken off, horses fall to the earth with a sound of thunder, and he rides on like a drunken man, amid the whistling of bullets and the flashing of swords, dealing blows to all, and heeding not those aimed at himself. More than once their father marvelled too at Andrii, seeing him, stirred only by a flash of impulse, dash at something which a sensible man in cold blood never would have attempted, and, by the sheer force of his mad attack, accomplish such wonders as could not but amaze even men grown old in battle. Old Taras admired and said, "And he too will make a good warrior if the enemy does not capture him meanwhile. He is not Ostap, but he is a dashing warrior, nevertheless."

The army decided to march straight on the city of Dubno, which, rumour said, contained much wealth and many rich inhabitants. The journey was accomplished in a day and a half, and the Zaporozhtzi appeared before the city. The inhabitants resolved to defend themselves to the utmost extent of their power, and to fight to the last extremity, preferring to die in their squares and streets, and on their thresholds, rather than admit the enemy to their houses. A high rampart of earth surrounded the city; and in places where it was low or weak, it was strengthened by a wall of stone, or a house which served as a redoubt, or even an oaken stockade. The garrison was strong and aware of the importance of their position. The Zaporozhtzi attacked the wall fiercely, but were met with a shower of grapeshot. The citizens and residents of the town evidently did not wish to remain idle, but gathered on the ramparts; in their eyes could be read desperate resistance. The women too were determined to take part in the fray, and upon the heads of the Zaporozhians rained down stones, casks of boiling water, and sacks of lime which blinded them. The Zaporozhtzi were not fond of having anything to do with fortified places: sieges were not in their line. The Koschevoi ordered them to retreat, saying, "It is useless, brother gentles; we will retire: but may I be a heathen Tatar, and not a Christian, if we do not clear them out of that town! may they all perish of hunger, the dogs!" The army retreated, surrounded the town, and, for lack of something to do, busied themselves with devastating the surrounding country, burning the neighbouring villages and the ricks of unthreshed grain, and turning their droves of horses loose in the cornfields, as yet untouched by the reaping-hook, where the plump ears waved, fruit, as luck would have it, of an unusually good harvest which should have liberally rewarded all tillers of the soil that season.

With horror those in the city beheld their means of subsistence destroyed. Meanwhile the Zaporozhtzi, having formed a double ring of their waggons around the city, disposed themselves as in the Setch in kurens, smoked their pipes, bartered their booty for weapons, played at leapfrog and odd-and-even, and gazed at the city with deadly cold-bloodedness. At night they lighted their camp fires, and the cooks boiled the porridge for each kuren in huge copper cauldrons; whilst an alert sentinel watched all night beside the blazing fire. But the Zaporozhtzi soon began to tire of inactivity and prolonged sobriety, unaccompanied by any fighting. The Koschevoi even ordered the allowance of wine to be doubled, which was sometimes done in the army when no difficult enterprises or movements were on hand. The young men, and Taras Bulba's sons in particular, did not like this life. Andrii was visibly bored. "You silly fellow!" said Taras to him, "be patient, you will be hetman one day. He is not a good warrior who loses heart in an important enterprise; but he who is not tired even of inactivity, who endures all, and who even if he likes a thing can give it up." But hot youth cannot agree with age; the two have different natures, and look at the same thing with different eyes.

But in the meantime Taras's band, led by Tovkatch, arrived; with him were also two osauls, the secretary, and other regimental officers: the Cossacks numbered over four thousand in all. There were among them many volunteers, who had risen of their own free will, without any summons, as soon as they had heard what the matter was. The osauls brought to Taras's sons the blessing of their aged mother, and to each a picture in a cypress-wood frame from the Mezhigorski monastery at Kief. The two brothers hung the pictures round their necks, and involuntarily grew pensive as they remembered their old mother. What did this blessing prophecy? Was it a blessing for their victory over the enemy, and then a joyous return to their home with booty and glory, to be everlastingly commemorated in the songs of guitar-players? or was it . . . ? But the future is unknown, and stands before a man like autumnal fogs rising from the swamps; birds fly foolishly up and down in it with flapping wings, never recognising each other, the dove seeing not the vulture, nor the vulture the dove, and no one knowing how far he may be flying from destruction.

 Ostap had long since attended to his duties and gone to the kuren. Andrii, without knowing why, felt a kind of oppression at his heart. The Cossacks had finished their evening meal; the wonderful July night had completely fallen; still he did not go to the kuren, nor lie down to sleep, but gazed unconsciously at the whole scene before him. In the sky innumerable stars twinkled brightly. The plain was covered far and wide with scattered waggons with swinging tar-buckets, smeared with tar, and loaded with every description of goods and provisions captured from the foe. Beside the waggons, under the waggons, and far beyond the waggons, Zaporozhtzi were everywhere visible, stretched upon the grass. They all slumbered in picturesque attitudes; one had thrust a sack under his head, another his cap, and another simply made use of his comrade's side. Swords, guns, matchlocks, short pipe-stems with copper mountings, iron awls, and a flint and steel were inseparable from every Cossack. The heavy oxen lay with their feet doubled under them like huge whitish masses, and at a distance looked like gray stones scattered on the slopes of the plain. On all sides the heavy snores of sleeping warriors began to arise from the grass, and were answered from the plain by the ringing neighs of their steeds, chafing at their hobbled feet. Meanwhile a certain threatening magnificence had mingled with the beauty of the July night. It was the distant glare of the burning district afar. In one place the flames spread quietly and grandly over the sky; in another, suddenly bursting into a whirlwind, they hissed and flew upwards to the very stars, and floating fragments died away in the most distant quarter of the heavens. Here the black, burned monastery like a grim Carthusian monk stood threatening, and displaying its dark magnificence at every flash; there blazed the monastery garden. It seemed as though the trees could be heard hissing as they stood wrapped in smoke; and when the fire burst forth, it suddenly lighted up the ripe plums with a phosphoric lilac-coloured gleam, or turned the yellowing pears here and there to pure gold. In the midst of them hung black against the wall of the building, or the trunk of a tree, the body of some poor Jew or monk who had perished in the flames with the structure. Above the distant fires hovered a flock of birds, like a cluster of tiny black crosses upon a fiery field. The town thus laid bare seemed to sleep; the spires and roofs, and its palisade and walls, gleamed quietly in the glare of the distant conflagrations. Andrii went the rounds of the Cossack ranks. The camp-fires, beside which the sentinels sat, were ready to go out at any moment; and even the sentinels slept, having devoured oatmeal and dumplings with true Cossack appetites. He was astonished at such carelessness, thinking, "It is well that there is no strong enemy at hand and nothing to fear." Finally he went to one of the waggons, climbed into it, and lay down upon his back, putting his clasped hands under his head; but he could not sleep, and gazed long at the sky. It was all open before him; the air was pure and transparent; the dense clusters of stars in the Milky Way, crossing the sky like a belt, were flooded with light. From time to time Andrii in some degree lost consciousness, and a light mist of dream veiled the heavens from him for a moment; but then he awoke, and they became visible again.

During one of these intervals it seemed to him that some strange human figure flitted before him. Thinking it to be merely a vision which would vanish at once, he opened his eyes, and beheld a withered, emaciated face bending over him, and gazing straight into his own. Long coal-black hair, unkempt, dishevelled, fell from beneath a dark veil which had been thrown over the head; whilst the strange gleam of the eyes, and the death-like tone of the sharp-cut features, inclined him to think that it was an apparition. His hand involuntarily grasped his gun; and he exclaimed almost convulsively: "Who are you? If you are an evil spirit, avaunt! If you are a living being, you have chosen an ill time for your jest. I will kill you with one shot."

In answer to this, the apparition laid its finger upon its lips and seemed to entreat silence. He dropped his hands and began to look more attentively. He recognised it to be a woman from the long hair, the brown neck, and the half-concealed bosom. But she was not a native of those regions: her wide cheek-bones stood out prominently over her hollow cheeks; her small eyes were obliquely set. The more he gazed at her features, the more he found them familiar. Finally he could restrain himself no longer, and said, "Tell me, who are you? It seems to me that I know you, or have seen you somewhere."

"Two years ago in Kief."

"Two years ago in Kief!" repeated Andrii, endeavouring to collect in his mind all that lingered in his memory of his former student life. He looked intently at her once more, and suddenly exclaimed at the top of his voice, "You are the Tatar! the servant of the lady, the Waiwode's daughter!"

"Sh!" cried the Tatar, clasping her hands with a supplicating glance, trembling all over, and turning her head round in order to see whether any one had been awakened by Andrii's loud exclamation.

"Tell me, tell me, why are you here?" said Andrii almost breathlessly, in a whisper, interrupted every moment by inward emotion. "Where is the lady? is she alive?"

"She is now in the city."

"In the city!" he exclaimed, again almost in a shriek, and feeling all the blood suddenly rush to his heart. "Why is she in the city?"

"Because the old lord himself is in the city: he has been Waiwode of Dubno for the last year and a half."

"Is she married? How strange you are! Tell me about her."

"She has eaten nothing for two days."

"What!"

"And not one of the inhabitants has had a morsel of bread for a long while; all have long been eating earth."

Andrii was astounded.

"The lady saw you from the city wall, among the Zaporozhtzi. She said to me, 'Go tell the warrior: if he remembers me, let him come to me; and do not forget to make him give you a bit of bread for my aged mother, for I do not wish to see my mother die before my very eyes. Better that I should die first, and she afterwards! Beseech him; clasp his knees, his feet: he also has an aged mother, let him give you the bread for her sake!'"

Many feelings awoke in the young Cossack's breast.

"But how came you here? how did you get here?"

"By an underground passage."

"Is there an underground passage?"

"Yes."

"Where?"

"You will not betray it, warrior?"

"I swear it by the holy cross!"

"You descend into a hole, and cross the brook, yonder among the reeds."

"And it leads into the city?"

"Straight into the monastery."

"Let us go, let us go at once."

"A bit of bread, in the name of Christ and of His holy mother!"

"Good, so be it. Stand here beside the waggon, or, better still, lie down in it: no one will see you, all are asleep. I will return at once."

And he set off for the baggage waggons, which contained the provisions belonging to their kuren. His heart beat. All the past, all that had been extinguished by the Cossack bivouacks, and by the stern battle of life, flamed out at once on the surface and drowned the present in its turn. Again, as from the dark depths of the sea, the noble lady rose before him: again there gleamed in his memory her beautiful arms, her eyes, her laughing mouth, her thick dark-chestnut hair, falling in curls upon her shoulders, and the firm, well-rounded limbs of her maiden form. No, they had not been extinguished in his breast, they had not vanished, they had simply been laid aside, in order, for a time, to make way for other strong emotions; but often, very often, the young Cossack's deep slumber had been troubled by them, and often he had lain sleepless on his couch, without being able to explain the cause.

His heart beat more violently at the thought of seeing her again, and his young knees shook. On reaching the baggage waggons, he had quite forgotten what he had come for; he raised his hand to his brow and rubbed it long, trying to recollect what he was to do. At length he shuddered, and was filled with terror as the thought suddenly occurred to him that she was dying of hunger. He jumped upon the waggon and seized several large loaves of black bread; but then he thought, "Is this not food, suited to a robust and easily satisfied Zaporozhetz, too coarse and unfit for her delicate frame?" Then he recollected that the Koschevoi, on the previous evening, had reproved the cooks for having cooked up all the oatmeal into porridge at once, when there was plenty for three times. Sure that he would find plenty of porridge in the kettles, he drew out his father's travelling kettle and went with it to the cook of their kuren, who was sleeping beside two big cauldrons, holding about ten pailfuls, under which the ashes still glowed. Glancing into them, he was amazed to find them empty. It must have required supernatural powers to eat it all; the more so, as their kuren numbered fewer than the others. He looked into the cauldron of the other kurens--nothing anywhere. Involuntarily the saying recurred to his mind, "The Zaporozhtzi are like children: if there is little they eat it, if there is much they leave nothing." What was to be done? There was, somewhere in the waggon belonging to his father's band, a sack of white bread, which they had found when they pillaged the bakery of the monastery. He went straight to his father's waggon, but it was not there. Ostap had taken it and put it under his head; and there he lay, stretched out on the ground, snoring so that the whole plain rang again. Andrii seized the sack abruptly with one hand and gave it a jerk, so that Ostap's head fell to the ground. The elder brother sprang up in his sleep, and, sitting there with closed eyes, shouted at the top of his lungs, "Stop them! Stop the cursed Lyakhs! Catch the horses! catch the horses!"--"Silence! I'll kill you," shouted Andrii in terror, flourishing the sack over him. But Ostap did not continue his speech, sank down again, and gave such a snore that the grass on which he lay waved with his breath.

Andrii glanced timidly on all sides to see if Ostap's talking in his sleep had waked any of the Cossacks. Only one long-locked head was raised in the adjoining kuren, and after glancing about, was dropped back on the ground. After waiting a couple of minutes he set out with his load. The Tatar woman was lying where he had left her, scarcely breathing. "Come, rise up. Fear not, all are sleeping. Can you take one of these loaves if I cannot carry all?" So saying, he swung the sack on to his back, pulled out another sack of millet as he passed the waggon, took in his hands the loaves he had wanted to give the Tatar woman to carry, and, bending somewhat under the load, went boldly through the ranks of sleeping Zaporozhtzi.

"Andrii," said old Bulba, as he passed. His heart died within him. He halted, trembling, and said softly, "What is it?"

"There's a woman with you. When I get up I'll give you a sound thrashing. Women will lead you to no good." So saying, he leaned his hand upon his hand and gazed intently at the muffled form of the Tatar.

Andrii stood there, more dead than alive, not daring to look in his father's face. When he did raise his eyes and glance at him, old Bulba was asleep, with his head still resting in the palm of his hand.

Andrii crossed himself. Fear fled from his heart even more rapidly than it had assailed it. When he turned to look at the Tatar woman, she stood before him, muffled in her mantle, like a dark granite statue, and the gleam of the distant dawn lighted up only her eyes, dull as those of a corpse. He plucked her by the sleeve, and both went on together, glancing back continually. At length they descended the slope of a small ravine, almost a hole, along the bottom of which a brook flowed lazily, overgrown with sedge, and strewed with mossy boulders. Descending into this ravine, they were completely concealed from the view of all the plain occupied by the Zaporovian camp. At least Andrii, glancing back, saw that the steep slope rose behind him higher than a man. On its summit appeared a few blades of steppe-grass; and behind them, in the sky, hung the moon, like a golden sickle. The breeze rising on the steppe warned them that the dawn was not far off. But nowhere was the crow of the cock heard. Neither in the city nor in the devastated neighbourhood had there been a cock for a long time past. They crossed the brook on a small plank, beyond which rose the opposite bank, which appeared higher than the one behind them and rose steeply. It seemed as though this were the strong point of the citadel upon which the besieged could rely; at all events, the earthen wall was lower there, and no garrison appeared behind it. But farther on rose the thick monastery walls. The steep bank was overgrown with steppe-grass, and in the narrow ravine between it and the brook grew tall reeds almost as high as a man. At the summit of the bank were the remains of a wattled fence, which had formerly surrounded some garden, and in front of it were visible the wide leaves of the burdock, from among which rose blackthorn, and sunflowers lifting their heads high above all the rest. Here the Tatar flung off her slippers and went barefoot, gathering her clothes up carefully, for the spot was marshy and full of water. Forcing their way among the reeds, they stopped before a ruined outwork. Skirting this outwork, they found a sort of earthen arch--an opening not much larger than the opening of an oven. The Tatar woman bent her head and went first. Andrii followed, bending low as he could, in order to pass with his sacks; and both soon found themselves in total darkness.

CHAPTER VI

Andrii could hardly move in the dark and narrow earthen burrow, as he followed the Tatar, dragging after him his sacks of bread. "It will soon be light," said his guide: "we are approaching the spot where I placed a light." And in fact the dark earthen walls began to be gradually lit up. They reached a widening in the passage where, it seemed, there had once been a chapel; at least, there was a small table against the wall, like an altar, and above, the faded, almost entirely obliterated picture of a Catholic Madonna. A small silver lamp hanging before it barely illumined it. The Tatar stooped and picked up from the ground a copper candlestick which she had left there, a candlestick with a tall, slender stem, and snuffers, pin, and extinguisher hanging about it on chains. She lighted it at the silver lamp. The light grew stronger; and as they went on, now illumined by it, and again enveloped in pitchy shadow, they suggested a picture by Gerard Dow.

The warrior's fresh, handsome countenance, overflowing with health and youth, presented a strong contrast to the pale, emaciated face of his companion. The passage grew a little higher, so that Andrii could hold himself erect. He gazed with curiosity at the earthen walls. Here and there, as in the catacombs at Kief, were niches in the walls; and in some places coffins were standing. Sometimes they came across human bones which had become softened with the dampness and were crumbling into dust. It was evident that pious folk had taken refuge here from the storms, sorrows, and seductions of the world. It was extremely damp in some places; indeed there was water under their feet at intervals. Andrii was forced to halt frequently to allow his companion to rest, for her fatigue kept increasing. The small piece of bread she had swallowed only caused a pain in her stomach, of late unused to food; and she often stood motionless for minutes together in one spot.

At length a small iron door appeared before them. "Glory be to God, we have arrived!" said the Tatar in a faint voice, and tried to lift her hand to knock, but had no strength to do so. Andrii knocked hard at the door in her stead. There was an echo as though a large space lay beyond the door; then the echo changed as if resounding through lofty arches. In a couple of minutes, keys rattled, and steps were heard descending some stairs. At length the door opened, and a monk, standing on the narrow stairs with the key and a light in his hands, admitted them. Andrii involuntarily halted at the sight of a Catholic monk--one of those who had aroused such hate and disdain among the Cossacks that they treated them even more inhumanly than they treated the Jews.

The monk, on his part, started back on perceiving a Zaporovian Cossack, but a whisper from the Tatar reassured him. He lighted them in, fastened the door behind them, and led them up the stairs. They found themselves beneath the dark and lofty arches of the monastery church. Before one of the altars, adorned with tall candlesticks and candles, knelt a priest praying quietly. Near him on each side knelt two young choristers in lilac cassocks and white lace stoles, with censers in their hands. He prayed for the performance of a miracle, that the city might be saved; that their souls might be strengthened; that patience might be given them; that doubt and timid, weak-spirited mourning over earthly misfortunes might be banished. A few women, resembling shadows, knelt supporting themselves against the backs of the chairs and dark wooden benches before them, and laying their exhausted heads upon them. A few men stood sadly, leaning against the columns upon which the wide arches rested. The stained-glass window above the altar suddenly glowed with the rosy light of dawn; and from it, on the floor, fell circles of blue, yellow, and other colours, illuminating the dim church. The whole altar was lighted up; the smoke from the censers hung a cloudy rainbow in the air. Andrii gazed from his dark corner, not without surprise, at the wonders worked by the light. At that moment the magnificent swell of the organ filled the whole church. It grew deeper and deeper, expanded, swelled into heavy bursts of thunder; and then all at once, turning into heavenly music, its ringing tones floated high among the arches, like clear maiden voices, and again descended into a deep roar and thunder, and then ceased. The thunderous pulsations echoed long and tremulously among the arches; and Andrii, with half-open mouth, admired the wondrous music.

Then he felt some one plucking the shirt of his caftan. "It is time," said the Tatar. They traversed the church unperceived, and emerged upon the square in front. Dawn had long flushed the heavens; all announced sunrise. The square was empty: in the middle of it still stood wooden pillars, showing that, perhaps only a week before, there had been a market here stocked with provisions. The streets, which were unpaved, were simply a mass of dried mud. The square was surrounded by small, one-storied stone or mud houses, in the walls of which were visible wooden stakes and posts obliquely crossed by carved wooden beams, as was the manner of building in those days. Specimens of it can still be seen in some parts of Lithuania and Poland. They were all covered with enormously high roofs, with a multitude of windows and air-holes. On one side, close to the church, rose a building quite detached from and taller than the rest, probably the town-hall or some official structure. It was two stories high, and above it, on two arches, rose a belvedere where a watchman stood; a huge clock-face was let into the roof.

The square seemed deserted, but Andrii thought he heard a feeble groan. Looking about him, he perceived, on the farther side, a group of two or three men lying motionless upon the ground. He fixed his eyes more intently on them, to see whether they were asleep or dead; and, at the same moment, stumbled over something lying at his feet. It was the dead body of a woman, a Jewess apparently. She appeared to be young, though it was scarcely discernible in her distorted and emaciated features. Upon her head was a red silk kerchief; two rows of pearls or pearl beads adorned the beads of her head-dress, from beneath which two long curls hung down upon her shrivelled neck, with its tightly drawn veins. Beside her lay a child, grasping convulsively at her shrunken breast, and squeezing it with involuntary ferocity at finding no milk there. He neither wept nor screamed, and only his gently rising and falling body would have led one to guess that he was not dead, or at least on the point of breathing his last. They turned into a street, and were suddenly stopped by a madman, who, catching sight of Andrii's precious burden, sprang upon him like a tiger, and clutched him, yelling, "Bread!" But his strength was not equal to his madness. Andrii repulsed him and he fell to the ground. Moved with pity, the young Cossack flung him a loaf, which he seized like a mad dog, gnawing and biting it; but nevertheless he shortly expired in horrible suffering, there in the street, from the effect of long abstinence. The ghastly victims of hunger startled them at every step. Many, apparently unable to endure their torments in their houses, seemed to run into the streets to see whether some nourishing power might not possibly descend from the air. At the gate of one house sat an old woman, and it was impossible to say whether she was asleep or dead, or only unconscious; at all events, she no longer saw or heard anything, and sat immovable in one spot, her head drooping on her breast. From the roof of another house hung a worn and wasted body in a rope noose. The poor fellow could not endure the tortures of hunger to the last, and had preferred to hasten his end by a voluntary death.

At the sight of such terrible proofs of famine, Andrii could not refrain from saying to the Tatar, "Is there really nothing with which they can prolong life? If a man is driven to extremities, he must feed on what he has hitherto despised; he can sustain himself with creatures which are forbidden by the law. Anything can be eaten under such circumstances."

"They have eaten everything," said the Tatar, "all the animals. Not a horse, nor a dog, nor even a mouse is to be found in the whole city. We never had any store of provisions in the town: they were all brought from the villages."

"But how can you, while dying such a fearful death, still dream of defending the city?"

"Possibly the Waiwode might have surrendered; but yesterday morning the commander of the troops at Buzhana sent a hawk into the city with a note saying that it was not to be given up; that he was coming to its rescue with his forces, and was only waiting for another leader, that they might march together. And now they are expected every moment. But we have reached the house."

Andrii had already noticed from a distance this house, unlike the others, and built apparently by some Italian architect. It was constructed of thin red bricks, and had two stories. The windows of the lower story were sheltered under lofty, projecting granite cornices. The upper story consisted entirely of small arches, forming a gallery; between the arches were iron gratings enriched with escutcheons; whilst upon the gables of the house more coats-of-arms were displayed. The broad external staircase, of tinted bricks, abutted on the square. At the foot of it sat guards, who with one hand held their halberds upright, and with the other supported their drooping heads, and in this attitude more resembled apparitions than living beings. They neither slept nor dreamed, but seemed quite insensible to everything; they even paid no attention to who went up the stairs. At the head of the stairs, they found a richly-dressed warrior, armed cap-a-pie, and holding a breviary in his hand. He turned his dim eyes upon them; but the Tatar spoke a word to him, and he dropped them again upon the open pages of his breviary. They entered the first chamber, a large one, serving either as a reception-room, or simply as an ante-room; it was filled with soldiers, servants, secretaries, huntsmen, cup-bearers, and the other servitors indispensable to the support of a Polish magnate's estate, all seated along the walls. The reek of extinguished candles was perceptible; and two were still burning in two huge candlesticks, nearly as tall as a man, standing in the middle of the room, although morning had long since peeped through the wide grated window. Andrii wanted to go straight on to the large oaken door adorned with a coat-of-arms and a profusion of carved ornaments, but the Tatar pulled his sleeve and pointed to a small door in the side wall. Through this they gained a corridor, and then a room, which he began to examine attentively. The light which filtered through a crack in the shutter fell upon several objects--a crimson curtain, a gilded cornice, and a painting on the wall. Here the Tatar motioned to Andrii to wait, and opened the door into another room from which flashed the light of a fire. He heard a whispering, and a soft voice which made him quiver all over. Through the open door he saw flit rapidly past a tall female figure, with a long thick braid of hair falling over her uplifted hands. The Tatar returned and told him to go in.

 He could never understand how he entered and how the door was shut behind him. Two candles burned in the room and a lamp glowed before the images: beneath the lamp stood a tall table with steps to kneel upon during prayer, after the Catholic fashion. But his eye did not seek this. He turned to the other side and perceived a woman, who appeared to have been frozen or turned to stone in the midst of some quick movement. It seemed as though her whole body had sought to spring towards him, and had suddenly paused. And he stood in like manner amazed before her. Not thus had he pictured to himself that he should find her. This was not the same being he had formerly known; nothing about her resembled her former self; but she was twice as beautiful, twice as enchanting, now than she had been then. Then there had been something unfinished, incomplete, about her; now here was a production to which the artist had given the finishing stroke of his brush. That was a charming, giddy girl; this was a woman in the full development of her charms. As she raised her eyes, they were full of feeling, not of mere hints of feeling. The tears were not yet dry in them, and framed them in a shining dew which penetrated the very soul. Her bosom, neck, and arms were moulded in the proportions which mark fully developed loveliness. Her hair, which had in former days waved in light ringlets about her face, had become a heavy, luxuriant mass, a part of which was caught up, while part fell in long, slender curls upon her arms and breast. It seemed as though her every feature had changed. In vain did he seek to discover in them a single one of those which were engraved in his memory--a single one. Even her great pallor did not lessen her wonderful beauty; on the contrary, it conferred upon it an irresistible, inexpressible charm. Andrii felt in his heart a noble timidity, and stood motionless before her. She, too, seemed surprised at the appearance of the Cossack, as he stood before her in all the beauty and might of his young manhood, and in the very immovability of his limbs personified the utmost freedom of movement. His eyes beamed with clear decision; his velvet brows curved in a bold arch; his sunburnt cheeks glowed with all the ardour of youthful fire; and his downy black moustache shone like silk.

"No, I have no power to thank you, noble sir," she said, her silvery voice all in a tremble. "God alone can reward you, not I, a weak woman." She dropped her eyes, her lids fell over them in beautiful, snowy semicircles, guarded by lashes long as arrows; her wondrous face bowed forward, and a delicate flush overspread it from within. Andrii knew not what to say; he wanted to say everything. He had in his mind to say it all ardently as it glowed in his heart--and could not. He felt something confining his mouth; voice and words were lacking; he felt that it was not for him, bred in the seminary and in the tumult of a roaming life, to reply fitly to such language, and was angry with his Cossack nature.

At that moment the Tatar entered the room. She had cut up the bread which the warrior had brought into small pieces on a golden plate, which she placed before her mistress. The lady glanced at her, at the bread, at her again, and then turned her eyes towards Andrii. There was a great deal in those eyes. That gentle glance, expressive of her weakness and her inability to give words to the feeling which overpowered her, was far more comprehensible to Andrii than any words. His heart suddenly grew light within him, all seemed made smooth. The mental emotions and the feelings which up to that moment he had restrained with a heavy curb, as it were, now felt themselves released, at liberty, and anxious to pour themselves out in a resistless torrent of words. Suddenly the lady turned to the Tatar, and said anxiously, "But my mother? you took her some?"

"She is asleep."

"And my father?"

"I carried him some; he said that he would come to thank the young lord in person."

She took the bread and raised it to her mouth. With inexpressible delight Andrii watched her break it with her shining fingers and eat it; but all at once he recalled the man mad with hunger, who had expired before his eyes on swallowing a morsel of bread. He turned pale and, seizing her hand, cried, "Enough! eat no more! you have not eaten for so long that too much bread will be poison to you now." And she at once dropped her hand, laid her bread upon the plate, and gazed into his eyes like a submissive child. And if any words could express-- But neither chisel, nor brush, nor mighty speech is capable of expressing what is sometimes seen in glances of maidens, nor the tender feeling which takes possession of him who receives such maiden glances.

"My queen!" exclaimed Andrii, his heart and soul filled with emotion, "what do you need? what do you wish? command me! Impose on me the most impossible task in all the world: I fly to fulfil it! Tell me to do that which it is beyond the power of man to do: I will fulfil it if I destroy myself. I will ruin myself. And I swear by the holy cross that ruin for your sake is as sweet--but no, it is impossible to say how sweet! I have three farms; half my father's droves of horses are mine; all that my mother brought my father, and which she still conceals from him--all this is mine! Not one of the Cossacks owns such weapons as I; for the pommel of my sword alone they would give their best drove of horses and three thousand sheep. And I renounce all this, I discard it, I throw it aside, I will burn and drown it, if you will but say the word, or even move your delicate black brows! But I know that I am talking madly and wide of the mark; that all this is not fitting here; that it is not for me, who have passed my life in the seminary and among the Zaporozhtzi, to speak as they speak where kings, princes, and all the best of noble knighthood have been. I can see that you are a different being from the rest of us, and far above all other boyars' wives and maiden daughters."

With growing amazement the maiden listened, losing no single word, to the frank, sincere language in which, as in a mirror, the young, strong spirit reflected itself. Each simple word of this speech, uttered in a voice which penetrated straight to the depths of her heart, was clothed in power. She advanced her beautiful face, pushed back her troublesome hair, opened her mouth, and gazed long, with parted lips. Then she tried to say something and suddenly stopped, remembering that the warrior was known by a different name; that his father, brothers, country, lay beyond, grim avengers; that the Zaporozhtzi besieging the city were terrible, and that the cruel death awaited all who were within its walls, and her eyes suddenly filled with tears. She seized a silk embroidered handkerchief and threw it over her face. In a moment it was all wet; and she sat for some time with her beautiful head thrown back, and her snowy teeth set on her lovely under-lip, as though she suddenly felt the sting of a poisonous serpent, without removing the handkerchief from her face, lest he should see her shaken with grief.

"Speak but one word to me," said Andrii, and he took her satin-skinned hand. A sparkling fire coursed through his veins at the touch, and he pressed the hand lying motionless in his.

But she still kept silence, never taking the kerchief from her face, and remaining motionless.

"Why are you so sad? Tell me, why are you so sad?"

She cast away the handkerchief, pushed aside the long hair which fell over her eyes, and poured out her heart in sad speech, in a quiet voice, like the breeze which, rising on a beautiful evening, blows through the thick growth of reeds beside the stream. They rustle, murmur, and give forth delicately mournful sounds, and the traveller, pausing in inexplicable sadness, hears them, and heeds not the fading light, nor the gay songs of the peasants which float in the air as they return from their labours in meadow and stubble-field, nor the distant rumble of the passing waggon.

"Am not I worthy of eternal pity? Is not the mother that bore me unhappy? Is it not a bitter lot which has befallen me? Art not thou a cruel executioner, fate? Thou has brought all to my feet--the highest nobles in the land, the richest gentlemen, counts, foreign barons, all the flower of our knighthood. All loved me, and any one of them would have counted my love the greatest boon. I had but to beckon, and the best of them, the handsomest, the first in beauty and birth would have become my husband. And to none of them didst thou incline my heart, O bitter fate; but thou didst turn it against the noblest heroes of our land, and towards a stranger, towards our enemy. O most holy mother of God! for what sin dost thou so pitilessly, mercilessly, persecute me? In abundance and superfluity of luxury my days were passed, the richest dishes and the sweetest wine were my food. And to what end was it all? What was it all for? In order that I might at last die a death more cruel than that of the meanest beggar in the kingdom? And it was not enough that I should be condemned to so horrible a fate; not enough that before my own end I should behold my father and mother perish in intolerable torment, when I would have willingly given my own life twenty times over to save them; all this was not enough, but before my own death I must hear words of love such as I had never before dreamed of. It was necessary that he should break my heart with his words; that my bitter lot should be rendered still more bitter; that my young life should be made yet more sad; that my death should seem even more terrible; and that, dying, I should reproach thee still more, O cruel fate! and thee--forgive my sin--O holy mother of God!"

As she ceased in despair, her feelings were plainly expressed in her face. Every feature spoke of gnawing sorrow and, from the sadly bowed brow and downcast eyes to the tears trickling down and drying on her softly burning cheeks, seemed to say, "There is no happiness in this face."

"Such a thing was never heard of since the world began. It cannot be," said Andrii, "that the best and most beautiful of women should suffer so bitter a fate, when she was born that all the best there is in the world should bow before her as before a saint. No, you will not die, you shall not die! I swear by my birth and by all there is dear to me in the world that you shall not die. But if it must be so; if nothing, neither strength, nor prayer, nor heroism, will avail to avert this cruel fate--then we will die together, and I will die first. I will die before you, at your beauteous knees, and even in death they shall not divide us."

"Deceive not yourself and me, noble sir," she said, gently shaking her beautiful head; "I know, and to my great sorrow I know but too well, that it is impossible for you to love me. I know what your duty is, and your faith. Your father calls you, your comrades, your country, and we are your enemies."

"And what are my father, my comrades, my country to me?" said Andrii, with a quick movement of his head, and straightening up his figure like a poplar beside the river. "Be that as it may, I have no one, no one!" he repeated, with that movement of the hand with which the Cossack expresses his determination to do some unheard-of deed, impossible to any other man. "Who says that the Ukraine is my country? Who gave it to me for my country? Our country is the one our soul longs for, the one which is dearest of all to us. My country is--you! That is my native land, and I bear that country in my heart. I will bear it there all my life, and I will see whether any of the Cossacks can tear it thence. And I will give everything, barter everything, I will destroy myself, for that country!"

Astounded, she gazed in his eyes for a space, like a beautiful statue, and then suddenly burst out sobbing; and with the wonderful feminine impetuosity which only grand-souled, uncalculating women, created for fine impulses of the heart, are capable of, threw herself upon his neck, encircling it with her wondrous snowy arms, and wept. At that moment indistinct shouts rang through the street, accompanied by the sound of trumpets and kettledrums; but he heard them not. He was only conscious of the beauteous mouth bathing him with its warm, sweet breath, of the tears streaming down his face, and of her long, unbound perfumed hair, veiling him completely in its dark and shining silk.

At that moment the Tatar ran in with a cry of joy. "Saved, saved!" she cried, beside herself. "Our troops have entered the city. They have brought corn, millet, flour, and Zaporozhtzi in chains!" But no one heard that "our troops" had arrived in the city, or what they had brought with them, or how they had bound the Zaporozhtzi. Filled with feelings untasted as yet upon earth, Andrii kissed the sweet mouth which pressed his cheek, and the sweet mouth did not remain unresponsive. In this union of kisses they experienced that which it is given to a man to feel but once on earth.

And the Cossack was ruined. He was lost to Cossack chivalry. Never again will Zaporozhe, nor his father's house, nor the Church of God, behold him. The Ukraine will never more see the bravest of the children who have undertaken to defend her. Old Taras may tear the grey hair from his scalp-lock, and curse the day and hour in which such a son was born to dishonour him.

CHAPTER VII

Noise and movement were rife in the Zaporozhian camp. At first, no one could account for the relieving army having made its way into the city; but it afterwards appeared that the Pereyaslavsky kuren, encamped before the wide gate of the town, had been dead drunk. It was no wonder that half had been killed, and the other half bound, before they knew what it was all about. Meantime the neighbouring kurens, aroused by the tumult, succeeded in grasping their weapons; but the relieving force had already passed through the gate, and its rear ranks fired upon the sleepy and only half-sober Zaporozhtzi who were pressing in disorder upon them, and kept them back.

The Koschevoi ordered a general assembly; and when all stood in a ring and had removed their caps and became quiet, he said: "See what happened last night, brother gentles! See what drunkenness has led to! See what shame the enemy has put upon us! It is evident that, if your allowances are kindly doubled, then you are ready to stretch out at full length, and the enemies of Christ can not only take your very trousers off you, but sneeze in your faces without your hearing them!"

The Cossacks all stood with drooping heads, knowing that they were guilty; only Kukubenko, the hetman of the Nezamisky kuren, answered back. "Stop, father!" said he; "although it is not lawful to make a retort when the Koschevoi speaks before the whole army, yet it is necessary to say that that was not the state of the case. You have not been quite just in your reprimand. The Cossacks would have been guilty, and deserving of death, had they got drunk on the march, or when engaged on heavy toilsome labour during war; but we have been sitting here unoccupied, loitering in vain before the city. There was no fast or other Christian restraint; how then could it be otherwise than that a man should get drunk in idleness? There is no sin in that. But we had better show them what it is to attack innocent people. They first beat us well, and now we will beat them so that not half a dozen of them will ever see home again."

The speech of the hetman of the kuren pleased the Cossacks. They raised their drooping heads upright and many nodded approvingly, muttering, "Kukubenko has spoken well!" And Taras Bulba, who stood not far from the Koschevoi, said: "How now, Koschevoi? Kukubenko has spoken truth. What have you to say to this?"

"What have I to say? I say, Blessed be the father of such a son! It does not need much wisdom to utter words of reproof; but much wisdom is needed to find such words as do not embitter a man's misfortune, but encourage him, restore to him his spirit, put spurs to the horse of his soul, refreshed by water. I meant myself to speak words of comfort to you, but Kukubenko has forestalled me."

"The Koschevoi has also spoken well!" rang through the ranks of the Zaporozhtzi. "His words are good," repeated others. And even the greyheads, who stood there like dark blue doves, nodded their heads and, twitching their grey moustaches, muttered softly, "That was well said."

"Listen now, gentles," continued the Koschevoi. "To take the city, by scaling its walls, or undermining them as the foreign engineers do, is not proper, not Cossack fashion. But, judging from appearances, the enemy entered the city without many provisions; they had not many waggons with them. The people in the city are hungry; they will all eat heartily, and the horses will soon devour the hay. I don't know whether their saints will fling them down anything from heaven with hayforks; God only knows that though there are a great many Catholic priests among them. By one means or another the people will seek to leave the city. Divide yourselves, therefore, into three divisions, and take up your posts before the three gates; five kurens before the principal gate, and three kurens before each of the others. Let the Dadikivsky and Korsunsky kurens go into ambush and

Taras and his men into ambush too. The Titarevsky and Timoschevsky kurens are to guard the baggage train on the right flank, the Scherbinovsky and Steblikivsky on the left, and to select from their ranks the most daring young men to face the foe. The Lyakhs are of a restless nature and cannot endure a siege, and perhaps this very day they will sally forth from the gates. Let each hetman inspect his kuren; those whose ranks are not full are to be recruited from the remains of the Pereyaslavsky kuren. Inspect them all anew. Give a loaf and a beaker to each Cossack to strengthen him. But surely every one must be satiated from last night; for all stuffed themselves so that, to tell the truth, I am only surprised that no one burst in the night. And here is one further command: if any Jew spirit-seller sells a Cossack so much as a single jug of brandy, I will nail pig's ears to his very forehead, the dog, and hang him up by his feet. To work, brothers, to work!"

Thus did the Koschevoi give his orders. All bowed to their girdles, and without putting on their caps set out for their waggons and camps. It was only when they had gone some distance that they covered themselves. All began to equip themselves: they tested their swords, poured powder from the sacks into their powder-flasks, drew up and arranged the waggons, and looked to their horses.

On his way to his band, Taras wondered what had become of Andrii; could he have been captured and found while asleep with the others? But no, Andrii was not the man to go alive into captivity. Yet he was not to be seen among the slaughtered Cossacks. Taras pondered deeply and went past his men without hearing that some one had for some time been calling him by name. "Who wants me?" he said, finally arousing himself from his reflections. Before him stood the Jew, Yankel. "Lord colonel! lord colonel!" said the Jew in a hasty and broken voice, as though desirous of revealing something not utterly useless, "I have been in the city, lord colonel!"

Taras looked at the Jew, and wondered how he had succeeded in getting into the city. "What enemy took you there?"

"I will tell you at once," said Yankel. "As soon as I heard the uproar this morning, when the Cossacks began to fire, I seized my caftan and, without stopping to put it on, ran at the top of my speed, thrusting my arms in on the way, because I wanted to know as soon as possible the cause of the noise and why the Cossacks were firing at dawn. I ran to the very gate of the city, at the moment when the last of the army was passing through. I looked, and in command of the rearguard was Cornet Galyandovitch. He is a man well known to me; he has owed me a hundred ducats these three years past. I ran after him, as though to claim the debt of him, and so entered the city with them."

"You entered the city, and wanted him to settle the debt!" said Bulba; "and he did not order you to be hung like a dog on the spot?"

"By heavens, he did want to hang me," replied the Jew; "his servants had already seized me and thrown a rope about my neck. But I besought the noble lord, and said that I would wait for the money as long as his lordship liked, and promised to lend him more if he would only help me to collect my debts from the other nobles; for I can tell my lord that the noble cornet had not a ducat in his pocket, although he has farms and estates and four castles and steppe-land that extends clear to Schklof; but he has not a penny, any more than a Cossack. If the Breslau Jews had not equipped him, he would never have gone on this campaign. That was the reason he did not go to the Diet."

"What did you do in the city? Did you see any of our people?"

"Certainly, there are many of them there: Itzok, Rachum, Samuel, Khaivalkh, Evrei the pawnbroker--"

"May they die, the dogs!" shouted Taras in a rage. "Why do you name your Jewish tribe to me? I ask you about our Zaporozhtzi."

"I saw none of our Zaporozhtzi; I saw only Lord Andrii."

"You saw Andrii!" shouted Bulba. "What is he doing? Where did you see him? In a dungeon? in a pit? dishonoured? bound?"

"Who would dare to bind Lord Andrii? now he is so grand a knight. I hardly recognised him. Gold on his shoulders and his belt, gold everywhere about him; as the sun shines in spring, when every bird twitters and sings in the orchard, so he shines, all gold. And his horse, which the Waiwode himself gave him, is the very best; that horse alone is worth two hundred ducats."

Bulba was petrified. "Why has he put on foreign garments?"

"He put them on because they were finer. And he rides about, and the others ride about, and he teaches them, and they teach him; like the very grandest Polish noble."

"Who forced him to do this?"

"I should not say that he had been forced. Does not my lord know that he went over to them of his own free will?"

"Who went over?"

"Lord Andrii."

"Went where?"

"Went over to their side; he is now a thorough foreigner."

"You lie, you hog's ear!"

"How is it possible that I should lie? Am I a fool, that I should lie? Would I lie at the risk of my head? Do not I know that Jews are hung like dogs if they lie to nobles?"

"Then it means, according to you, he has betrayed his native land and his faith?"

"I do not say that he has betrayed anything; I merely said that he had gone over to the other side."

"You lie, you imp of a Jew! Such a deed was never known in a Christian land. You are making a mistake, dog!"

"May the grass grow upon the threshold of my house if I am mistaken! May every one spit upon the grave of my father, my mother, my father's father, and my mother's father, if I am mistaken! If my lord wished I can even tell him why he went over to them."

"Why?"

"The Waiwode has a beautiful daughter. Holy Father! what a beauty!" Here the Jew tried his utmost to express beauty by extending his hands, screwing up his eyes, and twisting his mouth to one side as though tasting something on trial.

"Well, what of that?"

"He did it all for her, he went there for her sake. When a man is in love, then all things are the same to him; like the sole of a shoe which you can bend in any direction if you soak it in water."

Bulba reflected deeply. He remembered the power of weak woman--how she had ruined many a strong man, and that this was the weak point in Andrii's nature--and stood for some time in one spot, as though rooted there. "Listen, my lord, I will tell my lord all," said the Jew. "As soon as I heard the uproar, and saw them going through the city gate, I seized a string of pearls, in case of any emergency. For there are beauties and noble-women there; 'and if there are beauties and noble-women,' I said to myself, 'they will buy pearls, even if they have nothing to eat.' And, as soon as ever the cornet's servants had set me at liberty, I hastened to the Waiwode's residence to sell my pearls. I asked all manner of questions of the lady's Tatar maid; the wedding is to take place immediately, as soon as they have driven off the Zaporozhtzi. Lord Andrii has promised to drive off the Zaporovians."

"And you did not kill him on the spot, you devil's brat?" shouted Bulba.

"Why should I kill him? He went over of his own free will. What is his crime? He liked it better there, so he went there."

"And you saw him face to face?"

"Face to face, by heavens! such a magnificent warrior! more splendid than all the rest. God bless him, he knew me, and when I approached him he said at once--"

"What did he say?"

"He said-- First he beckoned me with his finger, and then he said, 'Yankel!' Lord Andrii said, 'Yankel, tell my father, tell my brother, tell all the Cossacks, all the Zaporozhtzi, everybody, that my father is no longer my father, nor my brother my brother, nor my comrades my comrades; and that I will fight them all, all.'"

"You lie, imp of a Jew!" shouted Taras, beside himself. "You lie, dog! I will kill you, Satan! Get away from here! if not, death awaits you!" So saying, Taras drew his sword.

The terrified Jew set off instantly, at the full speed of his thin, shrunken legs. He ran for a long time, without looking back, through the Cossack camp, and then far out on the deserted plain, although Taras did not chase him at all, reasoning that it was foolish to thus vent his rage on the first person who presented himself.

Then he recollected that he had seen Andrii on the previous night traversing the camp with some woman, and he bowed his grey head. Still he would not believe that so disgraceful a thing could have happened, and that his own son had betrayed his faith and soul.

Finally he placed his men in ambush in a wood--the only one which had not been burned by the Cossacks--whilst the Zaporozhians, foot and horse, set out for the three gates by three different roads. One after another the kurens turned out: Oumansky, Popovichesky, Kanevsky, Steblikovsky, Nezamaikovsky, Gurgazif, Titarevsky, Tomischevsky. The Pereyaslavsky kuren alone was wanting. Its Cossacks had smoked and drank to their destruction. Some awoke to find themselves bound in the enemy's hands; others never woke at all but passed in their sleep into the damp earth; and the hetman Khlib himself, minus his trousers and accoutrements, found himself in the camp of the Lyakhs.

The uproar among the Zaporozhtzi was heard in the city. All the besieged hastened to the ramparts, and a lively scene was presented to the Cossacks. The handsome Polish heroes thronged on the wall. The brazen helmets of some shone like the sun, and were adorned with feathers white as swans. Others wore pink and blue caps, drooping over one ear, and caftans with the sleeves thrown back, embroidered with gold. Their weapons were richly mounted and very costly, as were their equipments. In the front rank the Budzhakovsky colonel stood proudly in his red cap ornamented with gold. He was a tall, stout man, and his rich and ample caftan hardly covered him. Near the side gate stood another colonel. He was a dried-up little man, but his small, piercing eyes gleamed sharply from under his thick and shaggy brows, and as he turned quickly on all sides, motioning boldly with his thin, withered hand, and giving out his orders, it was evident that, in spite of his little body, he understood military science thoroughly. Not far from him stood a very tall cornet, with thick moustaches and a highly-coloured complexion--a noble fond of strong mead and hearty revelry. Behind them were many nobles who had equipped themselves, some with their own ducats, some from the royal treasury, some with money obtained from the Jews, by pawning everything they found in their ancestral castles. Many too were parasites, whom the senators took with them to dinners for show, and who stole silver cups from the table and the sideboard, and when the day's display was over mounted some noble's coach-box and drove his horses. There were folk of all kinds there. Sometimes they had not enough to drink, but all were equipped for war.

The Cossack ranks stood quietly before the walls. There was no gold about them, save where it shone on the hilt of a sword or the mountings of a gun. The Zaporozhtzi were not given to decking themselves out gaily for battle: their coats-of-mail and garments were plain, and their black-bordered red-crowned caps showed darkly in the distance.

Two men--Okhrim Nasch and Mikiga Golokopuitenko--advanced from the Zaporozhian ranks. One was quite young, the other older; both fierce in words, and not bad specimens of Cossacks in action. They were followed by Demid Popovitch, a strongly built Cossack who had been hanging about the Setch for a long time, after having been in Adrianople and undergoing a great deal in the course of his life. He had been burned, and had escaped to the Setch with blackened head and singed moustaches. But Popovitch recovered, let his hair grow, raised moustaches thick and black as pitch, and was a stout fellow, according to his own biting speech.

"Red jackets on all the army, but I should like to know what sort of men are under them," he cried.

"I will show you," shouted the stout colonel from above. "I will capture the whole of you. Surrender your guns and horses, slaves. Did you see how I caught your men?--Bring out a Zaporozhetz on the wall for them to see."

And they let out a Zaporozhetz bound with stout cords.

Before them stood Khlib, the hetman of the Pereyaslavsky kuren, without his trousers or accoutrements, just as they had captured him in his drunken sleep. He bowed his head in shame before the Cossacks at his nakedness, and at having been thus taken like a dog, while asleep. His hair had turned grey in one night.

"Grieve not, Khlib: we will rescue you," shouted the Cossacks from below.

"Grieve not, friend," cried the hetman Borodaty. "It is not your fault that they caught you naked: that misfortune might happen to any man. But it is a disgrace to them that they should have exposed you to dishonour, and not covered your nakedness decently."

"You seem to be a brave army when you have people who are asleep to fight," remarked Golokopuitenko, glancing at the ramparts.

"Wait a bit, we'll singe your top-knots for you!" was the reply.

"I should like to see them singe our scalp locks!" said Popovitch, prancing about before them on his horse; and then, glancing at his comrades, he added, "Well, perhaps the Lyakhs speak the truth: if that fat-bellied fellow leads them, they will all find a good shelter."

"Why do you think they will find a good shelter?" asked the Cossacks, knowing that Popovitch was probably preparing some repartee.

"Because the whole army will hide behind him; and the devil himself couldn't help you to reach any one with your spear through that belly of his!"

The Cossacks laughed, some of them shaking their heads and saying, "What a fellow Popovitch is for a joke! but now--" But the Cossacks had not time to explain what they meant by that "now."

"Fall back, fall back quickly from the wall!" shouted the Koschevoi, seeing that the Lyakhs could not endure these biting words, and that the colonel was waving his hand.

The Cossacks had hardly retreated from the wall before the grape-shot rained down. On the ramparts all was excitement, and the grey-haired Waiwode himself appeared on horseback. The gates opened and the garrison sallied forth. In the van came hussars in orderly ranks, behind them the horsemen in armour, and then the heroes in brazen helmets; after whom rode singly the highest nobility, each man accoutred as he pleased. These haughty nobles would not mingle in the ranks with others, and such of them as had no commands rode apart with their own immediate following. Next came some more companies, and after these the cornet, then more files of men, and the stout colonel; and in the rear of the whole force the little colonel.

"Keep them from forming in line!" shouted the Koschevoi; "let all the kurens attack them at once! Block the other gate! Titarevsky kuren, fall on one flank! Dyadovsky kuren, charge on the other! Attack them in the rear, Kukubenko and Palivod! Check them, break them!" The Cossacks attacked on all sides, throwing the Lyakhs into confusion and getting confused themselves. They did not even give the foe time to fire, it came to swords and spears at once. All fought hand to hand, and each man had an opportunity to distinguish himself.

Demid Popovitch speared three soldiers, and struck two of the highest nobles from their saddles, saying, "Good horses! I have long wanted just such horses." And he drove the horses far afield, shouting to the Cossacks standing about to catch them. Then he rushed again into the fray, fell upon the dismounted nobles, slew one, and throwing his lasso round the neck of the other, tied him to his saddle and dragged him over the plain, after having taken from him his sword from its rich hilt and removed from his girdle a whole bag of ducats.

Kobita, a good Cossack, though still very young, attacked one of the bravest men in the Polish army, and they fought long together. They grappled, and the Cossack mastering his foe, and throwing him down, stabbed him in the breast with his sharp Turkish knife. But he did not look out for himself, and a bullet struck him on the temple. The man who struck him down was the most distinguished of the nobles, the handsomest scion of an ancient and princely race. Like a stately poplar, he bestrode his dun-coloured steed, and many heroic deeds did he perform. He cut two Cossacks in twain. Fedor Korzh, the brave Cossack, he overthrew together with his horse, shooting the steed and picking off the rider with his spear. Many heads and hands did he hew off; and slew Kobita by sending a bullet through his temple.

"There's a man I should like to measure strength with!" shouted Kukubenko, the hetman of the Nezamaikovsky kuren. Spurring his horse, he dashed straight at the Pole's back, shouting loudly, so that all who stood near shuddered at the unearthly yell. The boyard tried to wheel his horse suddenly and face him, but his horse would not obey him; scared by the terrible cry, it bounded aside, and the Lyakh received Kukubenko's fire. The ball struck him in the shoulder-blade, and he rolled from his saddle. Even then he did not surrender and strove to deal his enemy a blow, but his hand was weak. Kukubenko, taking his heavy sword in both hands, thrust it through his mouth. The sword, breaking out two teeth, cut the tongue in twain, pierced the windpipe, and penetrated deep into the earth, nailing him to the ground. His noble blood, red as viburnum berries beside the river, welled forth in a stream staining his yellow, gold-embroidered caftan. But Kukubenko had already left him, and was forcing his way, with his Nezamaikovsky kuren, towards another group.

"He has left untouched rich plunder," said Borodaty, hetman of the Oumansky kuren, leaving his men and going to the place where the nobleman killed by Kukubenko lay. "I have killed seven nobles with my own hand, but such spoil I never beheld on any one." Prompted by greed, Borodaty bent down to strip off the rich armour, and had already secured the Turkish knife set with precious stones, and taken from the foe's belt a purse of ducats, and from his breast a silver case containing a maiden's curl, cherished tenderly as a love-token. But he heeded not how the red-faced cornet, whom he had already once hurled from the saddle and given a good blow as a remembrance, flew upon him from behind. The cornet swung his arm with all his might, and brought his sword down upon Borodaty's bent neck. Greed led to no good: the head rolled off, and the body fell headless, sprinkling the earth with blood far and wide; whilst the Cossack soul ascended, indignant and surprised at having so soon quitted so stout a frame. The cornet had not succeeded in seizing the hetman's head by its scalp-lock, and fastening it to his saddle, before an avenger had arrived.

As a hawk floating in the sky, sweeping in great circles with his mighty wings, suddenly remains poised in air, in one spot, and thence darts down like an arrow upon the shrieking quail, so Taras's son Ostap darted suddenly upon the cornet and flung a rope about his neck with one cast. The cornet's red face became a still deeper purple as the cruel noose compressed his throat, and he tried to use his pistol; but his convulsively quivering hand could not aim straight, and the bullet flew wild across the plain. Ostap immediately unfastened a silken cord which the cornet carried at his saddle bow to bind prisoners, and having with it bound him hand and foot, attached the cord to his saddle and dragged him across the field, calling on all the Cossacks of the Oumansky kuren to come and render the last honours to their hetman.

When the Oumantzi heard that the hetman of their kuren, Borodaty, was no longer among the living, they deserted the field of battle, rushed to secure his body, and consulted at once as to whom they should select as their leader. At length they said, "But why consult? It is impossible to find a better leader than Bulba's son, Ostap; he is younger than all the rest of us, it is true; but his judgment is equal to that of the eldest."

Ostap, taking off his cap, thanked his comrades for the honour, and did not decline it on the ground of youth or inexperience, knowing that war time is no fitting season for that; but instantly ordered them straight to the fray, and soon showed them that not in vain had they chosen him as hetman. The Lyakhs felt that the matter was growing too hot for them, and retreated across the plain in order to form again at its other end. But the little colonel signalled to the reserve of four hundred, stationed at the gate, and these rained shot upon the Cossacks. To little purpose, however, their shot only taking effect on the Cossack oxen, which were gazing wildly upon the battle. The frightened oxen, bellowing with fear, dashed into the camp, breaking the line of waggons and trampling on many. But Taras, emerging from ambush at the moment with his troops, headed off the infuriated cattle, which, startled by his yell, swooped down upon the Polish troops, overthrew the cavalry, and crushed and dispersed them all.

"Thank you, oxen!" cried the Zaporozhtzi; "you served us on the march, and now you serve us in war." And they attacked the foe with fresh vigour killing many of the enemy. Several distinguished themselves--Metelitza and Schilo, both of the Pisarenki, Vovtuzenko, and many others. The Lyakhs seeing that matters were going badly for them flung away their banners and shouted for the city gates to be opened. With a screeching sound the iron-bound gates swung open and received the weary and dust-covered riders, flocking like sheep into a fold. Many of the Zaporozhtzi would have pursued them, but Ostap stopped his Oumantzi, saying, "Farther, farther from the walls, brother gentles! it is not well to approach them too closely." He spoke truly; for from the ramparts the foe rained and poured down everything which came to hand, and many were struck. At that moment the Koschevoi came up and congratulated him, saying, "Here is the new hetman leading the army like an old one!" Old Bulba glanced round to see the new hetman, and beheld Ostap sitting on his horse at the head of the Oumantzi, his cap on one side and the hetman's staff in his hand. "Who ever saw the like!" he exclaimed; and the old man rejoiced, and began to thank all the Oumantzi for the honour they had conferred upon his son.

The Cossacks retired, preparing to go into camp; but the Lyakhs showed themselves again on the city ramparts with tattered mantles. Many rich caftans were spotted with blood, and dust covered the brazen helmets.

"Have you bound us?" cried the Zaporozhtzi to them from below.

"We will do so!" shouted the big colonel from above, showing them a rope. The weary, dust-covered warriors ceased not to threaten, nor the most zealous on both sides to exchange fierce remarks.

At length all dispersed. Some, weary with battle, stretched themselves out to rest; others sprinkled their wounds with earth, and bound them with kerchiefs and rich stuffs captured from the enemy. Others, who were fresher, began to inspect the corpses and to pay them the last honours. They dug graves with swords and spears, brought earth in their caps and the skirts of their garments, laid the Cossacks' bodies out decently, and covered them up in order that the ravens and eagles might not claw out their eyes. But binding the bodies of the Lyakhs, as they came to hand, to the tails of horses, they let these loose on the plain, pursuing them and beating them for some time. The infuriated horses flew over hill and hollow, through ditch and brook, dragging the bodies of the Poles, all covered with blood and dust, along the ground.

All the kurens sat down in circles in the evening, and talked for a long time of their deeds, and of the achievements which had fallen to the share of each, for repetition by strangers and posterity. It was long before they lay down to sleep; and longer still before old Taras, meditating what it might signify that Andrii was not among the foe, lay down. Had the Judas been ashamed to come forth against his own countrymen? or had the Jew been deceiving him, and had he simply gone into the city against his will? But then he recollected that there were no bounds to a woman's influence upon Andrii's heart; he felt ashamed, and swore a mighty oath to himself against the fair Pole who had bewitched his son. And he would have kept his oath. He would not have looked at her beauty; he would have dragged her forth by her thick and splendid hair; he would have trailed her after him over all the plain, among all the Cossacks. Her beautiful shoulders and bosom, white as fresh-fallen snow upon the mountain-tops, would have been crushed to earth and covered with blood and dust. Her lovely body would have been torn to pieces. But Taras, who did not foresee what God prepares for man on the morrow, began to grow drowsy, and finally fell asleep. The Cossacks still talked among themselves; and the sober sentinel stood all night long beside the fire without blinking and keeping a good look out on all sides.

CHAPTER VIII

The sun had not ascended midway in the heavens when all the army assembled in a group. News had come from the Setch that during the

Cossacks' absence the Tatars had plundered it completely, unearthed the treasures which were kept concealed in the ground, killed or carried into captivity all who had remained behind, and straightway set out, with all the flocks and droves of horses they had collected, for Perekop. One Cossack only, Maksin Galodukha, had broken loose from the Tatars' hands, stabbed the Mirza, seized his bag of sequins, and on a Tatar horse, in Tatar garments, had fled from his pursuers for two nights and a day and a half, ridden his horse to death, obtained another, killed that one too, and arrived at the Zaporozhian camp upon a third, having learned upon the road that the Zaporozhtzi were before Dubno. He could only manage to tell them that this misfortune had taken place; but as to how it happened--whether the remaining Zaporozhtzi had been carousing after Cossack fashion, and had been carried drunk into captivity, and how the Tatars were aware of the spot where the treasures of the army were concealed--he was too exhausted to say. Extremely fatigued, his body swollen, and his face scorched and weatherbeaten, he had fallen down, and a deep sleep had overpowered him.

In such cases it was customary for the Cossacks to pursue the robbers at once, endeavouring to overtake them on the road; for, let the prisoners once be got to the bazaars of Asia Minor, Smyrna, or the island of Crete, and God knows in what places the tufted heads of Zaporozhtzi might not be seen. This was the occasion of the Cossacks' assembling. They all stood to a man with their caps on; for they had not met to listen to the commands of their hetman, but to take counsel together as equals among equals. "Let the old men first advise," was shouted to the crowd. "Let the Koschevoi give his opinion," cried others.

The Koschevoi, taking off his cap and speaking not as commander, but as a comrade among comrades, thanked all the Cossacks for the honour, and said, "There are among us many experienced men and much wisdom; but since you have thought me worthy, my counsel is not to lose time in pursuing the Tatars, for you know yourselves what the Tatar is. He will not pause with his stolen booty to await our coming, but will vanish in a twinkling, so that you can find no trace of him. Therefore my advice is to go. We have had good sport here. The Lyakhs now know what Cossacks are. We have avenged our faith to the extent of our ability; there is not much to satisfy greed in the famished city, and so my advice is to go."

"To go," rang heavily through the Zaporozhian kurens. But such words did not suit Taras Bulba at all; and he brought his frowning, iron-grey brows still lower down over his eyes, brows like bushes growing on dark mountain heights, whose crowns are suddenly covered with sharp northern frost.

"No, Koschevoi, your counsel is not good," said he. "You cannot say that. You have evidently forgotten that those of our men captured by the Lyakhs will remain prisoners. You evidently wish that we should not heed the first holy law of comradeship; that we should leave our brethren to be flayed alive, or carried about through the towns and villages after their Cossack bodies have been quartered, as was done with the hetman and the bravest Russian warriors in the Ukraine. Have the enemy not desecrated the holy things sufficiently without that? What are we? I ask you all what sort of a Cossack is he who would desert his comrade in misfortune, and let him perish like a dog in a foreign land? If it has come to such a pass that no one has any confidence in Cossack honour, permitting men to spit upon his grey moustache, and upbraid him with offensive words, then let no one blame me; I will remain here alone."

All the Zaporozhtzi who were there wavered.

"And have you forgotten, brave comrades," said the Koschevoi, "that the Tatars also have comrades of ours in their hands; that if we do not rescue them now their lives will be sacrificed in eternal imprisonment among the infidels, which is worse than the most cruel death? Have you forgotten that they now hold all our treasure, won by Christian blood?"

The Cossacks reflected, not knowing what to say. None of them wished to deserve ill repute. Then there stepped out in front of them the oldest in years of all the Zaporozhian army, Kasyan Bovdug. He was respected by all the Cossacks. Twice had he been chosen Koschevoi, and had also been a stout warrior; but he had long been old, and had ceased to go upon raids. Neither did the old man like to give advice to any one; but loved to lie upon his side in the circle of Cossacks, listening to tales of every occurrence on the Cossack marches. He never joined in the conversation, but only listened, and pressed the ashes with his finger in his short pipe, which never left his mouth; and would sit so long with his eyes half open, that the Cossacks never knew whether he were asleep or still listening. He always stayed at home during their raids, but this time the old man had joined the army. He had waved his hand in Cossack fashion, and said, "Wherever you go, I am going too; perhaps I may be of some service to the Cossack nation." All the Cossacks became silent when he now stepped forward before the assembly, for it was long since any speech from him had been heard. Every one wanted to know what Bovdug had to say.

"It is my turn to speak a word, brother gentles," he began: "listen, my children, to an old man. The Koschevoi spoke well as the head of the Cossack army; being bound to protect it, and in respect to the treasures of the army he could say nothing wiser. That is so! Let that be my first remark; but now listen to my second. And this is my second remark: Taras spoke even more truly. God grant him many years, and that such leaders may be plentiful in the Ukraine! A Cossack's first duty and honour is to guard comradeship. Never in all my life, brother gentles, have I heard of any Cossack deserting or betraying any of his comrades. Both those made captive at the Setch and these taken here are our comrades. Whether they be few or many, it makes no difference; all are our comrades, and all are dear to us. So this is my speech: Let those to whom the prisoners captured by the Tatars are dear set out after the Tatars; and let those to whom the captives of the Poles are dear, and who do not care to desert a righteous cause, stay behind. The Koschevoi, in accordance with his duty, will accompany one half in pursuit of the Tatars, and the other half can choose a hetman to lead them. But if you will heed the words of an old man, there is no man fitter to be the commanding hetman than Taras Bulba. Not one of us is his equal in heroism."

Thus spoke Bovdug, and paused; and all the Cossacks rejoiced that the old man had in this manner brought them to an agreement. All flung up their caps and shouted, "Thanks, father! He kept silence for a long, long time, but he has spoken at last. Not in vain did he say, when we prepared for this expedition, that he might be useful to the Cossack nation: even so it has come to pass!"

"Well, are you agreed upon anything?" asked the Koschevoi.

"We are all agreed!" cried the Cossacks.

"Then the council is at an end?"

"At an end!" cried the Cossacks.

"Then listen to the military command, children," said the Koschevoi, stepping forward, and putting on his cap; whilst all the Cossacks took off theirs, and stood with uncovered heads, and with eyes fixed upon the earth, as was always the custom among them when the leader prepared to speak. "Now divide yourselves, brother gentles! Let those who wish to go stand on the right, and those who wish to stay, on the left. Where the majority of a kuren goes there its officers are to go: if the minority of a kuren goes over, it must be added to another kuren."

Then they began to take up their positions, some to the right and some to the left. Whither the majority of a kuren went thither the hetman went also; and the minority attached itself to another kuren. It came out pretty even on both sides. Those who wished to remain were nearly the whole of the Nezamaikovsky kuren, the entire Oumansky kuren, the entire Kanevsky kuren, and the larger half of the Popovitchsky, the Timoschevsky and the Steblikivsky kurens. All the rest preferred to go in pursuit of the Tatars. On both sides there were many stout and brave Cossacks. Among those who decided to follow the Tatars were Tcherevaty, and those good old Cossacks Pokotipole, Lemisch, and Prokopovitch Koma. Demid Popovitch also went with that party, because he could not sit long in one place: he had tried his hand on the Lyakhs and wanted to try it on the Tatars also. The hetmans of kurens were Nostiugan, Pokruischka, Nevnimsky, and numerous brave and renowned Cossacks who wished to test their swords and muscles in an encounter with the Tatars. There were likewise many brave Cossacks among those who preferred to remain, including the kuren hetmans, Demitrovitch, Kukubenko, Vertikhvist, Balan, and Ostap Bulba. Besides these there were plenty of stout and distinguished warriors: Vovtuzenko, Tcherevitchenko, Stepan Guska, Okhrim Guska, Vikola Gonstiy, Zadorozhniy, Metelitza, Ivan Zakrutiguba, Mosiy Pisarenko, and still another Pisarenko, and many others. They were all great travellers; they had visited the shores of Anatolia, the salt marshes and steppes of the Crimea, all the rivers great and small which empty into the Dnieper, and all the fords and islands of the Dnieper; they had been in Moldavia, Wallachia, and Turkey; they had sailed all over the Black Sea, in their double-ruddered Cossack boats; they had attacked with fifty skiffs in line the tallest and richest ships; they had sunk many a Turkish galley, and had burnt much, very much powder in their day; more than once they had made foot-bandages from velvets and rich stuffs; more than once they had beaten buckles for their girdles out of sequins. Every one of them had drunk and revelled away what would have sufficed any other for a whole lifetime, and had nothing to show for it. They spent it all, like Cossacks, in treating all the world, and in hiring music that every one might be merry. Even now few of them had amassed any property: some caskets, cups, and bracelets were hidden beneath the reeds on the islands of the Dnieper in order that the Tatars might not find them if by mishap they should succeed in falling suddenly on the Setch; but it would have been difficult for the Tatars to find them, for the owners themselves had forgotten where they had buried them. Such were the Cossacks who wished to remain and take vengeance on the Lyakhs for their trusty comrades and the faith of Christ. The old Cossack Bovdug wished also to remain with them, saying, "I am not of an age to pursue the Tatars, but this is a place to meet a good Cossack death. I have long prayed God that when my life was to end I might end it in battle for a holy and Christian cause. And so it has come to pass. There can be no more glorious end in any other place for the aged Cossack."

When they had all separated, and were ranged in two lines on opposite sides, the Koschevoi passed through the ranks, and said, "Well, brother gentles, are the two parties satisfied with each other?"

"All satisfied, father!" replied the Cossacks.

"Then kiss each other, and bid each other farewell; for God knows whether you will ever see each other alive again. Obey your hetman, but you know yourselves what you have to do: you know yourselves what Cossack honour requires."

And all the Cossacks kissed each other. The hetmans first began it. Stroking down their grey moustaches, they kissed each other, making the sign of the cross, and then, grasping hands firmly, wanted to ask of each other, "Well, brother, shall we see one another again or not?" But they did not ask the question: they kept silence, and both grey-heads were lost in thought. Then the Cossacks took leave of each other to the last man, knowing that there was a great deal of work before them all. Yet they were not obliged to part at once: they would have to wait until night in order not to let the Lyakhs perceive the diminution in the Cossack army. Then all went off, by kurens, to dine.

After dinner, all who had the prospect of the journey before them lay down to rest, and fell into a deep and long sleep, as though foreseeing that it was the last sleep they should enjoy in such security. They slept even until sunset; and when the sun had gone down and it had grown somewhat dusky, began to tar the waggons. All being in readiness, they sent the waggons ahead, and having pulled off their caps once more to their comrades, quietly followed the baggage train. The cavalry, without shouts or whistles to the horses, tramped lightly after the foot-soldiers, and all soon vanished in the darkness. The only sound was the dull thud of horses' hoofs, or the squeak of some wheel which had not got into working order, or had not been properly tarred amid the darkness.

Their comrades stood for some time waving their hands, though nothing was visible. But when they returned to their camping places and saw by the light of the gleaming stars that half the waggons were gone, and many of their comrades, each man's heart grew sad; all became involuntarily pensive, and drooped their heads towards the earth.

Taras saw how troubled were the Cossack ranks, and that sadness, unsuited to brave men, had begun to quietly master the Cossack hearts; but he remained silent. He wished to give them time to become accustomed to the melancholy caused by their parting from their comrades; but, meanwhile, he was preparing to rouse them at one blow, by a loud battle-cry in Cossack fashion, in order that good cheer might return to the soul of each with greater strength than before. Of this only the Slav nature, a broad, powerful nature, which is to others what the sea is to small rivulets, is capable. In stormy times it roars and thunders, raging, and raising such waves as weak rivers cannot throw up; but when it is windless and quiet, it spreads its boundless glassy surface, clearer than any river, a constant delight to the eye.

Taras ordered his servants to unload one of the waggons which stood apart. It was larger and stronger than any other in the Cossack camp; two stout tires encircled its mighty wheels. It was heavily laden, covered with horsecloths and strong wolf-skins, and firmly bound with tightly drawn tarred ropes. In the waggon were flasks and casks of good old wine, which had long lain in Taras's cellar. He had brought it along, in case a moment should arrive when some deed awaited them worthy of being handed down to posterity, so that each Cossack, to the very last man, might quaff it, and be inspired with sentiments fitting to the occasion. On receiving his command, the servants hastened to the waggon, hewed asunder the stout ropes with their swords, removed the thick wolf-skins and horsecloths, and drew forth the flasks and casks.

"Take them all," said Bulba, "all there are; take them, that every one may be supplied. Take jugs, or the pails for watering the horses; take sleeve or cap; but if you have nothing else, then hold your two hands under."

All the Cossacks seized something: one took a jug, another a pail, another a sleeve, another a cap, and another held both hands. Taras's servants, making their way among the ranks, poured out for all from the casks and flasks. But Taras ordered them not to drink until he should give the signal for all to drink together. It was evident that he wished to say something. He knew that however good in itself the wine might be and however fitted to strengthen the spirit of man, yet, if a suitable speech were linked with it, then the strength of the wine and of the spirit would be doubled.

"I treat you, brother gentles," thus spoke Bulba, "not in honour of your having made me hetman, however great such an honour may be, nor in honour of our parting from our comrades. To do both would be fitting at a fitting time; but the moment before us is not such a time. The work before us is great both in labour and in glory for the Cossacks. Therefore let us drink all together, let us drink before all else to the holy orthodox faith, that the day may finally come when it may be spread over all the world, and that everywhere there may be but one faith, and that all Mussulmans may become Christians. And let us also drink together to the Setch, that it may stand long for the ruin of the Mussulmans, and that every year there may issue forth from it young men, each better, each handsomer than the other. And let us drink to our own glory, that our grandsons and their sons may say that there were once men who were not ashamed of comradeship, and who never betrayed each other. Now to the faith, brother gentles, to the faith!"

"To the faith!" cried those standing in the ranks hard by, with thick voices. "To the faith!" those more distant took up the cry; and all, both young and old, drank to the faith.

"To the Setch!" said Taras, raising his hand high above his head.

"To the Setch!" echoed the foremost ranks. "To the Setch!" said the old men, softly, twitching their grey moustaches; and eagerly as young hawks, the youths repeated, "To the Setch!" And the distant plain heard how the Cossacks mentioned their Setch.

"Now a last draught, comrades, to the glory of all Christians now living in the world!"

And every Cossack drank a last draught to the glory of all Christians in the world. And among all the ranks in the kurens they long repeated, "To all the Christians in the world!"

The pails were empty, but the Cossacks still stood with their hands uplifted. Although the eyes of all gleamed brightly with the wine, they were thinking deeply. Not of greed or the spoils of war were they thinking now, nor of who would be lucky enough to get ducats, fine weapons, embroidered caftans, and Tcherkessian horses; but they meditated like eagles perched upon the rocky crests of mountains, from which the distant sea is visible, dotted, as with tiny birds, with galleys, ships, and every sort of vessel, bounded only by the scarcely visible lines of shore, with their ports like gnats and their forests like fine grass. Like eagles they gazed out on all the plain, with their fate darkling in the distance. All the plain, with its slopes and roads, will be covered with their white projecting bones, lavishly washed with their Cossack blood, and strewn with shattered waggons and with broken swords and spears; the eagles will swoop down and tear out their Cossack eyes. But there is one grand advantage: not a single noble deed will be lost, and the Cossack glory will not vanish like the tiniest grain of powder from a gun-barrel. The guitar-player with grey beard falling upon his breast, and perhaps a white-headed old man still full of ripe, manly strength will come, and will speak his low, strong words of them. And their glory will resound through all the world, and all who are born thereafter will speak of them; for the word of power is carried afar, ringing like a booming brazen bell, in which the maker has mingled much rich, pure silver, that is beautiful sound may be borne far and wide through the cities, villages, huts, and palaces, summoning all betimes to holy prayer.

CHAPTER IX

In the city, no one knew that one-half of the Cossacks had gone in pursuit of the Tatars. From the tower of the town hall the sentinel only perceived that a part of the waggons had been dragged into the forest; but it was thought that the Cossacks were preparing an ambush--a view taken by the French engineer also. Meanwhile, the Koschevoi's words proved not unfounded, for a scarcity of provisions arose in the city. According to a custom of past centuries, the army did not separate as much as was necessary. They tried to make a sortie; but half of those who did so were instantly killed by the Cossacks, and the other half driven back into the city with no results. But the Jews availed themselves of the opportunity to find out everything; whither and why the Zaporozhtzi had departed, and with what leaders, and which particular kurens, and their number, and how many had remained on the spot, and what they intended to do; in short, within a few minutes all was known in the city.

The besieged took courage, and prepared to offer battle. Taras had already divined it from the noise and movement in the city, and hastened about, making his arrangements, forming his men, and giving orders and instructions. He ranged the kurens in three camps, surrounding them with the waggons as bulwarks--a formation in which the Zaporozhtzi were invincible--ordered two kurens into ambush, and drove sharp stakes, broken guns, and fragments of spears into a part of the plain, with a view to forcing the enemy's cavalry upon it if an opportunity should present itself. When all was done which was necessary, he made a speech to the Cossacks, not for the purpose of encouraging and freshening up their spirits--he knew their souls were strong without that--but simply because he wished to tell them all he had upon his heart.

"I want to tell you, brother gentles, what our brotherhood is. You have heard from your fathers and grandfathers in what honour our land has always been held by all. We made ourselves known to the Greeks, and we took gold from Constantinople, and our cities were luxurious, and we had, too, our temples, and our princes--the princes of the Russian people, our own princes, not Catholic unbelievers. But the Mussulmans took all; all vanished, and we remained defenceless; yea, like a widow after the death of a powerful husband: defenceless was our land as well as ourselves! Such was the time, comrades, when we joined hands in a brotherhood: that is what our fellowship consists in. There is no more sacred brotherhood. The father loves his children, the mother loves her children, the children love their father and mother; but this is not like that, brothers. The wild beast also loves its young. But a man can be related only by similarity of mind and not of blood. There have been brotherhoods in other lands, but never any such brotherhoods as on our Russian soil. It has happened to many of you to be in foreign lands. You look: there are people there also, God's creatures, too; and you talk with them as with the men of your own country. But when it comes to saying a hearty word--you will see. No! they are sensible people, but not the same; the same kind of people, and yet not the same! No, brothers, to love as the Russian soul loves, is to love not with the mind or anything else, but with all that God has given, all that is within you. Ah!" said Taras, and waved his hand, and wiped his grey head, and twitched his moustache, and then went on: "No, no one else can love in that way! I know that baseness has now made its way into our land. Men care only to have their ricks of grain and hay, and their droves of horses, and that their mead may be safe in their cellars; they adopt, the devil only knows what Mussulman customs. They speak scornfully with their tongues. They care not to speak their real thoughts with their own countrymen. They sell their own things to their own comrades, like soulless creatures in the market-place. The favour of a foreign king, and not even a king, but the poor favour of a Polish magnate, who beats them on the mouth with his yellow shoe, is dearer to them than all brotherhood. But the very meanest of these vile men, whoever he may be, given over though he be to vileness and slavishness, even he, brothers, has some grains of Russian feeling; and they will assert themselves some day. And then the wretched man will beat his breast with his hands; and will tear his hair, cursing his vile life loudly, and ready to expiate his disgraceful deeds with torture. Let them know what brotherhood means on Russian soil! And if it has come to the point that a man must die for his brotherhood, it is not fit that any of them should die so. No! none of them. It is not a fit thing for their mouse-like natures."

Thus spoke the hetman; and after he had finished his speech he still continued to shake his head, which had grown grey in Cossack service. All who stood there were deeply affected by his speech, which went to their very hearts. The oldest in the ranks stood motionless, their grey heads drooping. Tears trickled quietly from their aged eyes; they wiped them slowly away with their sleeves, and then all, as if with one consent, waved their hands in the air at the same moment, and shook their experienced heads. For it was evident that old Taras recalled to them many of the best-known and finest traits of the heart in a man who has become wise through suffering, toil, daring, and every earthly misfortune, or, though unknown to them, of many things felt by young, pure spirits, to the eternal joy of the parents who bore them.

But the army of the enemy was already marching out of the city, sounding drums and trumpets; and the nobles, with their arms akimbo, were riding forth too, surrounded by innumerable servants. The stout colonel gave his orders, and they began to advance briskly on the Cossack camps, pointing their matchlocks threateningly. Their eyes flashed, and they were brilliant with brass armour. As soon as the Cossacks saw that they had come within gunshot, their matchlocks thundered all together, and they continued to fire without cessation.

The detonations resounded through the distant fields and meadows, merging into one continuous roar. The whole plain was shrouded in smoke, but the Zaporozhtzi continued to fire without drawing breath--the rear ranks doing nothing but loading the guns and handing them to those in front, thus creating amazement among the enemy, who could not understand how the Cossacks fired without reloading. Amid the dense smoke which enveloped both armies, it could not be seen how first one and then another dropped: but the Lyakhs felt that the balls flew thickly, and that the affair was growing hot; and when they retreated to escape from the smoke and see how matters stood, many were missing from their ranks, but only two or three out of a hundred were killed on the Cossack side. Still the Cossacks went on firing off their matchlocks without a moment's intermission. Even the foreign engineers were amazed at tactics heretofore unknown to them, and said then and there, in the presence of all, "These

Zaporozhtzi are brave fellows. That is the way men in other lands ought to fight." And they advised that the cannons should at once be turned on the camps. Heavily roared the iron cannons with their wide throats; the earth hummed and trembled far and wide, and the smoke lay twice as heavy over the plain. They smelt the reek of the powder among the squares and streets in the most distant as well as the nearest quarters of the city. But those who laid the cannons pointed them too high, and the shot describing too wide a curve flew over the heads of the camps, and buried themselves deep in the earth at a distance, tearing the ground, and throwing the black soil high in the air. At the sight of such lack of skill the French engineer tore his hair, and undertook to lay the cannons himself, heeding not the Cossack bullets which showered round him.

Taras saw from afar that destruction menaced the whole Nezamaikovsky and Steblikivsky kurens, and gave a ringing shout, "Get away from the waggons instantly, and mount your horses!" But the Cossacks would not have succeeded in effecting both these movements if Ostap had not dashed into the middle of the foe and wrenched the linstocks from six cannoneers. But he could not wrench them from the other four, for the Lyakhs drove him back. Meanwhile the foreign captain had taken the lunt in his own hand to fire the largest cannon, such a cannon as none of the Cossacks had ever beheld before. It looked horrible with its wide mouth, and a thousand deaths poured forth from it. And as it thundered, the three others followed, shaking in fourfold earthquake the dully responsive earth. Much woe did they cause. For more than one Cossack wailed the aged mother, beating with bony hands her feeble breast; more than one widow was left in Glukhof, Nemirof, Chernigof, and other cities. The loving woman will hasten forth every day to the bazaar, grasping at all passers-by, scanning the face of each to see if there be not among them one dearer than all; but though many an army will pass through the city, never among them will a single one of all their dearest be.

Half the Nezamaikovsky kuren was as if it had never been. As the hail suddenly beats down a field where every ear of grain shines like purest gold, so were they beaten down.

How the Cossacks hastened thither! How they all started up! How raged Kukubenko, the hetman, when he saw that the best half of his kuren was no more! He fought his way with his remaining Nezamaikovtzi to the very midst of the fray, cut down in his wrath, like a cabbage, the first man he met, hurled many a rider from his steed, piercing both horse and man with his lance; and making his way to the gunners, captured some of the cannons. Here he found the hetman of the Oumansky kuren, and Stepan Guska, hard at work, having already seized the largest cannon. He left those Cossacks there, and plunged with his own into another mass of the foe, making a lane through it. Where the Nezamaikovtzi passed there was a street; where they turned about there was a square as where streets meet. The foemen's ranks were visibly thinning, and the Lyakhs falling in sheaves. Beside the waggons stood Vovtuzenko, and in front Tcherevitchenko, and by the more distant ones Degtyarenko; and behind them the kuren hetman, Vertikhvist. Degtyarenko had pierced two Lyakhs with his spear, and now attacked a third, a stout antagonist. Agile and strong was the Lyakh, with glittering arms, and accompanied by fifty followers. He fell fiercely upon Degtyarenko, struck him to the earth, and, flourishing his sword above him, cried, "There is not one of you Cossack dogs who has dared to oppose me."

"Here is one," said Mosiy Schilo, and stepped forward. He was a muscular Cossack, who had often commanded at sea, and undergone many vicissitudes. The Turks had once seized him and his men at Trebizond, and borne them captives to the galleys, where they bound them hand and foot with iron chains, gave them no food for a week at a time, and made them drink sea-water. The poor prisoners endured and suffered all, but would not renounce their orthodox faith. Their hetman, Mosiy Schilo, could not bear it: he trampled the Holy Scriptures under foot, wound the vile turban about his sinful head, and became the favourite of a pasha, steward of a ship, and ruler over all the galley slaves. The poor slaves sorrowed greatly thereat, for they knew that if he had renounced his faith he would be a tyrant, and his hand would be the more heavy and severe upon them. So it turned out. Mosiy Schilo had them put in new chains, three to an oar. The cruel fetters cut to the very bone; and he beat them upon the back. But when the Turks, rejoicing at having obtained such a servant, began to carouse, and, forgetful of their law, got all drunk, he distributed all the sixty-four keys among the prisoners, in order that they might free themselves, fling their chains and manacles into the sea, and, seizing their swords, in turn kill the Turks. Then the Cossacks collected great booty, and returned with glory to their country; and the guitar-players celebrated Mosiy Schilo's exploits for a long time. They would have elected him Koschevoi, but he was a very eccentric Cossack. At one time he would perform some feat which the most sagacious would never have dreamed of. At another, folly simply took possession of him, and he drank and squandered everything away, was in debt to every one in the Setch, and, in addition to that, stole like a street thief. He carried off a whole Cossack equipment from a strange kuren by night and pawned it to the tavern-keeper. For this dishonourable act they bound him to a post in the bazaar, and laid a club beside him, in order that every one who passed should, according to the measure of his strength, deal him a blow. But there was not one Zaporozhetz out of them all to be found who would raise the club against him, remembering his former services. Such was the Cossack, Mosiy Schilo.

"Here is one who will kill you, dog!" he said, springing upon the Lyakh. How they hacked away! their shoulder-plates and breast-plates bent under their blows. The hostile Lyakh cut through Schilo's shirt of mail, reaching the body itself with his blade. The Cossack's shirt was dyed purple: but Schilo heeded it not. He brandished his brawny hand, heavy indeed was that mighty fist, and brought the pommel of his sword down unexpectedly upon his foeman's head. The brazen helmet flew into pieces and the Lyakh staggered and fell; but Schilo went on hacking and cutting gashes in the body of the stunned man. Kill not utterly thine enemy, Cossack: look back rather! The Cossack did not turn, and one of the dead man's servants plunged a knife into his neck. Schilo turned and tried to seize him, but he disappeared amid the smoke of the powder. On all sides rose the roar of matchlocks. Schilo knew that his wound was mortal. He fell with his hand upon his wound, and said, turning to his comrades, "Farewell, brother gentles, my comrades! may the holy Russian land stand forever, and may it be eternally honoured!" And as he closed his failing eyes, the Cossack soul fled from his grim body. Then Zadorozhniy came forward with his men, Vertikhvist issued from the ranks, and Balaban stepped forth.

"What now, gentles?" said Taras, calling to the hetmans by name: "there is yet powder in the power-flasks? The Cossack force is not weakened? the Cossacks do not yield?"

"There is yet powder in the flasks, father; the Cossack force is not weakened yet: the Cossacks yield not!"

And the Cossacks pressed vigorously on: the foemen's ranks were disordered. The short colonel beat the assembly, and ordered eight painted standards to be displayed to collect his men, who were scattered over all the plain. All the Lyakhs hastened to the standards. But they had not yet succeeded in ranging themselves in order, when the hetman Kukubenko attacked their centre again with his Nezamaikovtzi and fell straight upon the stout colonel. The colonel could not resist the attack, and, wheeling his horse about, set out at a gallop; but Kukubenko pursued him for a considerable distance cross the plain and prevented him from joining his regiment.

Perceiving this from the kuren on the flank, Stepan Guska set out after him, lasso in hand, bending his head to his horse's neck. Taking advantage of an opportunity, he cast his lasso about his neck at the first attempt. The colonel turned purple in the face, grasped the cord with both hands, and tried to break it; but with a powerful thrust Stepan drove his lance through his body, and there he remained pinned to the earth. But Guska did not escape his fate. The Cossacks had but time to look round when they beheld Stepan Guska elevated on four spears. All the poor fellow succeeded in saying was, "May all our enemies perish, and may the Russian land rejoice forever!" and then he yielded up his soul.

The Cossacks glanced around, and there was Metelitza on one side, entertaining the Lyakhs by dealing blows on the head to one and another; on the other side, the hetman Nevelitchkiy was attacking with his men; and Zakrutibuga was repulsing and slaying the enemy by the waggons. The third Pisarenko had repulsed a whole squadron from the more distant waggons; and they were still fighting and killing amongst the other waggons, and even upon them.

"How now, gentles?" cried Taras, stepping forward before them all: "is there still powder in your flasks? Is the Cossack force still strong? do the Cossacks yield?"

"There is still powder in the flasks, father; the Cossack force is still strong: the Cossacks yield not!"

But Bovdug had already fallen from the waggons; a bullet had struck him just below the heart. The old man collected all his strength, and said, "I sorrow not to part from the world. God grant every man such an end! May the Russian land be forever glorious!" And Bovdug's spirit flew above, to tell the old men who had gone on long before that men still knew how to fight on Russian soil, and better still, that they knew how to die for it and the holy faith.

Balaban, hetman of a kuren, soon after fell to the ground also from a waggon. Three mortal wounds had he received from a lance, a bullet, and a sword. He had been one of the very best of Cossacks, and had accomplished a great deal as a commander on naval expeditions; but more glorious than all the rest was his raid on the shores of Anatolia. They collected many sequins, much valuable Turkish plunder, caftans, and adornments of every description. But misfortune awaited them on their way back. They came across the Turkish fleet, and were fired on by the ships. Half the boats were crushed and overturned, drowning more than one; but the bundles of reeds bound to the sides, Cossack fashion, saved the boats from completely sinking. Balaban rowed off at full speed, and steered straight in the face of the sun, thus rendering himself invisible to the Turkish ships. All the following night they spent in baling out the water with pails and their caps, and in repairing the damaged places. They made sails out of their Cossack trousers, and, sailing off, escaped from the fastest Turkish vessels. And not only did they arrive unharmed at the Setch, but they brought a gold-embroidered vesture for the archimandrite at the Mezhigorsky Monastery in Kief, and an ikon frame of pure silver for the church in honour of the Intercession of the Virgin Mary, which is in Zaporozhe. The guitar-players celebrated the daring of Balaban and his Cossacks for a long time afterwards. Now he bowed his head, feeling the pains which precede death, and said quietly, "I am permitted, brother gentles, to die a fine death. Seven have I hewn in pieces, nine have I pierced with my lance, many have I trampled upon with my horse's hoofs; and I no longer remember how many my bullets have slain. May our Russian land flourish forever!" and his spirit fled.

Cossacks, Cossacks! abandon not the flower of your army. Already was Kukubenko surrounded, and seven men only remained of all the Nezamaikovsky kuren, exhausted and with garments already stained with their blood. Taras himself, perceiving their straits, hastened to their rescue; but the Cossacks arrived too late. Before the enemies who surrounded him could be driven off, a spear was buried just below Kukubenko's heart. He sank into the arms of the Cossacks who caught him, and his young blood flowed in a stream, like precious wine brought from the cellar in a glass vessel by careless servants, who, stumbling at the entrance, break the rich flask. The wine streams over the ground, and the master, hastening up, tears his hair, having reserved it, in order that if God should grant him, in his old age, to meet again the comrade of his youth, they might over it recall together former days, when a man enjoyed himself otherwise and better than now. Kukubenko cast his eyes around, and said, "I thank God that it has been my lot to die before your eyes, comrades. May they live better who come after us than we have lived; and may our Russian land, beloved by Christ, flourish forever!" and his young spirit fled. The angels took it in their arms and bore it to heaven: it will be well with him there. "Sit down at my right hand, Kukubenko," Christ will say to him: "you never betrayed your comrades, you never committed a dishonourable act, you never sold a man into misery, you preserved and defended my church." The death of Kukubenko saddened them all. The Cossack ranks were terribly thinned. Many brave men were missing, but the Cossacks still stood their ground.

"How now, gentles," cried Taras to the remaining kurens: "is there still powder in your flasks? Are your swords blunted? Are the Cossack forces wearied? Have the Cossacks given way?"

"There is still an abundance of powder; our swords are still sharp; the Cossack forces are not wearied, and the Cossacks have not yet yielded."

And the Cossacks again strained every nerve, as though they had suffered no loss. Only three kuren hetmans still remained alive. Red blood flowed in streams everywhere; heaps of their bodies and of those of the enemy were piled high. Taras looked up to heaven, and there already hovered a flock of vultures. Well, there would be prey for some one. And there the foe were raising Metelitza on their lances, and the head of the second Pisarenko was dizzily opening and shutting its eyes; and the mangled body of Okhrim Guska fell upon the ground. "Now," said Taras, and waved a cloth on high. Ostap understood this signal and springing quickly from his ambush attacked sharply. The Lyakhs could not withstand this onslaught; and he drove them back, and chased them straight to the spot where the stakes and fragments of spears were driven into the earth. The horses began to stumble and fall and the Lyakhs to fly over their heads. At that moment the Korsuntzi, who had stood till the last by the baggage waggons, perceived that they still had some bullets left, and suddenly fired a volley from their matchlocks. The Lyakhs became confused, and lost their presence of mind; and the Cossacks took courage. "The victory is ours!" rang Cossack voices on all sides; the trumpets sounded and the banner of victory was unfurled. The beaten Lyakhs ran in all directions and hid themselves. "No, the victory is not yet complete," said Taras, glancing at the city gate; and he was right.

The gates opened, and out dashed a hussar band, the flower of all the cavalry. Every rider was mounted on a matched brown horse from the Kabardei; and in front rode the handsomest, the most heroic of them all. His black hair streamed from beneath his brazen helmet; and from his arm floated a rich scarf, embroidered by the hands of a peerless beauty. Taras sprang back in horror when he saw that it was Andrii. And the latter meanwhile, enveloped in the dust and heat of battle, eager to deserve the scarf which had been bound as a gift upon his arm, flew on like a greyhound; the handsomest, most agile, and youngest of all the band. The experienced huntsman urges on the greyhound, and he springs forward, tossing up the snow, and a score of times outrunning the hare, in the ardour of his course. And so it was with Andrii. Old Taras paused and observed how he cleared a path before him, hewing away and dealing blows to the right and the left. Taras could not restrain himself, but shouted: "Your comrades! your comrades! you devil's brat, would you kill your own comrades?" But Andrii distinguished not who stood before him, comrades or strangers; he saw nothing. Curls, long curls, were what he saw; and a bosom like that of a river swan, and a snowy neck and shoulders, and all that is created for rapturous kisses.

"Hey there, lads! only draw him to the forest, entice him to the forest for me!" shouted Taras. Instantly thirty of the smartest Cossacks volunteered to entice him thither; and setting their tall caps firmly spurred their horses straight at a gap in the hussars. They attacked the front ranks in flank, beat them down, cut them off from the rear ranks, and slew many of them. Goloshchenko struck Andrii on the back with his sword, and immediately set out to ride away at the top of his speed. How Andrii flew after him! How his young blood coursed through all his veins! Driving his sharp spurs into his horse's flanks, he tore along after the Cossacks, never glancing back, and not perceiving that only twenty men at the most were following him. The Cossacks fled at full gallop, and directed their course straight for the forest. Andrii overtook them, and was on the point of catching Goloshchenko, when a powerful hand seized his horse's bridle. Andrii looked; before him stood Taras! He trembled all over, and turned suddenly pale, like a student who, receiving a blow on the forehead with a ruler, flushes up like fire, springs in wrath from his seat to chase his comrade, and suddenly encounters his teacher entering the classroom; in the instant his wrathful impulse calms down and his futile anger vanishes. In this wise, in an instant, Andrii's wrath was as if it had never existed. And he beheld before him only his terrible father.

"Well, what are we going to do now?" said Taras, looking him straight in the eyes. But Andrii could make no reply to this, and stood with his eyes fixed on the ground.

"Well, son; did your Lyakhs help you?"

Andrii made no answer.

"To think that you should be such a traitor! that you should betray your faith! betray your comrades! Dismount from your horse!"

Obedient as a child, he dismounted, and stood before Taras more dead than alive.

"Stand still, do not move! I gave you life, I will also kill you!" said Taras, and, retreating a step backwards, he brought his gun up to his shoulder. Andrii was white as a sheet; his lips moved gently, and he uttered a name; but it was not the name of his native land, nor of his mother, nor his brother; it was the name of the beautiful Pole. Taras fired.

Like the ear of corn cut down by the reaping-hook, like the young lamb when it feels the deadly steel in its heart, he hung his head and rolled upon the grass without uttering a word.

The murderer of his son stood still, and gazed long upon the lifeless body. Even in death he was very handsome; his manly face, so short a time ago filled with power, and with an irresistible charm for every woman, still had a marvellous beauty; his black brows, like sombre velvet, set off his pale features.

"Is he not a true Cossack?" said Taras; "he is tall of stature, and black-browed, his face is that of a noble, and his hand was strong in battle! He is fallen! fallen without glory, like a vile dog!"

"Father, what have you done? Was it you who killed him?" said Ostap, coming up at this moment.

Taras nodded.

Ostap gazed intently at the dead man. He was sorry for his brother, and said at once: "Let us give him honourable burial, father, that the foe may not dishonour his body, nor the birds of prey rend it."

"They will bury him without our help," said Taras; "there will be plenty of mourners and rejoicers for him."

And he reflected for a couple of minutes, whether he should fling him to the wolves for prey, or respect in him the bravery which every brave man is bound to honour in another, no matter whom? Then he saw Golopuitenko galloping towards them and crying: "Woe, hetman, the Lyakhs have been reinforced, a fresh force has come to their rescue!" Golopuitenko had not finished speaking when Vovtuzenko galloped up: "Woe, hetman! a fresh force is bearing down upon us."

Vovtuzenko had not finished speaking when Pisarenko rushed up without his horse: "Where are you, father? The Cossacks are seeking for you. Hetman Nevelitchkiy is killed, Zadorozhniy is killed, and Tcherevitchenko: but the Cossacks stand their ground; they will not die without looking in your eyes; they want you to gaze upon them once more before the hour of death arrives."

"To horse, Ostap!" said Taras, and hastened to find his Cossacks, to look once more upon them, and let them behold their hetman once more before the hour of death. But before they could emerge from the wood, the enemy's force had already surrounded it on all sides, and horsemen armed with swords and spears appeared everywhere between the trees. "Ostap, Ostap! don't yield!" shouted Taras, and grasping his sword he began to cut down all he encountered on every side. But six suddenly sprang upon Ostap. They did it in an unpropitious hour: the head of one flew off, another turned to flee, a spear pierced the ribs of a third; a fourth, more bold, bent his head to escape the bullet, and the bullet striking his horse's breast, the maddened animal reared, fell back upon the earth, and crushed his rider under him. "Well done, son! Well done, Ostap!" cried Taras: "I am following you." And he drove off those who attacked him. Taras hewed and fought, dealing blows at one after another, but still keeping his eye upon Ostap ahead. He saw that eight more were falling upon his son. "Ostap, Ostap! don't yield!" But they had already overpowered Ostap; one had flung his lasso about his neck, and they had bound him, and were carrying him away. "Hey, Ostap, Ostap!" shouted Taras, forcing his way towards him, and cutting men down like cabbages to right and left. "Hey, Ostap, Ostap!" But something at that moment struck him like a heavy stone. All grew dim and confused before his eyes. In one moment there flashed confusedly before him heads, spears, smoke, the gleam of fire, tree-trunks, and leaves; and then he sank heavily to the earth like a felled oak, and darkness covered his eyes.

CHAPTER X

"I have slept a long while!" said Taras, coming to his senses, as if after a heavy drunken sleep, and trying to distinguish the objects about him. A terrible weakness overpowered his limbs. The walls and corners of a strange room were dimly visible before him. At length he perceived that Tovkatch was seated beside him, apparently listening to his every breath.

"Yes," thought Tovkatch, "you might have slept forever." But he said nothing, only shook his finger, and motioned him to be silent.

"But tell me where I am now?" asked Taras, straining his mind, and trying to recollect what had taken place.

"Be silent!" cried his companion sternly. "Why should you want to know? Don't you see that you are all hacked to pieces? Here I have been galloping with you for two weeks without taking a breath; and you have been burnt up with fever and talking nonsense. This is the first time you have slept quietly. Be silent if you don't wish to do yourself an injury."

But Taras still tried to collect his thoughts and to recall what had passed. "Well, the Lyakhs must have surrounded and captured me. I had no chance of fighting my way clear from the throng."

"Be silent, I tell you, you devil's brat!" cried Tovkatch angrily, as a nurse, driven beyond her patience, cries out at her unruly charge. "What good will it do you to know how you got away? It is enough that you did get away. Some people were found who would not abandon you; let that be enough for you. It is something for me to have ridden all night with you. You think that you passed for a common Cossack? No, they have offered a reward of two thousand ducats for your head."

"And Ostap!" cried Taras suddenly, and tried to rise; for all at once he recollected that Ostap had been seized and bound before his very eyes, and that he was now in the hands of the Lyakhs. Grief overpowered him. He pulled off and tore in pieces the bandages from his wounds, and threw them far from him; he tried to say something, but only articulated some incoherent words. Fever and delirium seized upon him afresh, and he uttered wild and incoherent speeches. Meanwhile his faithful comrade stood beside him, scolding and showering harsh, reproachful words upon him without stint. Finally, he seized him by the arms and legs, wrapped him up like a child, arranged all his bandages, rolled him in an ox-hide, bound him with bast, and, fastening him with ropes to his saddle, rode with him again at full speed along the road.

"I'll get you there, even if it be not alive! I will not abandon your body for the Lyakhs to make merry over you, and cut your body in twain and fling it into the water. Let the eagle tear out your eyes if it must be so; but let it be our eagle of the steppe and not a Polish eagle, not one which has flown hither from Polish soil. I will bring you, though it be a corpse, to the Ukraine!"

Thus spoke his faithful companion. He rode without drawing rein, day and night, and brought Taras still insensible into the Zaporozhian Setch itself. There he undertook to cure him, with unswerving care, by the aid of herbs and liniments. He sought out a skilled Jewess, who made Taras drink various potions for a whole month, and at length he improved. Whether it was owing to the medicine or to his iron constitution gaining the upper hand, at all events, in six weeks he was on his feet. His wounds had closed, and only the scars of the sabre-cuts showed how deeply injured the old Cossack had been. But he was markedly sad and morose. Three deep wrinkles engraved themselves upon his brow and never more departed thence. Then he looked around him. All was new in the Setch; all his old companions were dead. Not one was left of those who had stood up for the right, for faith and brotherhood. And those who had gone forth with the Koschevoi in pursuit of the Tatars, they also had long since disappeared. All had perished. One had lost his head in battle; another had died for lack of food, amid the salt marshes of the Crimea; another had fallen in captivity and been unable to survive the disgrace. Their former Koschevoi was no longer living, nor any of his old companions, and the grass was growing over those once alert with power. He felt as one who had given a feast, a great noisy feast. All the dishes had been smashed in pieces; not a drop of wine was left anywhere; the guests and servants had all stolen valuable cups and platters; and he, like the master of the house, stood sadly thinking that it would have been no feast. In vain did they try to cheer Taras and to divert his mind; in vain did the long-bearded, grey-haired guitar-players come by twos and threes to glorify his Cossack deeds. He gazed grimly and indifferently at everything, with inappeasable grief printed on his stolid face; and said softly, as he drooped his head, "My son, my Ostap!"

The Zaporozhtzi assembled for a raid by sea. Two hundred boats were launched on the Dnieper, and Asia Minor saw those who manned them, with their shaven heads and long scalp-locks, devote her thriving shores to fire and sword; she saw the turbans of her Mahometan inhabitants strewn, like her innumerable flowers, over the blood-sprinkled fields, and floating along her river banks; she saw many tarry Zaporozhian trousers, and strong hands with black hunting-whips. The Zaporozhtzi ate up and laid waste all the vineyards. In the mosques they left heaps of dung. They used rich Persian shawls for sashes, and girded their dirty gaberdines with them. Long afterwards, short Zaporozhian pipes were found in those regions.

They sailed merrily back. A ten-gun Turkish ship pursued them and scattered their skiffs, like birds, with a volley from its guns. A third part of them sank in the depths of the sea; but the rest again assembled, and gained the mouth of the Dnieper with twelve kegs full of sequins. But all this did not interest Taras. He went off upon the steppe as though to hunt; but the charge remained in his gun, and, laying down the weapon, he would seat himself sadly on the shores of the sea. He sat there long with drooping head, repeating continually, "My Ostap, my Ostap!" Before him spread the gleaming Black Sea; in the distant reeds the sea-gull screamed. His grey moustache turned to silver, and the tears fell one by one upon it.

At last Taras could endure it no longer. "Whatever happens, I must go and find out what he is doing. Is he alive, or in the grave? I will know, cost what it may!" Within a week he found himself in the city of Ouman, fully armed, and mounted, with lance, sword, canteen, pot of oatmeal, powder horn, cord to hobble his horse, and other equipments. He went straight to a dirty, ill-kept little house, the small windows of which were almost invisible, blackened as they were with some unknown dirt. The chimney was wrapped in rags; and the roof, which was full of holes, was covered with sparrows. A heap of all sorts of refuse lay before the very door. From the window peered the head of a Jewess, in a head-dress with discoloured pearls.

"Is your husband at home?" said Bulba, dismounting, and fastening his horse's bridle to an iron hook beside the door.

"He is at home," said the Jewess, and hastened out at once with a measure of corn for the horse, and a stoup of beer for the rider.

"Where is your Jew?"

"He is in the other room at prayer," replied the Jewess, bowing and wishing Bulba good health as he raised the cup to his lips.

"Remain here, feed and water my horse, whilst I go speak with him alone. I have business with him."

This Jew was the well-known Yankel. He was there as revenue-farmer and tavern-keeper. He had gradually got nearly all the neighbouring noblemen and gentlemen into his hands, had slowly sucked away most of their money, and had strongly impressed his presence on that locality. For a distance of three miles in all directions, not a single farm remained in a proper state. All were falling in ruins; all had been drunk away, and poverty and rags alone remained. The whole neighbourhood was depopulated, as if after a fire or an epidemic; and if Yankel had lived there ten years, he would probably have depopulated the Waiwode's whole domains.

Taras entered the room. The Jew was praying, enveloped in his dirty shroud, and was turning to spit for the last time, according to the forms of his creed, when his eye suddenly lighted on Taras standing behind him. The first thing that crossed Yankel's mind was the two thousand ducats offered for his visitor's head; but he was ashamed of his avarice, and tried to stifle within him the eternal thought of gold, which twines, like a snake, about the soul of a Jew.

"Listen, Yankel," said Taras to the Jew, who began to bow low before him, and as he spoke he shut the door so that they might not be seen, "I saved your life: the Zaporozhtzi would have torn you to pieces like a dog. Now it is your turn to do me a service."

The Jew's face clouded over a little.

"What service? If it is a service I can render, why should I not render it?"

"Ask no questions. Take me to Warsaw."

"To Warsaw? Why to Warsaw?" said the Jew, and his brows and shoulders rose in amazement.

"Ask me nothing. Take me to Warsaw. I must see him once more at any cost, and say one word to him."

"Say a word to whom?"

"To him--to Ostap--to my son."

"Has not my lord heard that already--"

"I know, I know all. They offer two thousand ducats for my head. They know its value, fools! I will give you five thousand. Here are two thousand on the spot," and Bulba poured out two thousand ducats from a leather purse, "and the rest when I return."

The Jew instantly seized a towel and concealed the ducats under it. "Ai, glorious money! ai, good money!" he said, twirling one gold piece in his hand and testing it with his teeth. "I don't believe the man from whom my lord took these fine gold pieces remained in the world an hour longer; he went straight to the river and drowned himself, after the loss of such magnificent gold pieces."

"I should not have asked you, I might possibly have found my own way to Warsaw; but some one might recognise me, and then the cursed Lyakhs would capture me, for I am not clever at inventions; whilst that is just what you Jews are created for. You would deceive the very devil. You know every trick: that is why I have come to you; and, besides, I could do nothing of myself in Warsaw. Harness the horse to your waggon at once and take me."

"And my lord thinks that I can take the nag at once, and harness him, and say 'Get up, Dapple!' My lord thinks that I can take him just as he is, without concealing him?"

"Well, hide me, hide me as you like: in an empty cask?"

"Ai, ai! and my lord thinks he can be concealed in an empty cask? Does not my lord know that every man thinks that every cast he sees contains brandy?"

"Well, let them think it is brandy."

"Let them think it is brandy?" said the Jew, and grasped his ear-locks with both hands, and then raised them both on high.

"Well, why are you so frightened?"

"And does not my lord know that God has made brandy expressly for every one to sip? They are all gluttons and fond of dainties there: a nobleman will run five versts after a cask; he will make a hole in it, and as soon as he sees that nothing runs out, he will say, 'A Jew does not carry empty casks; there is certainly something wrong. Seize the Jew, bind the Jew, take away all the Jew's money, put the Jew in prison!' Then all the vile people will fall upon the Jew, for every one takes a Jew for a dog; and they think he is not a man, but only a Jew."

"Then put me in the waggon with some fish over me."

"I cannot, my lord, by heaven, I cannot: all over Poland the people are as hungry as dogs now. They will steal the fish, and feel my lord."

"Then take me in the fiend's way, only take me."

"Listen, listen, my lord!" said the Jew, turning up the ends of his sleeves, and approaching him with extended arms. "This is what we will do. They are building fortresses and castles everywhere: French engineers have come from Germany, and so a great deal of brick and stone is being carried over the roads. Let my lord lie down in the bottom of the waggon, and over him I will pile bricks. My lord is strong and well, apparently, so he will not mind if it is a little heavy; and I will make a hole in the bottom of the waggon in order to feed my lord."

"Do what you will, only take me!"

In an hour, a waggon-load of bricks left Ouman, drawn by two sorry nags. On one of them sat tall Yankel, his long, curling ear-locks flowing from beneath his Jewish cap, as he bounced about on the horse, like a verst-mark planted by the roadside.

CHAPTER XI

At the time when these things took place, there were as yet on the frontiers neither custom-house officials nor guards--those bugbears of enterprising people--so that any one could bring across anything he fancied. If any one made a search or inspection, he did it chiefly for his own pleasure, especially if there happened to be in the waggon objects attractive to his eye, and if his own hand possessed a certain weight and power. But the bricks found no admirers, and they entered the principal gate unmolested. Bulba, in his narrow cage, could only hear the noise, the shouts of the driver, and nothing more. Yankel, bouncing up and down on his dust-covered nag, turned, after making several detours, into a dark, narrow street bearing the names of the Muddy and also of the Jews' street, because Jews from nearly every part of Warsaw were to be found here. This street greatly resembled a back-yard turned wrong side out. The sun never seemed to shine into it. The black wooden houses, with numerous poles projecting from the windows, still further increased the darkness. Rarely did a brick wall gleam red among them; for these too, in many places, had turned quite black. Here and there, high up, a bit of stuccoed wall illumined by the sun glistened with intolerable whiteness. Pipes, rags, shells, broken and discarded tubs: every one flung whatever was useless to him into the street, thus affording the passer-by an opportunity of exercising all his five senses with the rubbish. A man on horseback could almost touch with his hand the poles thrown across the street from one house to another, upon which hung Jewish stockings, short trousers, and smoked geese. Sometimes a pretty little Hebrew face, adorned with discoloured pearls, peeped out of an old window. A group of little Jews, with torn and dirty garments and curly hair, screamed and rolled about in the dirt. A red-haired Jew, with freckles all over his face which made him look like a sparrow's egg, gazed from a window. He addressed Yankel at once in his gibberish, and Yankel at once drove into a court-yard. Another Jew came along, halted, and entered into conversation. When Bulba finally emerged from beneath the bricks, he beheld three Jews talking with great warmth.

Yankel turned to him and said that everything possible would be done; that his Ostap was in the city jail, and that although it would be difficult to persuade the jailer, yet he hoped to arrange a meeting.

Bulba entered the room with the three Jews.

The Jews again began to talk among themselves in their incomprehensible tongue. Taras looked hard at each of them. Something seemed to have moved him deeply; over his rough and stolid countenance a flame of hope spread, of hope such as sometimes visits a man in the last depths of his despair; his aged heart began to beat violently as though he had been a youth.

"Listen, Jews!" said he, and there was a triumphant ring in his words. "You can do anything in the world, even extract things from the bottom of the sea; and it has long been a proverb, that a Jew will steal from himself if he takes a fancy to steal. Set my Ostap at liberty! give him a chance to escape from their diabolical hands. I promised this man five thousand ducats; I will add another five thousand: all that I have, rich cups, buried gold, houses, all, even to my last garment, I will part with; and I will enter into a contract with you for my whole life, to give you half of all the booty I may gain in war."

"Oh, impossible, dear lord, it is impossible!" said Yankel with a sigh.

"Impossible," said another Jew.

All three Jews looked at each other.

"We might try," said the third, glancing timidly at the other two. "God may favour us."

All three Jews discussed the matter in German. Bulba, in spite of his straining ears, could make nothing of it; he only caught the word "Mardokhai" often repeated.

"Listen, my lord!" said Yankel. "We must consult with a man such as there never was before in the world . . . ugh, ugh! as wise as Solomon; and if he will do nothing, then no one in the world can. Sit here: this is the key; admit no one." The Jews went out into the street.

Taras locked the door, and looked out from the little window upon the dirty Jewish street. The three Jews halted in the middle of the street and began to talk with a good deal of warmth: a fourth soon joined them, and finally a fifth. Again he heard repeated, "Mardokhai, Mardokhai!" The Jews glanced incessantly towards one side of the street; at length from a dirty house near the end of it emerged a foot in a Jewish shoe and the skirts of a caftan. "Ah! Mardokhai, Mardokhai!" shouted the Jews in one voice. A thin Jew somewhat shorter than Yankel, but even more wrinkled, and with a huge upper lip, approached the impatient group; and all the Jews made haste to talk to him, interrupting each other. During the recital, Mardokhai glanced several times towards the little window, and Taras divined that the conversation concerned him.

Mardokhai waved his hands, listened, interrupted, spat frequently to one side, and, pulling up the skirts of his caftan, thrust his hand into his pocket and drew out some jingling thing, showing very dirty trousers in the operation. Finally all the Jews set up such a shouting that the Jew who was standing guard was forced to make a signal for silence, and Taras began to fear for his safety; but when he remembered that Jews can only consult in the street, and that the demon himself cannot understand their language, he regained his composure.

Two minutes later the Jews all entered the room together. Mardokhai approached Taras, tapped him on the shoulder, and said, "When we set to work it will be all right." Taras looked at this Solomon whom the world had never known and conceived some hope: indeed, his face might well inspire confidence. His upper lip was simply an object of horror; its thickness being doubtless increased by adventitious circumstances. This

Solomon's beard consisted only of about fifteen hairs, and they were on the left side. Solomon's face bore so many scars of battle, received for his daring, that he had doubtless lost count of them long before, and had grown accustomed to consider them as birthmarks.

Mardokhai departed, accompanied by his comrades, who were filled with admiration at his wisdom. Bulba remained alone. He was in a strange, unaccustomed situation for the first time in his life; he felt uneasy. His mind was in a state of fever. He was no longer unbending, immovable, strong as an oak, as he had formerly been: but felt timid and weak. He trembled at every sound, at every fresh Jewish face which showed itself at the end of the street. In this condition he passed the whole day. He neither ate nor drank, and his eye never for a moment left the small window looking on the street. Finally, late at night, Mardokhai and Yankel made their appearance. Taras's heart died within him.

"What news? have you been successful?" he asked with the impatience of a wild horse.

But before the Jews had recovered breath to answer, Taras perceived that Mardokhai no longer had the locks, which had formerly fallen in greasy curls from under his felt cap. It was evident that he wished to say something, but he uttered only nonsense which Taras could make nothing of. Yankel himself put his hand very often to his mouth as though suffering from a cold.

"Oh, dearest lord!" said Yankel: "it is quite impossible now! by heaven, impossible! Such vile people that they deserve to be spit upon! Mardokhai here says the same. Mardokhai has done what no man in the world ever did, but God did not will that it should be so. Three thousand soldiers are in garrison here, and to-morrow the prisoners are all to be executed."

Taras looked the Jew straight in the face, but no longer with impatience or anger.

"But if my lord wishes to see his son, then it must be early to-morrow morning, before the sun has risen. The sentinels have consented, and one gaoler has promised. But may he have no happiness in the world, woe is me! What greedy people! There are none such among us: I gave fifty ducats to each sentinel and to the gaoler."

"Good. Take me to him!" exclaimed Taras, with decision, and with all his firmness of mind restored. He agreed to Yankel's proposition that he should disguise himself as a foreign count, just arrived from Germany, for which purpose the prudent Jew had already provided a costume. It was already night. The master of the house, the red-haired Jew with freckles, pulled out a mattress covered with some kind of rug, and spread it on a bench for Bulba. Yankel lay upon the floor on a similar mattress. The red-haired Jew drank a small cup of brandy, took off his caftan, and betook himself--looking, in his shoes and stockings, very like a lean chicken--with his wife, to something resembling a cupboard. Two little Jews lay down on the floor beside the cupboard, like a couple of dogs. But Taras did not sleep; he sat motionless, drumming on the table with his fingers. He kept his pipe in his mouth, and puffed out smoke, which made the Jew sneeze in his sleep and pull his coverlet over his nose. Scarcely was the sky touched with the first faint gleams of dawn than he pushed Yankel with his foot, saying: "Rise, Jew, and give me your count's dress!"

In a moment he was dressed. He blackened his moustache and eyebrows, put on his head a small dark cap; even the Cossacks who knew him best would not have recognised him. Apparently he was not more than thirty-five. A healthy colour glowed on his cheeks, and his scars lent him an air of command. The gold-embroidered dress became him extremely well.

The streets were still asleep. Not a single one of the market folk as yet showed himself in the city, with his basket on his arm. Yankel and Bulba made their way to a building which presented the appearance of a crouching stork. It was large, low, wide, and black; and on one side a long slender tower like a stork's neck projected above the roof. This building served for a variety of purposes; it was a barrack, a jail, and the criminal court. The visitors entered the gate and found themselves in a vast room, or covered courtyard. About a thousand men were sleeping here. Straight before them was a small door, in front of which sat two sentries playing at some game which consisted in one striking the palm of the other's hand with two fingers. They paid little heed to the new arrivals, and only turned their heads when Yankel said, "It is we, sirs; do you hear? it is we."

"Go in!" said one of them, opening the door with one hand, and holding out the other to his comrade to receive his blows.

They entered a low and dark corridor, which led them to a similar room with small windows overhead. "Who goes there?" shouted several voices, and Taras beheld a number of warriors in full armour. "We have been ordered to admit no one."

"It is we!" cried Yankel; "we, by heavens, noble sirs!" But no one would listen to him. Fortunately, at that moment a fat man came up, who appeared to be a commanding officer, for he swore louder than all the others.

"My lord, it is we! you know us, and the lord count will thank you."

"Admit them, a hundred fiends, and mother of fiends! Admit no one else. And no one is to draw his sword, nor quarrel."

The conclusion of this order the visitors did not hear. "It is we, it is I, it is your friends!" Yankel said to every one they met.

"Well, can it be managed now?" he inquired of one of the guards, when they at length reached the end of the corridor.

"It is possible, but I don't know whether you will be able to gain admission to the prison itself. Yana is not here now; another man is keeping watch in his place," replied the guard.

"Ai, ai!" cried the Jew softly: "this is bad, my dear lord!"

"Go on!" said Taras, firmly, and the Jew obeyed.

At the arched entrance of the vaults stood a heyduke, with a moustache trimmed in three layers: the upper layer was trained backwards, the second straight forward, and the third downwards, which made him greatly resemble a cat.

The Jew shrank into nothing and approached him almost sideways: "Your high excellency! High and illustrious lord!"

"Are you speaking to me, Jew?"

"To you, illustrious lord."

"Hm, but I am merely a heyduke," said the merry-eyed man with the triple-tiered moustache.

"And I thought it was the Waiwode himself, by heavens! Ai, ai, ai!" Thereupon the Jew twisted his head about and spread out his fingers. "Ai, what a fine figure! Another finger's-breadth and he would be a colonel. The lord no doubt rides a horse as fleet as the wind and commands the troops!"

The heyduke twirled the lower tier of his moustache, and his eyes beamed.

"What a warlike people!" continued the Jew. "Ah, woe is me, what a fine race! Golden cords and trappings that shine like the sun; and the maidens, wherever they see warriors--Ai, ai!" Again the Jew wagged his head.

The heyduke twirled his upper moustache and uttered a sound somewhat resembling the neighing of a horse.

"I pray my lord to do us a service!" exclaimed the Jew: "this prince has come hither from a foreign land, and wants to get a look at the Cossacks. He never, in all his life, has seen what sort of people the Cossacks are."

The advent of foreign counts and barons was common enough in Poland: they were often drawn thither by curiosity to view this half-Asiatic corner of Europe. They regarded Moscow and the Ukraine as situated in Asia. So the heyduke bowed low, and thought fit to add a few words of his own.

"I do not know, your excellency," said he, "why you should desire to see them. They are dogs, not men; and their faith is such as no one respects."

"You lie, you son of Satan!" exclaimed Bulba. "You are a dog yourself! How dare you say that our faith is not respected? It is your heretical faith which is not respected."

"Oho!" said the heyduke. "I can guess who you are, my friend; you are one of the breed of those under my charge. So just wait while I summon our men."

Taras realised his indiscretion, but vexation and obstinacy hindered him from devising a means of remedying it. Fortunately Yankel managed to interpose at this moment:--

"Most noble lord, how is it possible that the count can be a Cossack? If he were a Cossack, where could have he obtained such a dress, and such a count-like mien?"

"Explain that yourself." And the heyduke opened his wide mouth to shout.

"Your royal highness, silence, silence, for heaven's sake!" cried Yankel. "Silence! we will pay you for it in a way you never dreamed of: we will give you two golden ducats."

"Oho! two ducats! I can't do anything with two ducats. I give my barber two ducats for only shaving the half of my beard. Give me a hundred ducats, Jew." Here the heyduke twirled his upper moustache. "If you don't, I will shout at once."

"Why so much?" said the Jew, sadly, turning pale, and undoing his leather purse; but it was lucky that he had no more in it, and that the heyduke could not count over a hundred.

"My lord, my lord, let us depart quickly! Look at the evil-minded fellow!" said Yankel to Taras, perceiving that the heyduke was turning the money over in his hand as though regretting that he had not demanded more.

"What do you mean, you devil of a heyduke?" said Bulba. "What do you mean by taking our money and not letting us see the Cossacks? No, you must let us see them. Since you have taken the money, you have no right to refuse."

"Go, go to the devil! If you won't, I'll give the alarm this moment. Take yourselves off quickly, I say!"

"My lord, my lord, let us go! in God's name let us go! Curse him! May he dream such things that he will have to spit," cried poor Yankel.

Bulba turned slowly, with drooping head, and retraced his steps, followed by the complaints of Yankel who was sorrowing at the thought of the wasted ducats.

"Why be angry? Let the dog curse. That race cannot help cursing. Oh, woe is me, what luck God sends to some people! A hundred ducats merely for driving us off! And our brother: they have torn off his ear-locks, and they made wounds on his face that you cannot bear to look at, and yet no one will give him a hundred gold pieces. O heavens! Merciful God!"

But this failure made a much deeper impression on Bulba, expressed by a devouring flame in his eyes.

"Let us go," he said, suddenly, as if arousing himself; "let us go to the square. I want to see how they will torture him."

"Oh, my lord! why go? That will do us no good now."

"Let us go," said Bulba, obstinately; and the Jew followed him, sighing like a nurse.

The square on which the execution was to take place was not hard to find: for the people were thronging thither from all quarters. In that savage age such a thing constituted one of the most noteworthy spectacles, not only for the common people, but among the higher classes. A number of the most pious old men, a throng of young girls, and the most cowardly women, who dreamed the whole night afterwards of their bloody corpses, and shrieked as loudly in their sleep as a drunken hussar, missed, nevertheless, no opportunity of gratifying their curiosity. "Ah, what tortures!" many of them would cry, hysterically, covering their eyes and turning away; but they stood their ground for a good while, all the same. Many a one, with gaping mouth and outstretched hands, would have liked to jump upon other folk's heads, to get a better view. Above the crowd towered a bulky butcher, admiring the whole process with the air of a connoisseur, and exchanging brief remarks with a gunsmith, whom he addressed as "Gossip," because he got drunk in the same alehouse with him on holidays. Some entered into warm discussions, others even laid wagers. But the majority were of the species who, all the world over, look on at the world and at everything that goes on in it and merely scratch their noses. In the front ranks, close to the bearded civic-guards, stood a young noble, in warlike array, who had certainly put his whole wardrobe on his back, leaving only his torn shirt and old shoes at his quarters. Two chains, one above the other, hung around his neck. He stood beside his mistress, Usisya, and glanced about incessantly to see that no one soiled her silk gown. He explained everything to her so perfectly that no one could have added a word. "All these people whom you see, my dear Usisya," he said, "have come to see the criminals executed; and that man, my love, yonder, holding the axe and other instruments in his hands, is the executioner, who will despatch them. When he begins to break them on the wheel, and torture them in other ways, the criminals will still be alive; but when he cuts off their heads, then, my love, they will die at once. Before that, they will cry and move; but as soon as their heads are cut off, it will be impossible for them to cry, or to eat or drink, because, my dear, they will no longer have any head." Usisya listened to all this with terror and curiosity.

The upper stories of the houses were filled with people. From the windows in the roof peered strange faces with beards and something resembling caps. Upon the balconies, beneath shady awnings, sat the aristocracy. The hands of smiling young ladies, brilliant as white sugar, rested on the railings. Portly nobles looked on with dignity. Servants in rich garb, with flowing sleeves, handed round various refreshments. Sometimes a black-eyed young rogue would take her cake or fruit and fling it among the crowd with her own noble little hand. The crowd of hungry gentles held up their caps to receive it; and some tall noble, whose head rose amid the throng, with his faded red jacket and discoloured gold braid, and who was the first to catch it with the aid of his long arms, would kiss his booty, press it to his heart, and finally put it in his mouth. The hawk, suspended beneath the balcony in a golden cage, was also a spectator; with beak inclined to one side, and with one foot raised, he, too, watched the people attentively. But suddenly a murmur ran through the crowd, and a rumour spread, "They are coming! they are coming! the Cossacks!"

They were bare-headed, with their long locks floating in the air. Their beards had grown, and their once handsome garments were worn out, and hung about them in tatters. They walked neither timidly nor surlily, but with a certain pride, neither looking at nor bowing to the people. At the head of all came Ostap.

What were old Taras's feelings when thus he beheld his Ostap? What filled his heart then? He gazed at him from amid the crowd, and lost not a single movement of his. They reached the place of execution. Ostap stopped. He was to be the first to drink the bitter cup. He glanced at his comrades, raised his hand, and said in a loud voice: "God grant that none of the heretics who stand here may hear, the unclean dogs, how Christians suffer! Let none of us utter a single word." After this he ascended the scaffold.

"Well done, son! well done!" said Bulba, softly, and bent his grey head.

The executioner tore off his old rags; they fastened his hands and feet in stocks prepared expressly, and-- We will not pain the reader with a picture of the hellish tortures which would make his hair rise upright on his head. They were the outcome of that coarse, wild age, when men still led a life of warfare which hardened their souls until no sense of humanity was left in them. In vain did some, not many, in that age make a stand against such terrible measures. In vain did the king and many nobles, enlightened in mind and spirit, demonstrate that such severity of punishment could but fan the flame of vengeance in the Cossack nation. But the power of the king, and the opinion of the wise, was as nothing before the savage will of the magnates of the kingdom, who, by their thoughtlessness and unconquerable lack of all far-sighted policy, their childish self-love and miserable pride, converted the Diet into the mockery of a government. Ostap endured the torture like a giant. Not a cry, not a groan, was heard. Even when they began to break the bones in his hands and feet, when, amid the death-like stillness of the crowd, the horrible cracking was audible to the most distant spectators; when even his tormentors turned aside their eyes, nothing like a groan escaped his lips, nor did his face quiver. Taras stood in the crowd with bowed head; and, raising his eyes proudly at that moment, he said, approvingly, "Well done, boy! well done!"

But when they took him to the last deadly tortures, it seemed as though his strength were failing. He cast his eyes around.

O God! all strangers, all unknown faces! If only some of his relatives had been present at his death! He would not have cared to hear the sobs and anguish of his poor, weak mother, nor the unreasoning cries of a wife, tearing her hair and beating her white breast; but he would have liked to see a strong man who might refresh him with a word of wisdom, and cheer his end. And his strength failed him, and he cried in the weakness of his soul, "Father! where are you? do you hear?"

"I hear!" rang through the universal silence, and those thousands of people shuddered in concert. A detachment of cavalry hastened to search through the throng of people. Yankel turned pale as death, and when the horsemen had got within a short distance of him, turned round in terror to look for Taras; but Taras was no longer beside him; every trace of him was lost.

CHAPTER XII

They soon found traces of Taras. An army of a hundred and twenty thousand Cossacks appeared on the frontier of the Ukraine. This was no small detachment sallying forth for plunder or in pursuit of the Tatars. No: the whole nation had risen, for the measure of the people's patience was over-full; they had risen to avenge the disregard of their rights, the dishonourable humiliation of themselves, the insults to the faith of their fathers and their sacred customs, the outrages upon their church, the excesses of the foreign nobles, the disgraceful domination of the Jews on Christian soil, and all that had aroused and deepened the stern hatred of the Cossacks for a long time past. Hetman Ostranitza, young, but firm in mind, led the vast Cossack force. Beside him was seen his old and experienced friend and counsellor, Gunya. Eight leaders led bands of twelve thousand men each. Two osauls and a bunchuzhniy assisted the hetman. A cornet-general carried the chief standard, whilst many other banners and standards floated in the air; and the comrades of the staff bore the golden staff of the hetman, the symbol of his office. There were also many other officials belonging to the different bands, the baggage train and the main force with detachments of infantry and cavalry. There were almost as many free Cossacks and volunteers as there were registered Cossacks. The Cossacks had risen everywhere. They came from Tchigirin, from Pereyaslaf, from Baturin, from Glukhof, from the regions of the lower Dnieper, and from all its upper shores and islands. An uninterrupted stream of horses and herds of cattle stretched across the plain. And among all these Cossacks, among all these bands, one was the choicest; and that was the band led by Taras Bulba. All contributed to give him an influence over the others: his advanced years, his experience and skill in directing an army, and his bitter hatred of the foe. His unsparing fierceness and cruelty seemed exaggerated even to the Cossacks. His grey head dreamed of naught save fire and sword, and his utterances at the councils of war breathed only annihilation.

It is useless to describe all the battles in which the Cossacks distinguished themselves, or the gradual courses of the campaign. All this is set down in the chronicles. It is well known what an army raised on Russian soil, for the orthodox faith, is like. There is no power stronger than faith. It is threatening and invincible like a rock, and rising amidst the stormy, ever-changing sea. From the very bottom of the sea it rears to heaven its jagged sides of firm, impenetrable stone. It is visible from everywhere, and looks the waves straight in the face as they roll past. And woe to the ship which is dashed against it! Its frame flies into splinters, everything in it is split and crushed, and the startled air re-echoes the piteous cries of the drowning.

In the pages of the chronicles there is a minute description of how the Polish garrisons fled from the freed cities; how the unscrupulous Jewish tavern-keepers were hung; how powerless was the royal hetman, Nikolai Pototzky, with his numerous army, against this invincible force; how, routed and pursued, he lost the best of his troops by drowning in a small stream; how the fierce Cossack regiments besieged him in the little town of

Polon; and how, reduced to extremities, he promised, under oath, on the part of the king and the government, its full satisfaction to all, and the restoration of all their rights and privileges. But the Cossacks were not men to give way for this. They already knew well what a Polish oath was worth. And Pototzky would never more have pranced on his six-thousand ducat horse from the Kabardei, attracting the glances of distinguished ladies and the envy of the nobility; he would never more have made a figure in the Diet, by giving costly feasts to the senators--if the Russian priests who were in the little town had not saved him. When all the popes, in their brilliant gold vestments, went out to meet the Cossacks, bearing the holy pictures and the cross, with the bishop himself at their head, crosier in hand and mitre on his head, the Cossacks all bowed their heads and took off their caps. To no one lower than the king himself would they have shown respect at such an hour; but their daring fell before the Church of Christ, and they honoured their priesthood. The hetman and leaders agreed to release Pototzky, after having extracted from him a solemn oath to leave all the Christian churches unmolested, to forswear the ancient enmity, and to do no harm to the Cossack forces. One leader alone would not consent to such a peace. It was Taras. He tore a handful of hair from his head, and cried:

"Hetman and leaders! Commit no such womanish deed. Trust not the Lyakhs; slay the dogs!"

When the secretary presented the agreement, and the hetman put his hand to it, Taras drew a genuine Damascene blade, a costly Turkish sabre of the finest steel, broke it in twain like a reed, and threw the two pieces far away on each side, saying, "Farewell! As the two pieces of this sword will never reunite and form one sword again, so we, comrades, shall nevermore behold each other in this world. Remember my parting words." As he spoke his voice grew stronger, rose higher, and acquired a hitherto unknown power; and his prophetic utterances troubled them all. "Before the death hour you will remember me! Do you think that you have purchased peace and quiet? do you think that you will make a great show? You will make a great show, but after another fashion. They will flay the skin from your head, hetman, they will stuff it with bran, and long will it be exhibited at fairs. Neither will you retain your heads, gentles. You will be thrown into damp dungeons, walled about with stone, if they do not boil you alive in cauldrons like sheep. And you, men," he continued, turning to his followers, "which of you wants to die his true death? not through sorrows and the ale-house; but an honourable Cossack death, all in one bed, like bride and groom? But, perhaps, you would like to return home, and turn infidels, and carry Polish priests on your backs?"

"We will follow you, noble leader, we will follow you!" shouted all his band, and many others joined them.

"If it is to be so, then follow me," said Taras, pulling his cap farther over his brows. Looking menacingly at the others, he went to his horse, and cried to his men, "Let no one reproach us with any insulting speeches. Now, hey there, men! we'll call on the Catholics." And then he struck his horse, and there followed him a camp of a hundred waggons, and with them many Cossack cavalry and infantry; and, turning, he threatened with a glance all who remained behind, and wrath was in his eye. The band departed in full view of all the army, and Taras continued long to turn and glower.

The hetman and leaders were uneasy; all became thoughtful, and remained silent, as though oppressed by some heavy foreboding. Not in vain had Taras prophesied: all came to pass as he had foretold. A little later, after the treacherous attack at Kaneva, the hetman's head was mounted on a stake, together with those of many of his officers.

And what of Taras? Taras made raids all over Poland with his band, burned eighteen towns and nearly forty churches, and reached Cracow. He killed many nobles, and plundered some of the richest and finest castles. The Cossacks emptied on the ground the century-old mead and wine, carefully hoarded up in lordly cellars; they cut and burned the rich garments and equipments which they found in the wardrobes. "Spare nothing," was the order of Taras. The Cossacks spared not the black-browed gentlewomen, the brilliant, white-bosomed maidens: these could not save themselves even at the altar, for Taras burned them with the altar itself. Snowy hands were raised to heaven from amid fiery flames, with piteous shrieks which would have moved the damp earth itself to pity and caused the steppe-grass to bend with compassion at their fate. But the cruel Cossacks paid no heed; and, raising the children in the streets upon the points of their lances, they cast them also into the flames.

"This is a mass for the soul of Ostap, you heathen Lyakhs," was all that Taras said. And such masses for Ostap he had sung in every village, until the Polish Government perceived that Taras's raids were more than ordinary expeditions for plunder; and Pototzky was given five regiments, and ordered to capture him without fail.

Six days did the Cossacks retreat along the by-roads before their pursuers; their horses were almost equal to this unchecked flight, and nearly saved them. But this time Pototzky was also equal to the task intrusted to him; unweariedly he followed them, and overtook them on the bank of the Dniester, where Taras had taken possession of an abandoned and ruined castle for the purpose of resting.

On the very brink of the Dniester it stood, with its shattered ramparts and the ruined remnants of its walls. The summit of the cliff was strewn with ragged stones and broken bricks, ready at any moment to detach themselves. The royal hetman, Pototzky, surrounded it on the two sides which faced the plain. Four days did the Cossacks fight, tearing down bricks and stones for missiles. But their stones and their strength were at length exhausted, and Taras resolved to cut his way through the beleaguering forces. And the Cossacks would have cut their way through, and their swift steeds might again have served them faithfully, had not Taras halted suddenly in the very midst of their flight, and shouted, "Halt! my pipe has dropped with its tobacco: I won't let those heathen Lyakhs have my pipe!" And the old hetman stooped down, and felt in the grass for his pipe full of tobacco, his inseparable companion on all his expeditions by sea and land and at home.

But in the meantime a band of Lyakhs suddenly rushed up, and seized him by the shoulders. He struggled with all might; but he could not scatter on the earth, as he had been wont to do, the heydukes who had seized him. "Oh, old age, old age!" he exclaimed: and the stout old Cossack wept. But his age was not to blame: nearly thirty men were clinging to his arms and legs.

"The raven is caught!" yelled the Lyakhs. "We must think how we can show him the most honour, the dog!" They decided, with the permission of the hetman, to burn him alive in the sight of all. There stood hard by a leafless tree, the summit of which had been struck by lightning. They fastened him with iron chains and nails driven through his hands high up on the trunk of the tree, so that he might be seen from all sides; and began at once to place fagots at its foot. But Taras did not look at the wood, nor did he think of the fire with which they were preparing to roast him: he gazed anxiously in the direction whence his Cossacks were firing. From his high point of observation he could see everything as in the palm of his hand.

"Take possession, men," he shouted, "of the hillock behind the wood: they cannot climb it!" But the wind did not carry his words to them. "They are lost, lost!" he said in despair, and glanced down to where the water of the Dniester glittered. Joy gleamed in his eyes. He saw the sterns of four boats peeping out from behind some bushes; exerted all the power of his lungs, and shouted in a ringing tone, "To the bank, to the bank, men! descend the path to the left, under the cliff. There are boats on the bank; take all, that they may not catch you."

This time the breeze blew from the other side, and his words were audible to the Cossacks. But for this counsel he received a blow on the head with the back of an axe, which made everything dance before his eyes.

The Cossacks descended the cliff path at full speed, but their pursuers were at their heels. They looked: the path wound and twisted, and made many detours to one side. "Comrades, we are trapped!" said they. All halted for an instant, raised their whips, whistled, and their Tatar horses rose from the ground, clove the air like serpents, flew over the precipice, and plunged straight into the Dniester. Two only did not alight in the river, but thundered down from the height upon the stones, and perished there with their horses without uttering a cry. But the Cossacks had already swum shoreward from their horses, and unfastened the boats, when the Lyakhs halted on the brink of the precipice, astounded by this wonderful feat, and thinking, "Shall we jump down to them, or not?"

One young colonel, a lively, hot-blooded soldier, own brother to the beautiful Pole who had seduced poor Andrii, did not reflect long, but leaped with his horse after the Cossacks. He made three turns in the air with his steed, and fell heavily on the rocks. The sharp stones tore him in pieces; and his brains, mingled with blood, bespattered the shrubs growing on the uneven walls of the precipice.

When Taras Bulba recovered from the blow, and glanced towards the Dniester, the Cossacks were already in the skiffs and rowing away. Balls were showered upon them from above but did not reach them. And the old hetman's eyes sparkled with joy.

"Farewell, comrades!" he shouted to them from above; "remember me, and come hither again next spring and make merry in the same fashion! What! cursed Lyakhs, have ye caught me? Think ye there is anything in the world that a Cossack fears? Wait; the time will come when ye shall learn what the orthodox Russian faith is! Already the people scent it far and near.

A czar shall arise from Russian soil, and there shall not be a power in the world which shall not submit to him!" But fire had already risen from the fagots; it lapped his feet, and the flame spread to the tree. . . . But can any fire, flames, or power be found on earth which are capable of overpowering Russian strength?

Broad is the river Dniester, and in it are many deep pools, dense reed-beds, clear shallows and little bays; its watery mirror gleams, filled with the melodious plaint of the swan, the proud wild goose glides swiftly over it; and snipe, red-throated ruffs, and other birds are to be found among the reeds and along the banks. The Cossacks rowed swiftly on in the narrow double-ruddered boats--rowed stoutly, carefully shunning the sand bars, and cleaving the ranks of the birds, which took wing--rowed, and talked of their hetman.

ST. JOHN'S EVE

A STORY TOLD BY THE SACRISTAN OF THE DIKANKA CHURCH

Thoma Grigroovitch had one very strange eccentricity: to the day of his death he never liked to tell the same thing twice. There were times when, if you asked him to relate a thing afresh, he would interpolate new matter, or alter it so that it was impossible to recognise it. Once upon a time, one of those gentlemen who, like the usurers at our yearly fairs, clutch and beg and steal every sort of frippery, and issue mean little volumes, no thicker than an A B C book, every month, or even every week, wormed this same story out of Thoma Grigorovitch, and the latter completely forgot about it. But that same young gentleman, in the pea-green caftan, came from Poltava, bringing with him a little book, and, opening it in the middle, showed it to us. Thoma Grigorovitch was on the point of setting his spectacles astride of his nose, but recollected that he had forgotten to wind thread about them and stick them together with wax, so he passed it over to me. As I understand nothing about reading and writing, and do not wear spectacles, I undertook to read it. I had not turned two leaves when all at once he caught me by the hand and stopped me.

"Stop! tell me first what you are reading."

I confess that I was a trifle stunned by such a question.

"What! what am I reading, Thoma Grigorovitch? Why, your own words."

"Who told you that they were my words?"

"Why, what more would you have? Here it is printed: 'Related by such and such a sacristan.'"

"Spit on the head of the man who printed that! he lies, the dog of a Moscow pedlar! Did I say that? "Twas just the same as though one hadn't his wits about him!' Listen. I'll tell the tale to you on the spot."

We moved up to the table, and he began.

*

My grandfather (the kingdom of heaven be his! may he eat only wheaten rolls and poppy-seed cakes with honey in the other world!) could tell a story wonderfully well. When he used to begin a tale you could not stir from the spot all day, but kept on listening. He was not like the story-teller of the present day, when he begins to lie, with a tongue as though he had had nothing to eat for three days, so that you snatch your cap and flee from the house. I remember my old mother was alive then, and in the long winter evenings when the frost was crackling out of doors, and had sealed up hermetically the narrow panes of our cottage, she used to sit at her wheel, drawing out a long thread in her hand, rocking the cradle with her foot, and humming a song, which I seem to hear even now.

The lamp, quivering and flaring up as though in fear of something, lighted up our cottage; the spindle hummed; and all of us children, collected in a cluster, listened to grandfather, who had not crawled off the stove for more than five years, owing to his great age. But the wondrous tales of the incursions of the Zaporozhian Cossacks and the Poles, the bold deeds of Podkova, of Poltar-Kozhukh, and Sagaidatchnii, did not interest us so much as the stories about some deed of old which always sent a shiver through our frames and made our hair rise upright on our heads. Sometimes such terror took possession of us in consequence of them, that, from that evening forward, Heaven knows how wonderful everything seemed to us. If one chanced to go out of the cottage after nightfall for anything, one fancied that a visitor from the other world had lain down to sleep in one's bed; and I have often taken my own smock, at a distance, as it lay at the head of the bed, for the Evil One rolled up into a ball! But the chief thing about grandfather's stories was, that he never lied in all his life; and whatever he said was so, was so.

I will now tell you one of his wonderful tales. I know that there are a great many wise people who copy in the courts, and can even read civil documents, but who, if you were to put into their hand a simple prayer-book, could not make out the first letter in it, and would show all their teeth in derision. These people laugh at everything you tell them. Along comes one of them--and doesn't believe in witches! Yes, glory to God that I have lived so long in the world! I have seen heretics to whom it would be easier to lie in confession than it would be to our brothers and equals to take snuff, and these folk would deny the existence of witches! But let them just dream about something, and they won't even tell what it was! There, it is no use talking about them!

No one could have recognised the village of ours a little over a hundred years ago; it was a hamlet, the poorest kind of a hamlet. Half a score of miserable farmhouses, unplastered and badly thatched, were scattered here and there about the fields. There was not a yard or a decent shed to shelter animals or waggons. That was the way the wealthy lived: and if you had looked for our brothers, the poor--why, a hole in the ground--that was a cabin for you! Only by the smoke could you tell that a God-created man lived there. You ask why they lived so? It was not entirely through poverty: almost every one led a raiding Cossack life, and gathered not a little plunder in foreign lands; it was rather because it was little use building up a good wooden house. Many folk were engaged in raids all over the country--Crimeans, Poles, Lithuanians! It was quite possible that their own countrymen might make a descent and plunder everything. Anything was possible.

In this hamlet a man, or rather a devil in human form, often made his appearance. Why he came, and whence, no one knew. He prowled about, got drunk, and suddenly disappeared as if into the air, leaving no trace of his existence. Then, behold, he seemed to have dropped from the sky again, and went flying about the street of the village, of which no trace now remains, and which was not more than a hundred paces from Dikanka. He would collect together all the Cossacks he met; then there were songs, laughter, and cash in plenty, and vodka flowed like water. . . . He would address the pretty girls, and give them ribbons, earrings, strings of beads-- more than they knew what to do with. It is true that the pretty girls rather hesitated about accepting his presents: God knows, perhaps, what unclean hands they had passed through. My grandfather's aunt, who kept at that time a tavern, in which Basavriuk (as they called this devil-man) often caroused, said that no consideration on the earth would have induced her to accept a gift from him. But then, again, how avoid accepting? Fear seized on every one when he knit his shaggy brows, and gave a sidelong glance which might send your feet God knows whither: whilst if you did accept, then the next night some fiend from the swamp, with horns on his head, came and began to squeeze your neck, if there was a string of beads upon it; or bite your finger, if there was a ring upon it; or drag you by the hair, if ribbons were braided in it. God have mercy, then, on those who held such gifts! But here was the difficulty: it was impossible to get rid of them; if you threw them into the water, the diabolical ring or necklace would skim along the surface and into your hand.

There was a church in the village--St. Pantelei, if I remember rightly. There lived there a priest, Father Athanasii of blessed memory. Observing that Basavriuk did not come to church, even at Easter, he determined to reprove him and impose penance upon him. Well, he hardly escaped with his life. "Hark ye, sir!" he thundered in reply, "learn to mind your own business instead of meddling in other people's, if you don't want that throat of yours stuck with boiling kutya[1]." What was to be done with this unrepentant man? Father Athanasii contented himself with announcing that any one who should make the acquaintance of Basavriuk would be counted a Catholic, an enemy of Christ's orthodox church, not a member of the human race.

[1] A dish of rice or wheat flour, with honey and raisins, which is brought to the church on the celebration of memorial masses.

In this village there was a Cossack named Korzh, who had a labourer whom people called Peter the Orphan--perhaps because no one remembered either his father or mother. The church elder, it is true, said that they had died of the pest in his second year; but my grandfather's aunt would not hear of that, and tried with all her might to furnish him with parents, although poor Peter needed them about as much as we need last year's snow. She said that his father had been in Zaporozhe, and had been taken prisoner by the Turks, amongst whom he underwent God only knows what tortures, until having, by some miracle, disguised himself as a eunuch, he made his escape. Little cared the black-browed youths and maidens about Peter's parents. They merely remarked, that if he only had a new coat, a red sash, a black lambskin cap with a smart blue crown on his head, a Turkish sabre by his side, a whip in one hand and a pipe with handsome mountings in the other, he would surpass all the young men. But the pity was, that the only thing poor Peter had was a grey gaberdine with more holes in it than there are gold pieces in a Jew's pocket. But that was not the worst of it. Korzh had a daughter, such a beauty as I think you can hardly have chanced to see. My grandfather's aunt used to say--and you know that it is easier for a woman to kiss the Evil One than to call any one else a beauty--that this Cossack maiden's cheeks were as plump and fresh as the pinkest poppy when, bathed in God's dew, it unfolds its petals, and coquets with the rising sun; that her brows were evenly arched over her bright eyes like black cords, such as our maidens buy nowadays, for their crosses and ducats, off the Moscow pedlars who visit the villages with their baskets; that her little mouth, at sight of which the youths smacked their lips, seemed made to warble the songs of nightingales; that her hair, black as the raven's wing, and soft as young flax, fell in curls over her shoulders, for our maidens did not then plait their hair in pigtails interwoven with pretty, bright-hued ribbons. Eh! may I never intone another alleluia in the choir, if I would not have kissed her, in spite of the grey which is making its way through the old wool which covers my pate, and of the old woman beside me, like a thorn in my side! Well, you know what happens when young men and maidens live side by side. In the twilight the heels of red boots were always visible in the place where Pidorka chatted with her Peter. But Korzh would never have suspected anything out of the way, only one day-- it is evident that none but the Evil One could have inspired him--Peter took into his head to kiss the maiden's rosy lips with all his heart, without first looking well about him; and that same Evil One--may the son of a dog dream of the holy cross!--caused the old grey-beard, like a fool, to open the cottage door at that same moment. Korzh was petrified, dropped his jaw, and clutched at the door for support. Those unlucky kisses completely stunned him.

Recovering himself, he took his grandfather's hunting whip from the wall, and was about to belabour Peter's back with it, when Pidorka's little six-year-old brother Ivas rushed up from somewhere or other, and, grasping his father's legs with his little hands, screamed out, "Daddy, daddy! don't beat Peter!" What was to be done? A father's heart is not made of stone. Hanging the whip again on the wall, he led Peter quietly from the house. "If you ever show yourself in my cottage again, or even under the windows, look out, Peter, for, by heaven, your black moustache will disappear; and your black locks, though wound twice about your ears, will take leave of your pate, or my name is not Terentiy Korzh." So saying, he gave him such a taste of his fist in the nape of his neck, that all grew dark before Peter, and he flew headlong out of the place.

So there was an end of their kissing. Sorrow fell upon our turtle doves; and a rumour grew rife in the village that a certain Pole, all embroidered with gold, with moustaches, sabre, spurs, and pockets jingling like the bells of the bag with which our sacristan Taras goes through the church every day, had begun to frequent Korzh's house. Now, it is well known why a father has visitors when there is a black-browed daughter about. So, one day, Pidorka burst into tears, and caught the hand of her brother Ivas. "Ivas, my dear! Ivas, my love! fly to Peter, my child of gold, like an arrow from a bow. Tell him all: I would have loved his brown eyes, I would have kissed his fair face, but my fate decrees otherwise. More than one handkerchief have I wet with burning tears. I am sad and heavy at heart. And my own father is my enemy. I will not marry the Pole, whom I do not love. Tell him they are making ready for a wedding, but there will be no music at our wedding: priests will sing instead of pipes and viols. I shall not dance with my bridegroom: they will carry me out. Dark, dark will be my dwelling of maple wood; and, instead of chimneys, a cross will stand upon the roof."

Peter stood petrified, without moving from the spot, when the innocent child lisped out Pidorka's words to him. "And I, wretched man, had thought to go to the Crimea and Turkey, to win gold and return to thee, my beauty! But it may not be. We have been overlooked by the evil eye. I too shall have a wedding, dear one; but no ecclesiastics will be present at that wedding. The black crow instead of the pope will caw over me; the bare plain will be my dwelling; the dark blue cloud my roof-tree. The eagle will claw out my brown eyes: the rain will wash my Cossack bones, and the whirlwinds dry them. But what am I? Of what should I complain? 'Tis clear God willed it so. If I am to be lost, then so be it!" and he went straight to the tavern.

My late grandfather's aunt was somewhat surprised at seeing Peter at the tavern, at an hour when good men go to morning mass; and stared at him as though in a dream when he called for a jug of brandy, about half a pailful. But the poor fellow tried in vain to drown his woe. The vodka stung his tongue like nettles, and tasted more bitter than wormwood. He flung the jug from him upon the ground.

"You have sorrowed enough, Cossack," growled a bass voice behind him. He looked round--it was Basavriuk! Ugh, what a face! His hair was like a brush, his eyes like those of a bull. "I know what you lack: here it is." As he spoke he jingled a leather purse which hung from his girdle and smiled diabolically. Peter shuddered. "Ha, ha, ha! how it shines!" he roared, shaking out ducats into his hands: "ha, ha, ha! how it jingles! And I only ask one thing for a whole pile of such shiners."

"It is the Evil One!" exclaimed Peter. "Give me them! I'm ready for anything!"

They struck hands upon it, and Basavriuk said, "You are just in time, Peter: to-morrow is St. John the Baptist's day. Only on this one night in the year does the fern blossom. I will await you at midnight in the Bear's ravine."

I do not believe that chickens await the hour when the housewife brings their corn with as much anxiety as Peter awaited the evening. He kept looking to see whether the shadows of the trees were not lengthening, whether the sun was not turning red towards setting; and, the longer he watched, the more impatient he grew. How long it was! Evidently, God's day had lost its end somewhere. But now the sun has set. The sky is red only on one side, and it is already growing dark. It grows colder in the fields. It gets gloomier and gloomier, and at last quite dark. At last! With heart almost bursting from his bosom, he set out and cautiously made his way down through the thick woods into the deep hollow called the Bear's ravine. Basavriuk was already waiting there. It was so dark that you could not see a yard before you. Hand in hand they entered the ravine, pushing through the luxuriant thorn-bushes and stumbling at almost every step. At last they reached an open spot. Peter looked about him: he had never chanced to come there before. Here Basavriuk halted.

"Do you see before you three hillocks? There are a great many kinds of flowers upon them. May some power keep you from plucking even one of them. But as soon as the fern blossoms, seize it, and look not round, no matter what may seem to be going on behind thee."

Peter wanted to ask some questions, but behold Basavriuk was no longer there. He approached the three hillocks--where were the flowers? He saw none. The wild steppe-grass grew all around, and hid everything in its luxuriance. But the lightning flashed; and before him was a whole bed of flowers, all wonderful, all strange: whilst amongst them there were also the simple fronds of fern. Peter doubted his senses, and stood thoughtfully before them, arms akimbo.

"What manner of prodigy is this? why, one can see these weeds ten times a day. What is there marvellous about them? Devil's face must be mocking me!"

But behold! the tiny flower-bud of the fern reddened and moved as though alive. It was a marvel in truth. It grew larger and larger, and glowed like a burning coal. The tiny stars of light flashed up, something burst softly, and the flower opened before his eyes like a flame, lighting the others about it.

"Now is the time," thought Peter, and extended his hand. He saw hundreds of hairy hands reach also for the flower from behind him, and there was a sound of scampering in his rear. He half closed his eyes, and plucked sharply at the stalk, and the flower remained in his hand.

All became still.

Upon a stump sat Basavriuk, quite blue like a corpse. He did not move so much as a finger. Hi eyes were immovably fixed on something visible to him alone; his mouth was half open and speechless. Nothing stirred around. Ugh! it was horrible! But then a whistle was heard which made Peter's heart grow cold within him; and it seemed to him that the grass whispered, and the flowers began to talk among themselves in delicate voices, like little silver bells, while the trees rustled in murmuring contention;-- Basavriuk's face suddenly became full of life, and his eyes sparkled. "The witch has just returned," he muttered between his teeth. "Hearken, Peter: a charmer will stand before you in a moment; do whatever she commands; if not--you are lost forever."

Then he parted the thorn-bushes with a knotty stick and before him stood a tiny farmhouse. Basavriuk smote it with his fist, and the wall trembled. A large black dog ran out to meet them, and with a whine transformed itself into a cat and flew straight at his eyes.

"Don't be angry, don't be angry, you old Satan!" said Basavriuk, employing such words as would have made a good man stop his ears. Behold, instead of a cat, an old woman all bent into a bow, with a face wrinkled like a baked apple, and a nose and chin like a pair of nutcrackers.

"A fine charmer!" thought Peter; and cold chills ran down his back. The witch tore the flower from his hand, stooped and muttered over it for a long time, sprinkling it with some kind of water. Sparks flew from her mouth, and foam appeared on her lips.

"Throw it away," she said, giving it back to Peter.

Peter threw it, but what wonder was this? The flower did not fall straight to the earth, but for a long while twinkled like a fiery ball through the darkness, and swam through the air like a boat. At last it began to sink lower and lower, and fell so far away that the little star, hardly larger than a poppy-seed, was barely visible. "There!" croaked the old woman, in a dull voice: and Basavriuk, giving him a spade, said, "Dig here, Peter: you will find more gold than you or Korzh ever dreamed of."

Peter spat on his hands, seized the spade, pressed his foot on it, and turned up the earth, a second, a third, a fourth time. The spade clinked against something hard, and would go no further. Then his eyes began to distinguish a small, iron-bound coffer. He tried to seize it; but the chest began to sink into the earth, deeper, farther, and deeper still: whilst behind him he heard a laugh like a serpent's hiss.

"No, you shall not have the gold until you shed human blood," said the witch, and she led up to him a child of six, covered with a white sheet, and indicated by a sign that he was to cut off his head.

Peter was stunned. A trifle, indeed, to cut off a man's, or even an innocent child's, head for no reason whatever! In wrath he tore off the sheet enveloping the victim's head, and behold! before him stood Ivas. The poor child crossed his little hands, and hung his head. Peter flew at the witch with the knife like a madman, and was on the point of laying hands on her.

"What did you promise for the girl?" thundered Basavriuk; and like a shot he was on his back. The witch stamped her foot: a blue flame flashed from the earth and illumined all within it. The earth became transparent as if moulded of crystal; and all that was within it became visible, as if in the palm of the hand. Ducats, precious stones in chests and pots, were piled in heaps beneath the very spot they stood on. Peter's eyes flashed, his mind grew troubled. . . . He grasped the knife like a madman, and the innocent blood spurted into his eyes. Diabolical laughter resounded on all sides. Misshapen monsters flew past him in flocks. The witch, fastening her hands in the headless trunk, like a wolf, drank its blood. His head whirled. Collecting all his strength, he set out to run. Everything grew red before him. The trees seemed steeped in blood, and burned and groaned. The sky glowed and threatened. Burning points, like lightning, flickered before his eyes. Utterly exhausted, he rushed into his miserable hovel and fell to the ground like a log. A death-like sleep overpowered him.

Two days and two nights did Peter sleep, without once awakening. When he came to himself, on the third day, he looked long at all the corners of his hut, but in vain did he endeavour to recollect what had taken place; his memory was like a miser's pocket, from which you cannot entice a quarter of a kopek. Stretching himself, he heard something clash at his feet. He looked, there were two bags of gold. Then only, as if in a dream, he recollected that he had been seeking for treasure, and that something had frightened him in the woods.

Korzh saw the sacks--and was mollified. "A fine fellow, Peter, quite unequalled! yes, and did I not love him? Was he not to me as my own son?" And the old fellow repeated this fiction until he wept over it himself. Pidorka began to tell Peter how some passing gipsies had stolen Ivas; but he could not even recall him--to such a degree had the Devil's influence darkened his mind! There was no reason for delay. The Pole was dismissed, and the wedding-feast prepared; rolls were baked, towels and handkerchiefs embroidered; the young people were seated at table; the wedding-loaf was cut; guitars, cymbals, pipes, viols sounded, and pleasure was rife.

A wedding in the olden times was not like one of the present day. My grandfather's aunt used to tell how the maidens--in festive head-dresses of yellow, blue, and pink ribbons, above which they bound gold braid; in thin chemisettes embroidered on all the seams with red silk, and strewn with tiny silver flowers; in morocco shoes, with high iron heels--danced the gorlitza as swimmingly as peacocks, and as wildly as the whirlwind; how the youths--with their ship-shaped caps upon their heads, the crowns of gold brocade, and two horns projecting, one in front and another behind, of the very finest black lambskin; in tunics of the finest blue silk with red borders--stepped forward one by one, their arms akimbo in stately form, and executed the gopak; how the lads--in tall Cossack caps, and light cloth gaberdines, girt with silver embroidered belts, their short pipes in their teeth--skipped before them and talked nonsense. Even Korzh as he gazed at the young people could not help getting gay in his old age. Guitar in hand, alternately puffing at his pipe and singing, a brandy-glass upon his head, the greybeard began the national dance amid loud shouts from the merry-makers.

What will not people devise in merry mood? They even began to disguise their faces till they did not look like human beings. On such occasions one would dress himself as a Jew, another as the Devil: they would begin by kissing each other, and end by seizing each other by the hair. God be with them! you laughed till you held your sides. They dressed themselves in Turkish and Tatar garments. All upon them glowed like a conflagration, and then they began to joke and play pranks. . . .

An amusing thing happened to my grandfather's aunt, who was at this wedding. She was wearing an ample Tatar robe, and, wine-glass in hand, was entertaining the company. The Evil One instigated one man to pour vodka over her from behind. Another, at the same moment, evidently not by accident, struck a light, and held it to her. The flame flashed up, and poor aunt, in terror, flung her dress off, before them all. Screams, laughter, jests, arose as if at a fair. In a word, the old folks could not recall so merry a wedding.

Pidorka and Peter began to live like a gentleman and lady. There was plenty of everything and everything was fine. . . . But honest folk shook their heads when they marked their way of living. "From the Devil no good can come," they unanimously agreed. "Whence, except from the tempter of orthodox people, came this wealth? Where else could he have got such a lot of gold from? Why, on the very day that he got rich, did Basavriuk vanish as if into thin air?"

Say, if you can, that people only imagine things! A month had not passed, and no one would have recognised Peter. He sat in one spot, saying no word to any one; but continually thinking and seemingly trying to recall something. When Pidorka succeeded in getting him to speak, he appeared to forget himself, and would carry on a conversation, and even grow cheerful; but if he inadvertently glanced at the sacks, "Stop, stop! I have forgotten," he would cry, and again plunge into reverie and strive to recall something. Sometimes when he sat still a long time in one place, it seemed to him as though it were coming, just coming back to mind, but again all would fade away. It seemed as if he was sitting in the tavern: they brought him vodka; vodka stung him; vodka was repulsive to him. Some one came along and struck him on the shoulder; but beyond that everything was veiled in darkness before him. The perspiration would stream down his face, and he would sit exhausted in the same place.

What did not Pirdorka do? She consulted the sorceresses; and they poured out fear, and brewed stomach ache[2]--but all to no avail. And so the summer passed. Many a Cossack had mowed and reaped; many a Cossack, more enterprising than the rest, had set off upon an expedition. Flocks of ducks were already crowding the marshes, but there was not even a hint of improvement.

[2] "To pour out fear" refers to a practice resorted to in case of fear. When it is desired to know what caused this, melted lead or wax is poured into water, and the object whose form it assumes is the one which frightened

the sick person; after this, the fear departs. Sonyashnitza is brewed for giddiness and pain in the bowels. To this end, a bit of stump is burned, thrown into a jug, and turned upside down into a bowl filled with water, which is placed on the patient's stomach: after an incantation, he is given a spoonful of this water to drink.

It was red upon the steppes. Ricks of grain, like Cossack's caps, dotted the fields here and there. On the highway were to be encountered waggons loaded with brushwood and logs. The ground had become more solid, and in places was touched with frost. Already had the snow begun to fall and the branches of the trees were covered with rime like rabbit-skin. Already on frosty days the robin redbreast hopped about on the snow-heaps like a foppish Polish nobleman, and picked out grains of corn; and children, with huge sticks, played hockey upon the ice; while their fathers lay quietly on the stove, issuing forth at intervals with lighted pipes in their lips, to growl, in regular fashion, at the orthodox frost, or to take the air, and thresh the grain spread out in the barn. At last the snow began to melt, and the ice slipped away: but Peter remained the same; and, the more time went on, the more morose he grew. He sat in the cottage as though nailed to the spot, with the sacks of gold at his feet. He grew averse to companionship, his hair grew long, he became terrible to look at; and still he thought of but one thing, still he tried to recall something, and got angry and ill-tempered because he could not. Often, rising wildly from his seat, he gesticulated violently and fixed his eyes on something as though desirous of catching it: his lips moving as though desirous of uttering some long-forgotten word, but remaining speechless. Fury would take possession of him: he would gnaw and bite his hands like a man half crazy, and in his vexation would tear out his hair by the handful, until, calming down, he would relapse into forgetfulness, as it were, and then would again strive to recall the past and be again seized with fury and fresh tortures. What visitation of God was this?

Pidorka was neither dead not alive. At first it was horrible for her to remain alone with him in the cottage; but, in course of time, the poor woman grew accustomed to her sorrow. But it was impossible to recognise the Pidorka of former days. No blushes, no smiles: she was thin and worn with grief, and had wept her bright eyes away. Once some one who took pity on her advised her to go to the witch who dwelt in the Bear's ravine, and enjoyed the reputation of being able to cure every disease in the world. She determined to try that last remedy: and finally persuaded the old woman to come to her. This was on St. John's Eve, as it chanced. Peter lay insensible on the bench, and did not observe the newcomer. Slowly he rose, and looked about him. Suddenly he trembled in every limb, as though he were on the scaffold: his hair rose upon his head, and he laughed a laugh that filled Pidorka's heart with fear.

"I have remembered, remembered!" he cried, in terrible joy; and, swinging a hatchet round his head, he struck at the old woman with all his might. The hatchet penetrated the oaken door nearly four inches. The old woman disappeared; and a child of seven, covered in a white sheet, stood in the middle of the cottage. . . . The sheet flew off. "Ivas!" cried Pidorka, and ran to him; but the apparition became covered from head to foot with blood, and illumined the whole room with red light. . . .

She ran into the passage in her terror, but, on recovering herself a little, wished to help Peter. In vain! the door had slammed to behind her, so that she could not open it. People ran up, and began to knock: they broke in the door, as though there were but one mind among them. The whole cottage was full of smoke; and just in the middle, where Peter had stood, was a heap of ashes whence smoke was still rising. They flung themselves upon the sacks: only broken potsherds lay there instead of ducats. The Cossacks stood with staring eyes and open mouths, as if rooted to the earth, not daring to move a hair, such terror did this wonder inspire in them.

I do not remember what happened next. Pidorka made a vow to go upon a pilgrimage, collected the property left her by her father, and in a few days it was as if she had never been in the village. Whither she had gone, no one could tell. Officious old women would have despatched her to the same place whither Peter had gone; but a Cossack from Kief reported that he had seen, in a cloister, a nun withered to a mere skeleton who prayed unceasingly. Her fellow-villagers recognised her as Pidorka by the tokens-- that no one heard her utter a word; and that she had come on foot, and had brought a frame for the picture of God's mother, set with such brilliant stones that all were dazzled at the sight.

But this was not the end, if you please. On the same day that the Evil One made away with Peter, Basavriuk appeared again; but all fled from him. They knew what sort of a being he was--none else than Satan, who had assumed human form in order to unearth treasures; and, since treasures do not yield to unclean hands, he seduced the young. That same year, all deserted their earthen huts and collected in a village; but even there there was no peace on account of that accursed Basavriuk.

My late grandfather's aunt said that he was particularly angry with her because she had abandoned her former tavern, and tried with all his might to revenge himself upon her. Once the village elders were assembled in the tavern, and, as the saying goes, were arranging the precedence at the table, in the middle of which was placed a small roasted lamb, shame to say. They chattered about this, that, and the other--among the rest about various marvels and strange things. Well, they saw something; it would have been nothing if only one had seen it, but all saw it, and it was this: the sheep raised his head, his goggling eyes became alive and sparkled; and the black, bristling moustache, which appeared for one instant, made a significant gesture at those present. All at once recognised Basavriuk's countenance in the sheep's head; my grandfather's aunt thought it was on the point of asking for vodka. The worthy elders seized their hats and hastened home.

Another time, the church elder himself, who was fond of an occasional private interview with my grandfather's brandy-glass, had not succeeded in getting to the bottom twice, when he beheld the glass bowing very low to him. "Satan take you, let us make the sign of the cross over you!"--And the same marvel happened to his better half. She had just begun to mix the dough in a huge kneading-trough when suddenly the trough sprang up. "Stop, stop! where are you going?" Putting its arms akimbo, with dignity, it went skipping all about the cottage--you may laugh, but it was no laughing matter to our grandfathers. And in vain did Father Athanasii go through all the village with holy water, and chase the Devil through all the streets with his brush. My late grandfather's aunt long complained that, as soon as it was dark, some one came knocking at her door and scratching at the wall.

Well! All appears to be quiet now in the place where our village stands; but it was not so very long ago--my father was still alive--that I remember how a good man could not pass the ruined tavern which a dishonest race had long managed for their own interest. From the smoke-blackened chimneys smoke poured out in a pillar, and rising high in the air, rolled off like a cap, scattering burning coals over the steppe; and Satan (the son of a dog should not be mentioned) sobbed so pitifully in his lair that the startled ravens rose in flocks from the neighbouring oak-wood and flew through the air with wild cries.

THE CLOAK

In the department of--but it is better not to mention the department. There is nothing more irritable than departments, regiments, courts of justice, and, in a word, every branch of public service. Each individual attached to them nowadays thinks all society insulted in his person. Quite recently a complaint was received from a justice of the peace, in which he plainly demonstrated that all the imperial institutions were going to the dogs, and that the Czar's sacred name was being taken in vain; and in proof he appended to the complaint a romance in which the justice of the peace is made to appear about once every ten lines, and sometimes in a drunken condition. Therefore, in order to avoid all unpleasantness, it will be better to describe the department in question only as a certain department.

So, in a certain department there was a certain official--not a very high one, it must be allowed--short of stature, somewhat pock-marked, red-haired, and short-sighted, with a bald forehead, wrinkled cheeks, and a complexion of the kind known as sanguine. The St. Petersburg climate was responsible for this. As for his official status, he was what is called a perpetual titular councillor, over which, as is well known, some writers make merry, and crack their jokes, obeying the praiseworthy custom of attacking those who cannot bite back.

His family name was Bashmatchkin. This name is evidently derived from "bashmak" (shoe); but when, at what time, and in what manner, is not known. His father and grandfather, and all the Bashmatchkins, always wore boots, which only had new heels two or three times a year. His name was Akakiy Akakievitch. It may strike the reader as rather singular and far-fetched, but he may rest assured that it was by no means far-fetched, and that the circumstances were such that it would have been impossible to give him any other.

This is how it came about.

Akakiy Akakievitch was born, if my memory fails me not, in the evening of the 23rd of March. His mother, the wife of a Government official and a very fine woman, made all due arrangements for having the child baptised. She was lying on the bed opposite the door; on her right stood the godfather, Ivan Ivanovitch Eroshkin, a most estimable man, who served as presiding officer of the senate, while the godmother, Anna Semenovna Byelobrushkova, the wife of an officer of the quarter, and a woman of rare virtues. They offered the mother her choice of three names, Mokiya, Sossiya, or that the child should be called after the martyr Khozdazat. "No," said the good woman, "all those names are poor." In order to please her they opened the calendar to another place; three more names appeared, Triphiliy, Dula, and Varakhasiy. "This is a judgment," said the old woman. "What names! I truly never heard the like. Varada or Varukh might have been borne, but not Triphiliy and Varakhasiy!" They turned to another page and found Pavsikakhiy and Vakhtisiy. "Now I see," said the old woman, "that it is plainly fate. And since such is the case, it will be better to name him after his father. His father's name was Akakiy, so let his son's be Akakiy too." In this manner he became Akakiy Akakievitch. They christened the child, whereat he wept and made a grimace, as though he foresaw that he was to be a titular councillor.

 In this manner did it all come about. We have mentioned it in order that the reader might see for himself that it was a case of necessity, and that it was utterly impossible to give him any other name. When and how he entered the department, and who appointed him, no one could remember. However much the directors and chiefs of all kinds were changed, he was always to be seen in the same place, the same attitude, the same occupation; so that it was afterwards affirmed that he had been born in undress uniform with a bald head. No respect was shown him in the department. The porter not only did not rise from his seat when he passed, but never even glanced at him, any more than if a fly had flown through the reception-room. His superiors treated him in coolly despotic fashion. Some sub-chief would thrust a paper under his nose without so much as saying, "Copy," or "Here's a nice interesting affair," or anything else agreeable, as is customary amongst well-bred officials. And he took it, looking only at the paper and not observing who handed it to him, or whether he had the right to do so; simply took it, and set about copying it.

 The young officials laughed at and made fun of him, so far as their official wit permitted; told in his presence various stories concocted about him, and about his landlady, an old woman of seventy; declared that she beat him; asked when the wedding was to be; and strewed bits of paper over his head, calling them snow. But Akakiy Akakievitch answered not a word, any more than if there had been no one there besides himself. It even had no effect upon his work: amid all these annoyances he never made a single mistake in a letter. But if the joking became wholly unbearable, as when they jogged his hand and prevented his attending to his work, he would exclaim, "Leave me alone! Why do you insult me?" And there was something strange in the words and the voice in which they were uttered. There was in it something which moved to pity; so much that one young man, a new-comer, who, taking pattern by the others, had permitted himself to make sport of Akakiy, suddenly stopped short, as though all about him had undergone a transformation, and presented itself in a different aspect. Some unseen force repelled him from the comrades whose acquaintance he had made, on the supposition that they were well-bred and polite men. Long afterwards, in his gayest moments, there recurred to his mind the little official with the bald forehead, with his heart-rending words, "Leave me alone! Why do you insult me?" In these moving words, other words resounded--"I am thy brother." And the young man covered his face with his hand; and many a time afterwards, in the course of his life, shuddered at seeing how much inhumanity there is in man, how much savage coarseness is concealed beneath delicate, refined worldliness, and even, O God! in that man whom the world acknowledges as honourable and noble.

It would be difficult to find another man who lived so entirely for his duties. It is not enough to say that Akakiy laboured with zeal: no, he laboured with love. In his copying, he found a varied and agreeable employment. Enjoyment was written on his face: some letters were even favourites with him; and when he encountered these, he smiled, winked, and worked with his lips, till it seemed as though each letter might be read in his face, as his pen traced it. If his pay had been in proportion to his zeal, he would, perhaps, to his great surprise, have been made even a councillor of state. But he worked, as his companions, the wits, put it, like a horse in a mill.

Moreover, it is impossible to say that no attention was paid to him. One director being a kindly man, and desirous of rewarding him for his long service, ordered him to be given something more important than mere copying. So he was ordered to make a report of an already concluded affair to another department: the duty consisting simply in changing the heading and altering a few words from the first to the third person. This caused him so much toil that he broke into a perspiration, rubbed his forehead, and finally said, "No, give me rather something to copy." After that they let him copy on forever.

Outside this copying, it appeared that nothing existed for him. He gave no thought to his clothes: his undress uniform was not green, but a sort of rusty-meal colour. The collar was low, so that his neck, in spite of the fact that it was not long, seemed inordinately so as it emerged from it, like the necks of those plaster cats which wag their heads, and are carried about upon the heads of scores of image sellers. And something was always sticking to his uniform, either a bit of hay or some trifle. Moreover, he had a peculiar knack, as he walked along the street, of arriving beneath a window just as all sorts of rubbish were being flung out of it: hence he always bore about on his hat scraps of melon rinds and other such articles. Never once in his life did he give heed to what was going on every day in the street; while it is well known that his young brother officials train the range of their glances till they can see when any one's trouser straps come undone upon the opposite sidewalk, which always brings a malicious smile to their faces. But Akakiy Akakievitch saw in all things the clean, even strokes of his written lines; and only when a horse thrust his nose, from some unknown quarter, over his shoulder, and sent a whole gust of wind down his neck from his nostrils, did he observe that he was not in the middle of a page, but in the middle of the street.

On reaching home, he sat down at once at the table, supped his cabbage soup up quickly, and swallowed a bit of beef with onions, never noticing their taste, and gulping down everything with flies and anything else which the Lord happened to send at the moment. His stomach filled, he rose from the table, and copied papers which he had brought home. If there happened to be none, he took copies for himself, for his own gratification, especially if the document was noteworthy, not on account of its style, but of its being addressed to some distinguished person.

Even at the hour when the grey St. Petersburg sky had quite dispersed, and all the official world had eaten or dined, each as he could, in accordance with the salary he received and his own fancy; when all were resting from the departmental jar of pens, running to and fro from their own and other people's indispensable occupations, and from all the work that an uneasy man makes willingly for himself, rather than what is necessary; when officials hasten to dedicate to pleasure the time which is left to them, one bolder than the rest going to the theatre; another, into the street looking under all the bonnets; another wasting his evening in compliments to some pretty girl, the star of a small official circle; another--and this is the common case of all--visiting his comrades on the fourth or third floor, in two small rooms with an ante-room or kitchen, and some pretensions to fashion, such as a lamp or some other trifle which has cost many a sacrifice of dinner or pleasure trip; in a word, at the hour when all officials disperse among the contracted quarters of their friends, to play whist, as they sip their tea from glasses with a kopek's worth of sugar, smoke long pipes, relate at times some bits of gossip which a Russian man can never, under any circumstances, refrain from, and, when there is nothing else to talk of, repeat eternal anecdotes about the commandant to whom they had sent word that the tails of the horses on the Falconet Monument had been cut off, when all strive to divert themselves, Akakiy Akakievitch indulged in no kind of diversion. No one could ever say that he had seen him at any kind of evening party. Having written to his heart's content, he lay down to sleep, smiling at the thought of the coming day--of what God might send him to copy on the morrow.

Thus flowed on the peaceful life of the man, who, with a salary of four hundred rubles, understood how to be content with his lot; and thus it would have continued to flow on, perhaps, to extreme old age, were it not that there are various ills strewn along the path of life for titular councillors as well as for private, actual, court, and every other species of councillor, even for those who never give any advice or take any themselves.

There exists in St. Petersburg a powerful foe of all who receive a salary of four hundred rubles a year, or thereabouts. This foe is no other than the Northern cold, although it is said to be very healthy. At nine o'clock in the morning, at the very hour when the streets are filled with men bound for the various official departments, it begins to bestow such powerful and piercing nips on all noses impartially that the poor officials really do not know what to do with them. At an hour when the foreheads of even those who occupy exalted positions ache with the cold, and tears start to their eyes, the poor titular councillors are sometimes quite unprotected. Their only salvation lies in traversing as quickly as possible, in their thin little cloaks, five or six streets, and then warming their feet in the porter's room, and so thawing all their talents and qualifications for official service, which had become frozen on the way.

Akakiy Akakievitch had felt for some time that his back and shoulders suffered with peculiar poignancy, in spite of the fact that he tried to traverse the distance with all possible speed. He began finally to wonder whether the fault did not lie in his cloak. He examined it thoroughly at home, and discovered that in two places, namely, on the back and shoulders, it had become thin as gauze: the cloth was worn to such a degree that he could see through it, and the lining had fallen into pieces. You must know that Akakiy Akakievitch's cloak served as an object of ridicule to the officials: they even refused it the noble name of cloak, and called it a cape. In fact, it was of singular make: its collar diminishing year by year, but serving to patch its other parts. The patching did not exhibit great skill on the part of the tailor, and was, in fact, baggy and ugly. Seeing how the matter stood, Akakiy Akakievitch decided that it would be necessary to take the cloak to Petrovitch, the tailor, who lived somewhere on the fourth floor up a dark stair-case, and who, in spite of his having but one eye, and pock-marks all over his face, busied himself with considerable success in repairing the trousers and coats of officials and others; that is to say, when he was sober and not nursing some other scheme in his head.

It is not necessary to say much about this tailor; but, as it is the custom to have the character of each personage in a novel clearly defined, there is no help for it, so here is Petrovitch the tailor. At first he was called only Grigoriy, and was some gentleman's serf; he commenced calling himself Petrovitch from the time when he received his free papers, and further began to drink heavily on all holidays, at first on the great ones, and then on all church festivities without discrimination, wherever a cross stood in the calendar. On this point he was faithful to ancestral custom; and when quarrelling with his wife, he called her a low female and a German. As we have mentioned his wife, it will be necessary to say a word or two about her. Unfortunately, little is known of her beyond the fact that Petrovitch has a wife, who wears a cap and a dress; but cannot lay claim to beauty, at least, no one but the soldiers of the guard even looked under her cap when they met her.

Ascending the staircase which led to Petrovitch's room--which staircase was all soaked with dish-water, and reeked with the smell of spirits which affects the eyes, and is an inevitable adjunct to all dark stairways in St. Petersburg houses--ascending the stairs, Akakiy Akakievitch pondered how much Petrovitch would ask, and mentally resolved not to give more than two rubles. The door was open; for the mistress, in cooking some fish, had raised such a smoke in the kitchen that not even the beetles were visible. Akakiy Akakievitch passed through the kitchen unperceived, even by the housewife, and at length reached a room where he beheld Petrovitch seated on a large unpainted table, with his legs tucked under him like a Turkish pasha. His feet were bare, after the fashion of tailors who sit at work; and the first thing which caught the eye was his thumb, with a deformed nail thick and strong as a turtle's shell. About Petrovitch's neck hung a skein of silk and thread, and upon his knees lay some old garment. He had been trying unsuccessfully for three minutes to thread his needle, and was enraged at the darkness and even at the thread, growling in a low voice, "It won't go through, the barbarian! you pricked me, you rascal!"

Akakiy Akakievitch was vexed at arriving at the precise moment when Petrovitch was angry; he liked to order something of Petrovitch when the latter was a little downhearted, or, as his wife expressed it, "when he had settled himself with brandy, the one-eyed devil!" Under such circumstances, Petrovitch generally came down in his price very readily, and even bowed and returned thanks. Afterwards, to be sure, his wife would come, complaining that her husband was drunk, and so had fixed the price too low; but, if only a ten-kopek piece were added, then the matter was settled. But now it appeared that Petrovitch was in a sober condition, and therefore rough, taciturn, and inclined to demand, Satan only knows what price. Akakiy Akakievitch felt this, and would gladly have beat a retreat; but he was in for it. Petrovitch screwed up his one eye very intently at him, and Akakiy Akakievitch involuntarily said: "How do you do, Petrovitch?"

"I wish you a good morning, sir," said Petrovitch, squinting at Akakiy Akakievitch's hands, to see what sort of booty he had brought.

"Ah! I--to you, Petrovitch, this--" It must be known that Akakiy Akakievitch expressed himself chiefly by prepositions, adverbs, and scraps of phrases which had no meaning whatever. If the matter was a very difficult one, he had a habit of never completing his sentences; so that frequently, having begun a phrase with the words, "This, in fact, is quite--" he forgot to go on, thinking that he had already finished it.

"What is it?" asked Petrovitch, and with his one eye scanned Akakievitch's whole uniform from the collar down to the cuffs, the back, the tails and the button-holes, all of which were well known to him, since they were his own handiwork. Such is the habit of tailors; it is the first thing they do on meeting one.

"But I, here, this--Petrovitch--a cloak, cloth--here you see, everywhere, in different places, it is quite strong--it is a little dusty, and looks old, but it is new, only here in one place it is a little--on the back, and here on one of the shoulders, it is a little worn, yes, here on this shoulder it is a little--do you see? that is all. And a little work--"

Petrovitch took the cloak, spread it out, to begin with, on the table, looked hard at it, shook his head, reached out his hand to the window-sill for his snuff-box, adorned with the portrait of some general, though what general is unknown, for the place where the face should have been had been rubbed through by the finger, and a square bit of paper had been pasted over it. Having taken a pinch of snuff, Petrovitch held up the cloak, and inspected it against the light, and again shook his head once more. After which he again lifted the general-adorned lid with its bit of pasted paper, and having stuffed his nose with snuff, closed and put away the snuff-box, and said finally, "No, it is impossible to mend it; it's a wretched garment!"

Akakiy Akakievitch's heart sank at these words.

"Why is it impossible, Petrovitch?" he said, almost in the pleading voice of a child; "all that ails it is, that it is worn on the shoulders. You must have some pieces--"

"Yes, patches could be found, patches are easily found," said Petrovitch, "but there's nothing to sew them to. The thing is completely rotten; if you put a needle to it--see, it will give way."

"Let it give way, and you can put on another patch at once."

"But there is nothing to put the patches on to; there's no use in strengthening it; it is too far gone. It's lucky that it's cloth; for, if the wind were to blow, it would fly away."

"Well, strengthen it again. How will this, in fact--"

"No," said Petrovitch decisively, "there is nothing to be done with it. It's a thoroughly bad job. You'd better, when the cold winter weather comes on, make yourself some gaiters out of it, because stockings are not warm. The Germans invented them in order to make more money." Petrovitch loved, on all occasions, to have a fling at the Germans. "But it is plain you must have a new cloak."

At the word "new," all grew dark before Akakiy Akakievitch's eyes, and everything in the room began to whirl round. The only thing he saw clearly was the general with the paper face on the lid of Petrovitch's snuff-box. "A new one?" said he, as if still in a dream: "why, I have no money for that."

"Yes, a new one," said Petrovitch, with barbarous composure.

"Well, if it came to a new one, how would it--?"

"You mean how much would it cost?"

"Yes."

"Well, you would have to lay out a hundred and fifty or more," said Petrovitch, and pursed up his lips significantly. He liked to produce powerful effects, liked to stun utterly and suddenly, and then to glance sideways to see what face the stunned person would put on the matter.

"A hundred and fifty rubles for a cloak!" shrieked poor Akakiy Akakievitch, perhaps for the first time in his life, for his voice had always been distinguished for softness.

"Yes, sir," said Petrovitch, "for any kind of cloak. If you have a marten fur on the collar, or a silk-lined hood, it will mount up to two hundred."

"Petrovitch, please," said Akakiy Akakievitch in a beseeching tone, not hearing, and not trying to hear, Petrovitch's words, and disregarding all his "effects," "some repairs, in order that it may wear yet a little longer."

"No, it would only be a waste of time and money," said Petrovitch; and Akakiy Akakievitch went away after these words, utterly discouraged. But Petrovitch stood for some time after his departure, with significantly compressed lips, and without betaking himself to his work, satisfied that he would not be dropped, and an artistic tailor employed.

Akakiy Akakievitch went out into the street as if in a dream. "Such an affair!" he said to himself: "I did not think it had come to--" and then after a pause, he added, "Well, so it is! see what it has come to at last! and I never imagined that it was so!" Then followed a long silence, after which he exclaimed, "Well, so it is! see what already--nothing unexpected that--it would be nothing--what a strange circumstance!" So saying, instead of going home, he went in exactly the opposite direction without himself suspecting it. On the way, a chimney-sweep bumped up against him, and blackened his shoulder, and a whole hatful of rubbish landed on him from the top of a house which was building. He did not notice it; and only when he ran against a watchman, who, having planted his halberd beside him, was shaking some snuff from his box into his horny hand, did he recover himself a little, and that because the watchman said, "Why are you poking yourself into a man's very face? Haven't you the pavement?" This caused him to look about him, and turn towards home.

There only, he finally began to collect his thoughts, and to survey his position in its clear and actual light, and to argue with himself, sensibly and frankly, as with a reasonable friend with whom one can discuss private and personal matters. "No," said Akakiy Akakievitch, "it is impossible to reason with Petrovitch now; he is that--evidently his wife has been beating him. I'd better go to him on Sunday morning; after Saturday night he will be a little cross-eyed and sleepy, for he will want to get drunk, and his wife won't give him any money; and at such a time, a ten-kopek piece in his hand will--he will become more fit to reason with, and then the cloak, and that--" Thus argued Akakiy Akakievitch with himself, regained his courage, and waited until the first Sunday, when, seeing from afar that Petrovitch's wife had left the house, he went straight to him.

Petrovitch's eye was, indeed, very much askew after Saturday: his head drooped, and he was very sleepy; but for all that, as soon as he knew what it was a question of, it seemed as though Satan jogged his memory. "Impossible," said he: "please to order a new one." Thereupon Akakiy Akakievitch handed over the ten-kopek piece. "Thank you, sir; I will drink your good health," said Petrovitch: "but as for the cloak, don't trouble yourself about it; it is good for nothing. I will make you a capital new one, so let us settle about it now."

Akakiy Akakievitch was still for mending it; but Petrovitch would not hear of it, and said, "I shall certainly have to make you a new one, and you may depend upon it that I shall do my best. It may even be, as the fashion goes, that the collar can be fastened by silver hooks under a flap."

Then Akakiy Akakievitch saw that it was impossible to get along without a new cloak, and his spirit sank utterly. How, in fact, was it to be done? Where was the money to come from? He might, to be sure, depend, in part, upon his present at Christmas; but that money had long been allotted beforehand. He must have some new trousers, and pay a debt of long standing to the shoemaker for putting new tops to his old boots, and he must order three shirts from the seamstress, and a couple of pieces of linen. In short, all his money must be spent; and even if the director should be so kind as to order him to receive forty-five rubles instead of forty, or even fifty, it would be a mere nothing, a mere drop in the ocean towards the funds necessary for a cloak: although he knew that Petrovitch was often wrong-headed enough to blurt out some outrageous price, so that even his own wife could not refrain from exclaiming, "Have you lost your senses, you fool?" At one time he would not work at any price, and now it was quite likely that he had named a higher sum than the cloak would cost.

But although he knew that Petrovitch would undertake to make a cloak for eighty rubles, still, where was he to get the eighty rubles from? He might possibly manage half, yes, half might be procured, but where was the other half to come from? But the reader must first be told where the first half came from. Akakiy Akakievitch had a habit of putting, for every ruble he spent, a groschen into a small box, fastened with a lock and key, and with a slit in the top for the reception of money. At the end of every half-year he counted over the heap of coppers, and changed it for silver. This he had done for a long time, and in the course of years, the sum had mounted up to over forty rubles. Thus he had one half on hand; but where was he to find the other half? where was he to get another forty rubles from? Akakiy Akakievitch thought and thought, and decided that it would be necessary to curtail his ordinary expenses, for the space of one year at least, to dispense with tea in the evening; to burn no candles, and, if there was anything which he must do, to go into his landlady's room, and work by her light. When he went into the street, he must walk as lightly as he could, and as cautiously, upon the stones, almost upon tiptoe, in order not to wear his heels down in too short a time; he must give the laundress as little to wash as possible; and, in order not to wear out his clothes, he must take them off, as soon as he got home, and wear only his cotton dressing-gown, which had been long and carefully saved.

To tell the truth, it was a little hard for him at first to accustom himself to these deprivations; but he got used to them at length, after a fashion, and all went smoothly. He even got used to being hungry in the evening, but he made up for it by treating himself, so to say, in spirit, by bearing ever in mind the idea of his future cloak. From that time forth his existence seemed to become, in some way, fuller, as if he were married, or as if some other man lived in him, as if, in fact, he were not alone, and some pleasant friend had consented to travel along life's path with him, the friend being no other than the cloak, with thick wadding and a strong lining incapable of wearing out. He became more lively, and even his character grew firmer, like that of a man who has made up his mind, and set himself a goal. From his face and gait, doubt and indecision, all hesitating and wavering traits disappeared of themselves. Fire gleamed in his eyes, and occasionally the boldest and most daring ideas flitted through his mind; why not, for instance, have marten fur on the collar? The thought of this almost made him absent-minded. Once, in copying a letter, he nearly made a mistake, so that he exclaimed almost aloud, "Ugh!" and crossed himself. Once, in the course of every month, he had a conference with Petrovitch on the subject of the cloak, where it would be better to buy the cloth, and the colour, and the price. He always returned home satisfied, though troubled, reflecting that the time would come at last when it could all be bought, and then the cloak made.

The affair progressed more briskly than he had expected. Far beyond all his hopes, the director awarded neither forty nor forty-five rubles for Akakiy Akakievitch's share, but sixty. Whether he suspected that Akakiy Akakievitch needed a cloak, or whether it was merely chance, at all events, twenty extra rubles were by this means provided. This circumstance hastened matters. Two or three months more of hunger and Akakiy Akakievitch had accumulated about eighty rubles. His heart, generally so quiet, began to throb. On the first possible day, he went shopping in company with Petrovitch. They bought some very good cloth, and at a reasonable rate too, for they had been considering the matter for six months, and rarely let a month pass without their visiting the shops to inquire prices. Petrovitch himself said that no better cloth could be had. For lining, they selected a cotton stuff, but so firm and thick that Petrovitch declared it to be better than silk, and even prettier and more glossy. They did not buy the marten fur, because it was, in fact, dear, but in its stead, they picked out the very best of cat-skin which could be found in the shop, and which might, indeed, be taken for marten at a distance.

Petrovitch worked at the cloak two whole weeks, for there was a great deal of quilting: otherwise it would have been finished sooner. He charged twelve rubles for the job, it could not possibly have been done for less. It was all sewed with silk, in small, double seams; and Petrovitch went over each seam afterwards with his own teeth, stamping in various patterns.

It was--it is difficult to say precisely on what day, but probably the most glorious one in Akakiy Akakievitch's life, when Petrovitch at length brought home the cloak. He brought it in the morning, before the hour when it was necessary to start for the department. Never did a cloak arrive so exactly in the nick of time; for the severe cold had set in, and it seemed to threaten to increase. Petrovitch brought the cloak himself as befits a good tailor. On his countenance was a significant expression, such as Akakiy Akakievitch had never beheld there. He seemed fully sensible that he had done no small deed, and crossed a gulf separating tailors who only put in linings, and execute repairs, from those who make new things. He took the cloak out of the pocket handkerchief in which he had brought it. The handkerchief was fresh from the laundress, and he put it in his pocket for use. Taking out the cloak, he gazed proudly at it, held it up with both hands, and flung it skilfully over the shoulders of Akakiy Akakievitch. Then he pulled it and fitted it down behind with his hand, and he draped it around Akakiy Akakievitch without buttoning it. Akakiy Akakievitch, like an experienced man, wished to try the sleeves. Petrovitch helped him on with them, and it turned out that the sleeves were satisfactory also. In short, the cloak appeared to be perfect, and most seasonable. Petrovitch did not neglect to observe that it was only because he lived in a narrow street, and had no signboard, and had known Akakiy Akakievitch so long, that he had made it so cheaply; but that if he had been in business on the Nevsky Prospect, he would have charged seventy-five rubles for the making alone.

Akakiy Akakievitch did not care to argue this point with Petrovitch. He paid him, thanked him, and set out at once in his new cloak for the department. Petrovitch followed him, and, pausing in the street, gazed long at the cloak in the distance, after which he went to one side expressly to run through a crooked alley, and emerge again into the street beyond to gaze once more upon the cloak from another point, namely, directly in front.

Meantime Akakiy Akakievitch went on in holiday mood. He was conscious every second of the time that he had a new cloak on his shoulders; and several times he laughed with internal satisfaction. In fact, there were two advantages, one was its warmth, the other its beauty. He saw nothing of the road, but suddenly found himself at the department. He took off his cloak in the ante-room, looked it over carefully, and confided it to the especial care of the attendant. It is impossible to say precisely how it was that every one in the department knew at once that Akakiy Akakievitch had a new cloak, and that the "cape" no longer existed. All rushed at the same moment into the ante-room to inspect it. They congratulated him and said pleasant things to him, so that he began at first to smile and then to grow ashamed. When all surrounded him, and said that the new cloak must be "christened," and that he must give a whole evening at least to this, Akakiy Akakievitch lost his head completely, and did not know where he stood, what to answer, or how to get out of it. He stood blushing all over for several minutes, and was on the point of assuring them with great simplicity that it was not a new cloak, that it was so and so, that it was in fact the old "cape."

At length one of the officials, a sub-chief probably, in order to show that he was not at all proud, and on good terms with his inferiors, said, "So be it, only I will give the party instead of Akakiy Akakievitch; I invite you all to tea with me to-night; it happens quite a propos, as it is my name-day." The officials naturally at once offered the sub-chief their congratulations and accepted the invitations with pleasure. Akakiy Akakievitch would have declined, but all declared that it was discourteous, that it was simply a sin and a shame, and that he could not possibly refuse. Besides, the notion became pleasant to him when he recollected that he should thereby have a chance of wearing his new cloak in the evening also.

That whole day was truly a most triumphant festival day for Akakiy Akakievitch. He returned home in the most happy frame of mind, took off his cloak, and hung it carefully on the wall, admiring afresh the cloth and the lining. Then he brought out his old, worn-out cloak, for comparison. He looked at it and laughed, so vast was the difference. And long after dinner he laughed again when the condition of the "cape" recurred to his mind. He dined cheerfully, and after dinner wrote nothing, but took his ease for a while on the bed, until it got dark. Then he dressed himself leisurely, put on his cloak, and stepped out into the street. Where the host lived, unfortunately we cannot say: our memory begins to fail us badly; and the houses and streets in St. Petersburg have become so mixed up in our head that it is very difficult to get anything out of it again in proper form. This much is certain, that the official lived in the best part of the city; and therefore it must have been anything but near to Akakiy Akakievitch's residence. Akakiy Akakievitch was first obliged to traverse a kind of wilderness of deserted, dimly-lighted streets; but in proportion as he approached the official's quarter of the city, the streets became more lively, more populous, and more brilliantly illuminated. Pedestrians began to appear; handsomely dressed ladies were more frequently encountered; the men had otter skin collars to their coats; peasant waggoners, with their grate-like sledges stuck over with brass-headed nails, became rarer; whilst on the other hand, more and more drivers in red velvet caps, lacquered sledges and bear-skin coats began to appear, and carriages with rich hammer-cloths flew swiftly through the streets, their wheels scrunching the snow. Akakiy Akakievitch gazed upon all this as upon a novel sight. He had not been in the streets during the evening for years. He halted out of curiosity before a shop-window to look at a picture representing a handsome woman, who had thrown off her shoe, thereby baring her whole foot in a very pretty way; whilst behind her the head of a man with whiskers and a handsome moustache peeped through the doorway of another room. Akakiy Akakievitch shook his head and laughed, and then went on his way. Why did he laugh? Either because he had met with a thing utterly unknown, but for which every one cherishes, nevertheless, some sort of feeling; or else he thought, like many officials, as follows: "Well, those French! What is to be said? If they do go in anything of that sort, why--" But possibly he did not think at all.

Akakiy Akakievitch at length reached the house in which the sub-chief lodged. The sub-chief lived in fine style: the staircase was lit by a lamp; his apartment being on the second floor. On entering the vestibule, Akakiy Akakievitch beheld a whole row of goloshes on the floor. Among them, in the centre of the room, stood a samovar or tea-urn, humming and emitting clouds of steam. On the walls hung all sorts of coats and cloaks, among which there were even some with beaver collars or velvet facings. Beyond, the buzz of conversation was audible, and became clear and loud when the servant came out with a trayful of empty glasses, cream-jugs, and sugar-bowls. It was evident that the officials had arrived long before, and had already finished their first glass of tea.

Akakiy Akakievitch, having hung up his own cloak, entered the inner room. Before him all at once appeared lights, officials, pipes, and card-tables; and he was bewildered by the sound of rapid conversation rising from all the tables, and the noise of moving chairs. He halted very awkwardly in the middle of the room, wondering what he ought to do. But they had seen him. They received him with a shout, and all thronged at once into the ante-room, and there took another look at his cloak. Akakiy Akakievitch, although somewhat confused, was frank-hearted, and could not refrain from rejoicing when he saw how they praised his cloak. Then, of course, they all dropped him and his cloak, and returned, as was proper, to the tables set out for whist.

All this, the noise, the talk, and the throng of people was rather overwhelming to Akakiy Akakievitch. He simply did not know where he stood, or where to put his hands, his feet, and his whole body. Finally he sat down by the players, looked at the cards, gazed at the face of one and another, and after a while began to gape, and to feel that it was wearisome, the more so as the hour was already long past when he usually went to bed. He wanted to take leave of the host; but they would not let him go, saying that he must not fail to drink a glass of champagne in honour of his new garment. In the course of an hour, supper, consisting of vegetable salad, cold veal, pastry, confectioner's pies, and champagne, was served. They made Akakiy Akakievitch drink two glasses of champagne, after which he felt things grow livelier.

Still, he could not forget that it was twelve o'clock, and that he should have been at home long ago. In order that the host might not think of some excuse for detaining him, he stole out of the room quickly, sought out, in the ante-room, his cloak, which, to his sorrow, he found lying on the floor, brushed it, picked off every speck upon it, put it on his shoulders, and descended the stairs to the street.

In the street all was still bright. Some petty shops, those permanent clubs of servants and all sorts of folk, were open. Others were shut, but, nevertheless, showed a streak of light the whole length of the door-crack, indicating that they were not yet free of company, and that probably some domestics, male and female, were finishing their stories and conversations whilst leaving their masters in complete ignorance as to their whereabouts. Akakiy Akakievitch went on in a happy frame of mind: he even started to run, without knowing why, after some lady, who flew past like a flash of lightning. But he stopped short, and went on very quietly as before, wondering why he had quickened his pace. Soon there spread before him those deserted streets, which are not cheerful in the daytime, to say nothing of the evening. Now they were even more dim and lonely: the lanterns began to grow rarer, oil, evidently, had been less liberally supplied. Then came wooden houses and fences: not a soul anywhere; only the snow sparkled in the streets, and mournfully veiled the low-roofed cabins with their closed shutters. He approached the spot where the street crossed a vast square with houses barely visible on its farther side, a square which seemed a fearful desert.

Afar, a tiny spark glimmered from some watchman's box, which seemed to stand on the edge of the world. Akakiy Akakievitch's cheerfulness diminished at this point in a marked degree. He entered the square, not without an involuntary sensation of fear, as though his heart warned him of some evil. He glanced back and on both sides, it was like a sea about him. "No, it is better not to look," he thought, and went on, closing his eyes. When he opened them, to see whether he was near the end of the square, he suddenly beheld, standing just before his very nose, some bearded individuals of precisely what sort he could not make out. All grew dark before his eyes, and his heart throbbed.

"But, of course, the cloak is mine!" said one of them in a loud voice, seizing hold of his collar. Akakiy Akakievitch was about to shout "watch," when the second man thrust a fist, about the size of a man's head, into his mouth, muttering, "Now scream!"

Akakiy Akakievitch felt them strip off his cloak and give him a push with a knee: he fell headlong upon the snow, and felt no more. In a few minutes he recovered consciousness and rose to his feet; but no one was there. He felt that it was cold in the square, and that his cloak was gone; he began to shout, but his voice did not appear to reach to the outskirts of the square. In despair, but without ceasing to shout, he started at a run across the square, straight towards the watchbox, beside which stood the watchman, leaning on his halberd, and apparently curious to know what kind of a customer was running towards him and shouting. Akakiy Akakievitch ran up to him, and began in a sobbing voice to shout that he was asleep, and attended to nothing, and did not see when a man was robbed. The watchman replied that he had seen two men stop him in the middle of the square, but supposed that they were friends of his; and that, instead of scolding vainly, he had better go to the police on the morrow, so that they might make a search for whoever had stolen the cloak.

Akakiy Akakievitch ran home in complete disorder; his hair, which grew very thinly upon his temples and the back of his head, wholly disordered; his body, arms, and legs covered with snow. The old woman, who was mistress of his lodgings, on hearing a terrible knocking, sprang hastily from her bed, and, with only one shoe on, ran to open the door, pressing the sleeve of her chemise to her bosom out of modesty; but when she had opened it, she fell back on beholding Akakiy Akakievitch in such a state. When he told her about the affair, she clasped her hands, and said that he must go straight to the district chief of police, for his subordinate would turn up his nose, promise well, and drop the matter there. The very best thing to do, therefore, would be to go to the district chief, whom she knew, because Finnish Anna, her former cook, was now nurse at his house. She often saw him passing the house; and he was at church every Sunday, praying, but at the same time gazing cheerfully at everybody; so that he must be a good man, judging from all appearances. Having listened to this opinion, Akakiy Akakievitch betook himself sadly to his room; and how he spent the night there any one who can put himself in another's place may readily imagine.

Early in the morning, he presented himself at the district chief's; but was told that this official was asleep. He went again at ten and was again informed that he was asleep; at eleven, and they said: "The superintendent is not at home;" at dinner time, and the clerks in the ante-room would not admit him on any terms, and insisted upon knowing his business. So that at last, for once in his life, Akakiy Akakievitch felt an inclination to show some spirit, and said curtly that he must see the chief in person; that they ought not to presume to refuse him entrance; that he came from the department of justice, and that when he complained of them, they would see.

The clerks dared make no reply to this, and one of them went to call the chief, who listened to the strange story of the theft of the coat. Instead of directing his attention to the principal points of the matter, he began to question Akakiy Akakievitch: Why was he going home so late? Was he in the habit of doing so, or had he been to some disorderly house? So that Akakiy Akakievitch got thoroughly confused, and left him without knowing whether the affair of his cloak was in proper train or not.

All that day, for the first time in his life, he never went near the department. The next day he made his appearance, very pale, and in his old cape, which had become even more shabby. The news of the robbery of the cloak touched many; although there were some officials present who never lost an opportunity, even such a one as the present, of ridiculing Akakiy Akakievitch. They decided to make a collection for him on the spot, but the officials had already spent a great deal in subscribing for the director's portrait, and for some book, at the suggestion of the head of that division, who was a friend of the author; and so the sum was trifling.

One of them, moved by pity, resolved to help Akakiy Akakievitch with some good advice at least, and told him that he ought not to go to the police, for although it might happen that a police-officer, wishing to win the approval of his superiors, might hunt up the cloak by some means, still his cloak would remain in the possession of the police if he did not offer legal proof that it belonged to him. The best thing for him, therefore, would be to apply to a certain prominent personage; since this prominent personage, by entering into relations with the proper persons, could greatly expedite the matter.

As there was nothing else to be done, Akakiy Akakievitch decided to go to the prominent personage. What was the exact official position of the prominent personage remains unknown to this day. The reader must know that the prominent personage had but recently become a prominent personage, having up to that time been only an insignificant person. Moreover, his present position was not considered prominent in comparison with others still more so. But there is always a circle of people to whom what is insignificant in the eyes of others, is important enough. Moreover, he strove to increase his importance by sundry devices; for instance, he managed to have the inferior officials meet him on the staircase when he entered upon his service; no one was to presume to come directly to him, but the strictest etiquette must be observed; the collegiate recorder must make a report to the government secretary, the government secretary to the titular councillor, or whatever other man was proper, and all business must come before him in this manner. In Holy Russia all is thus contaminated with the love of imitation; every man imitates and copies his superior. They even say that a certain titular councillor, when promoted to the head of some small separate room, immediately partitioned off a private room for himself, called it the audience chamber, and posted at the door a lackey with red collar and braid, who grasped the handle of the door and opened to all comers; though the audience chamber could hardly hold an ordinary writing-table.

The manners and customs of the prominent personage were grand and imposing, but rather exaggerated. The main foundation of his system was strictness. "Strictness, strictness, and always strictness!" he generally said; and at the last word he looked significantly into the face of the person to whom he spoke. But there was no necessity for this, for the half-score of subordinates who formed the entire force of the office were properly afraid; on catching sight of him afar off they left their work and waited, drawn up in line, until he had passed through the room. His ordinary converse with his inferiors smacked of sternness, and consisted chiefly of three phrases: "How dare you?" "Do you know whom you are speaking to?" "Do you realise who stands before you?"

Otherwise he was a very kind-hearted man, good to his comrades, and ready to oblige; but the rank of general threw him completely off his balance. On receiving any one of that rank, he became confused, lost his way, as it were, and never knew what to do. If he chanced to be amongst his equals he was still a very nice kind of man, a very good fellow in many respects, and not stupid; but the very moment that he found himself in the society of people but one rank lower than himself he became silent; and his situation aroused sympathy, the more so as he felt himself that he might have been making an incomparably better use of his time. In his eyes there was sometimes visible a desire to join some interesting conversation or group; but he was kept back by the thought, "Would it not be a very great condescension on his part? Would it not be familiar? and would he not thereby lose his importance?" And in consequence of such reflections he always remained in the same dumb state, uttering from time to time a few monosyllabic sounds, and thereby earning the name of the most wearisome of men.

To this prominent personage Akakiy Akakievitch presented himself, and this at the most unfavourable time for himself though opportune for the prominent personage. The prominent personage was in his cabinet conversing gaily with an old acquaintance and companion of his childhood whom he had not seen for several years and who had just arrived when it was announced to him that a person named Bashmatchkin had come. He asked abruptly, "Who is he?"--"Some official," he was informed. "Ah, he can wait! this is no time for him to call," said the important man.

It must be remarked here that the important man lied outrageously: he had said all he had to say to his friend long before; and the conversation had been interspersed for some time with very long pauses, during which they merely slapped each other on the leg, and said, "You think so, Ivan Abramovitch!" "Just so, Stepan Varlamitch!" Nevertheless, he ordered that the official should be kept waiting, in order to show his friend, a man who had not been in the service for a long time, but had lived at home in the country, how long officials had to wait in his ante-room.

At length, having talked himself completely out, and more than that, having had his fill of pauses, and smoked a cigar in a very comfortable arm-chair with reclining back, he suddenly seemed to recollect, and said to the secretary, who stood by the door with papers of reports, "So it seems that there is a tchinovnik waiting to see me. Tell him that he may come in." On perceiving Akakiy Akakievitch's modest mien and his worn undress uniform, he turned abruptly to him and said, "What do you want?" in a curt hard voice, which he had practised in his room in private, and before the looking-glass, for a whole week before being raised to his present rank.

Akakiy Akakievitch, who was already imbued with a due amount of fear, became somewhat confused: and as well as his tongue would permit, explained, with a rather more frequent addition than usual of the word "that," that his cloak was quite new, and had been stolen in the most inhuman manner; that he had applied to him in order that he might, in some way, by his intermediation--that he might enter into correspondence with the chief of police, and find the cloak.

For some inexplicable reason this conduct seemed familiar to the prominent personage. "What, my dear sir!" he said abruptly, "are you not acquainted with etiquette? Where have you come from? Don't you know how such matters are managed? You should first have entered a complaint about this at the court below: it would have gone to the head of the department, then to the chief of the division, then it would have been handed over to the secretary, and the secretary would have given it to me."

"But, your excellency," said Akakiy Akakievitch, trying to collect his small handful of wits, and conscious at the same time that he was perspiring terribly, "I, your excellency, presumed to trouble you because secretaries--are an untrustworthy race."

"What, what, what!" said the important personage. "Where did you get such courage? Where did you get such ideas? What impudence towards their chiefs and superiors has spread among the young generation!" The prominent personage apparently had not observed that Akakiy Akakievitch was already in the neighbourhood of fifty. If he could be called a young man, it must have been in comparison with some one who was twenty. "Do you know to whom you speak? Do you realise who stands before you? Do you realise it? do you realise it? I ask you!" Then he stamped his foot and raised his voice to such a pitch that it would have frightened even a different man from Akakiy Akakievitch.

Akakiy Akakievitch's senses failed him; he staggered, trembled in every limb, and, if the porters had not run to support him, would have fallen to the floor. They carried him out insensible. But the prominent personage, gratified that the effect should have surpassed his expectations, and quite intoxicated with the thought that his word could even deprive a man of his senses, glanced sideways at his friend in order to see how he looked upon this, and perceived, not without satisfaction, that his friend was in a most uneasy frame of mind, and even beginning, on his part, to feel a trifle frightened.

Akakiy Akakievitch could not remember how he descended the stairs and got into the street. He felt neither his hands nor feet. Never in his life had he been so rated by any high official, let alone a strange one. He went staggering on through the snow-storm, which was blowing in the streets, with his mouth wide open; the wind, in St. Petersburg fashion, darted upon him from all quarters, and down every cross-street. In a twinkling it had blown a quinsy into his throat, and he reached home unable to utter a word. His throat was swollen, and he lay down on his bed. So powerful is sometimes a good scolding!

The next day a violent fever showed itself. Thanks to the generous assistance of the St. Petersburg climate, the malady progressed more rapidly than could have been expected: and when the doctor arrived, he found, on feeling the sick man's pulse, that there was nothing to be done, except to prescribe a fomentation, so that the patient might not be left entirely without the beneficent aid of medicine; but at the same time, he predicted his end in thirty-six hours. After this he turned to the landlady, and said, "And as for you, don't waste your time on him: order his pine coffin now, for an oak one will be too expensive for him." Did Akakiy Akakievitch hear these fatal words? and if he heard them, did they produce any overwhelming effect upon him? Did he lament the bitterness of his life?--We know not, for he continued in a delirious condition. Visions incessantly appeared to him, each stranger than the other. Now he saw Petrovitch, and ordered him to make a cloak, with some traps for robbers, who seemed to him to be always under the bed; and cried every moment to the landlady to pull one of them from under his coverlet. Then he inquired why his old mantle hung before him when he had a new cloak. Next he fancied that he was standing before the prominent person, listening to a thorough setting-down, and saying, "Forgive me, your excellency!" but at last he began to curse, uttering the most horrible words, so that his aged landlady crossed herself, never in her life having heard anything of the kind from him, the more so as those words followed directly after the words "your excellency." Later on he talked utter nonsense, of which nothing could be made: all that was evident being, that his incoherent words and thoughts hovered ever about one thing, his cloak.

 At length poor Akakiy Akakievitch breathed his last. They sealed up neither his room nor his effects, because, in the first place, there were no heirs, and, in the second, there was very little to inherit beyond a bundle of goose-quills, a quire of white official paper, three pairs of socks, two or three buttons which had burst off his trousers, and the mantle already known to the reader. To whom all this fell, God knows. I confess that the person who told me this tale took no interest in the matter. They carried Akakiy Akakievitch out and buried him.

 And St. Petersburg was left without Akakiy Akakievitch, as though he had never lived there. A being disappeared who was protected by none, dear to none, interesting to none, and who never even attracted to himself the attention of those students of human nature who omit no opportunity of thrusting a pin through a common fly, and examining it under the microscope. A being who bore meekly the jibes of the department, and went to his grave without having done one unusual deed, but to whom, nevertheless, at the close of his life appeared a bright visitant in the form of a cloak, which momentarily cheered his poor life, and upon whom, thereafter, an intolerable misfortune descended, just as it descends upon the mighty of this world!

 Several days after his death, the porter was sent from the department to his lodgings, with an order for him to present himself there immediately; the chief commanding it. But the porter had to return unsuccessful, with the answer that he could not come; and to the question, "Why?" replied, "Well, because he is dead! he was buried four days ago." In this manner did they hear of Akakiy Akakievitch's death at the department, and the next day a new official sat in his place, with a handwriting by no means so upright, but more inclined and slanting.

 But who could have imagined that this was not really the end of Akakiy Akakievitch, that he was destined to raise a commotion after death, as if in compensation for his utterly insignificant life? But so it happened, and our poor story unexpectedly gains a fantastic ending.

A rumour suddenly spread through St. Petersburg that a dead man had taken to appearing on the Kalinkin Bridge and its vicinity at night in the form of a tchinovnik seeking a stolen cloak, and that, under the pretext of its being the stolen cloak, he dragged, without regard to rank or calling, every one's cloak from his shoulders, be it cat-skin, beaver, fox, bear, sable; in a word, every sort of fur and skin which men adopted for their covering. One of the department officials saw the dead man with his own eyes and immediately recognised in him Akakiy Akakievitch. This, however, inspired him with such terror that he ran off with all his might, and therefore did not scan the dead man closely, but only saw how the latter threatened him from afar with his finger. Constant complaints poured in from all quarters that the backs and shoulders, not only of titular but even of court councillors, were exposed to the danger of a cold on account of the frequent dragging off of their cloaks.

Arrangements were made by the police to catch the corpse, alive or dead, at any cost, and punish him as an example to others in the most severe manner. In this they nearly succeeded; for a watchman, on guard in Kirushkin Alley, caught the corpse by the collar on the very scene of his evil deeds, when attempting to pull off the frieze coat of a retired musician. Having seized him by the collar, he summoned, with a shout, two of his comrades, whom he enjoined to hold him fast while he himself felt for a moment in his boot, in order to draw out his snuff-box and refresh his frozen nose. But the snuff was of a sort which even a corpse could not endure. The watchman having closed his right nostril with his finger, had no sooner succeeded in holding half a handful up to the left than the corpse sneezed so violently that he completely filled the eyes of all three. While they raised their hands to wipe them, the dead man vanished completely, so that they positively did not know whether they had actually had him in their grip at all. Thereafter the watchmen conceived such a terror of dead men that they were afraid even to seize the living, and only screamed from a distance, "Hey, there! go your way!" So the dead tchinovnik began to appear even beyond the Kalinkin Bridge, causing no little terror to all timid people.

But we have totally neglected that certain prominent personage who may really be considered as the cause of the fantastic turn taken by this true history. First of all, justice compels us to say that after the departure of poor, annihilated Akakiy Akakievitch he felt something like remorse.

Suffering was unpleasant to him, for his heart was accessible to many good impulses, in spite of the fact that his rank often prevented his showing his true self. As soon as his friend had left his cabinet, he began to think about poor Akakiy Akakievitch. And from that day forth, poor Akakiy Akakievitch, who could not bear up under an official reprimand, recurred to his mind almost every day. The thought troubled him to such an extent that a week later he even resolved to send an official to him, to learn whether he really could assist him; and when it was reported to him that Akakiy Akakievitch had died suddenly of fever, he was startled, hearkened to the reproaches of his conscience, and was out of sorts for the whole day.

 Wishing to divert his mind in some way, and drive away the disagreeable impression, he set out that evening for one of his friends' houses, where he found quite a large party assembled. What was better, nearly every one was of the same rank as himself, so that he need not feel in the least constrained. This had a marvellous effect upon his mental state. He grew expansive, made himself agreeable in conversation, in short, he passed a delightful evening. After supper he drank a couple of glasses of champagne--not a bad recipe for cheerfulness, as every one knows. The champagne inclined him to various adventures; and he determined not to return home, but to go and see a certain well-known lady of German extraction, Karolina Ivanovna, a lady, it appears, with whom he was on a very friendly footing.

 It must be mentioned that the prominent personage was no longer a young man, but a good husband and respected father of a family. Two sons, one of whom was already in the service, and a good-looking, sixteen-year-old daughter, with a rather retrousse but pretty little nose, came every morning to kiss his hand and say, "Bonjour, papa." His wife, a still fresh and good-looking woman, first gave him her hand to kiss, and then, reversing the procedure, kissed his. But the prominent personage, though perfectly satisfied in his domestic relations, considered it stylish to have a friend in another quarter of the city. This friend was scarcely prettier or younger than his wife; but there are such puzzles in the world, and it is not our place to judge them. So the important personage descended the stairs, stepped into his sledge, said to the coachman, "To Karolina Ivanovna's," and, wrapping himself luxuriously in his warm cloak, found himself in that delightful frame of mind than which a Russian can conceive no better, namely, when you think of nothing yourself, yet when the thoughts creep into your mind of their own accord, each more agreeable than the other, giving you no trouble either to drive them away or seek them. Fully satisfied, he recalled all the gay features of the evening just passed, and all the mots which had made the little circle laugh. Many of them he repeated in a low voice, and found them quite as funny as before; so it is not surprising that he should laugh heartily at them. Occasionally, however, he was interrupted by gusts of wind, which, coming suddenly, God knows whence or why, cut his face, drove masses of snow into it, filled out his cloak-collar like a sail, or suddenly blew it over his head with supernatural force, and thus caused him constant trouble to disentangle himself.

Suddenly the important personage felt some one clutch him firmly by the collar. Turning round, he perceived a man of short stature, in an old, worn uniform, and recognised, not without terror, Akakiy Akakievitch. The official's face was white as snow, and looked just like a corpse's. But the horror of the important personage transcended all bounds when he saw the dead man's mouth open, and, with a terrible odour of the grave, gave vent to the following remarks: "Ah, here you are at last! I have you, that--by the collar! I need your cloak; you took no trouble about mine, but reprimanded me; so now give up your own."

The pallid prominent personage almost died of fright. Brave as he was in the office and in the presence of inferiors generally, and although, at the sight of his manly form and appearance, every one said, "Ugh! how much character he had!" at this crisis, he, like many possessed of an heroic exterior, experienced such terror, that, not without cause, he began to fear an attack of illness. He flung his cloak hastily from his shoulders and shouted to his coachman in an unnatural voice, "Home at full speed!" The coachman, hearing the tone which is generally employed at critical moments and even accompanied by something much more tangible, drew his head down between his shoulders in case of an emergency, flourished his whip, and flew on like an arrow. In a little more than six minutes the prominent personage was at the entrance of his own house. Pale, thoroughly scared, and cloakless, he went home instead of to Karolina Ivanovna's, reached his room somehow or other, and passed the night in the direst distress; so that the next morning over their tea his daughter said, "You are very pale to-day, papa." But papa remained silent, and said not a word to any one of what had happened to him, where he had been, or where he had intended to go.

This occurrence made a deep impression upon him. He even began to say: "How dare you? do you realise who stands before you?" less frequently to the under-officials, and if he did utter the words, it was only after having first learned the bearings of the matter. But the most noteworthy point was, that from that day forward the apparition of the dead tchinovnik ceased to be seen. Evidently the prominent personage's cloak just fitted his shoulders;

at all events, no more instances of his dragging cloaks from people's shoulders were heard of. But many active and apprehensive persons could by no means reassure themselves, and asserted that the dead tchinovnik still showed himself in distant parts of the city.

In fact, one watchman in Kolomna saw with his own eyes the apparition come from behind a house. But being rather weak of body, he dared not arrest him, but followed him in the dark, until, at length, the apparition looked round, paused, and inquired, "What do you want?" at the same time showing a fist such as is never seen on living men. The watchman said, "It's of no consequence," and turned back instantly. But the apparition was much too tall, wore huge moustaches, and, directing its steps apparently towards the Obukhoff bridge, disappeared in the darkness of the night.

HOW THE TWO IVANS QUARRELLED

CHAPTER I

IVAN IVANOVITCH AND IVAN NIKIFOROVITCH

A fine pelisse has Ivan Ivanovitch! splendid! And what lambskin! deuce take it, what lambskin! blue-black with silver lights. I'll forfeit, I know not what, if you find any one else owning such a one. Look at it, for heaven's sake, especially when he stands talking with any one! look at him side-ways: what a pleasure it is! To describe it is impossible: velvet! silver! fire! Nikolai the Wonder-worker, saint of God! why have I not such a pelisse? He had it made before Agafya Fedosyevna went to Kief. You know Agafya Fedosyevna who bit the assessor's ear off?

Ivan Ivanovitch is a very handsome man. What a house he has in Mirgorod! Around it on every side is a balcony on oaken pillars, and on the balcony are benches. Ivan Ivanovitch, when the weather gets too warm, throws off his pelisse and his remaining upper garments, and sits, in his shirt sleeves, on the balcony to observe what is going on in the courtyard and the street. What apples and pears he has under his very windows! You have but to open the window and the branches force themselves through into the room. All this is in front of the house; but you should see what he has in the garden. What is there not there? Plums, cherries, every sort of vegetable, sunflowers, cucumbers, melons, peas, a threshing-floor, and even a forge.

A very fine man, Ivan Ivanovitch! He is very fond of melons: they are his favourite food. As soon as he has dined, and come out on his balcony, in his shirt sleeves, he orders Gapka to bring two melons, and immediately cuts them himself, collects the seeds in a paper, and begins to eat. Then he orders Gapka to fetch the ink-bottle, and, with his own hand, writes this inscription on the paper of seeds: "These melons were eaten on such and such a date." If there was a guest present, then it reads, "Such and such a person assisted."

The late judge of Mirgorod always gazed at Ivan Ivanovitch's house with pleasure. The little house is very pretty. It pleases me because sheds and other little additions are built on to it on all sides; so that, looking at it from a distance, only roofs are visible, rising one above another, and greatly resembling a plate full of pancakes, or, better still, fungi growing on the trunk of a tree. Moreover, the roof is all overgrown with weeds: a willow, an oak, and two apple-trees lean their spreading branches against it. Through the trees peep little windows with carved and white-washed shutters, which project even into the street.

A very fine man, Ivan Ivanovitch! The commissioner of Poltava knows him too. Dorosh Tarasovitch Pukhivotchka, when he leaves Khorola, always goes to his house. And when Father Peter, the Protopope who lives at Koliberdas, invites a few guests, he always says that he knows of no one who so well fulfils all his Christian duties and understands so well how to live as Ivan Ivanovitch.

How time flies! More than ten years have already passed since he became a widower. He never had any children. Gapka has children and they run about the court-yard. Ivan Ivanovitch always gives each of them a cake, or a slice of melon, or a pear.

Gapka carries the keys of the storerooms and cellars; but the key of the large chest which stands in his bedroom, and that of the centre storeroom, Ivan Ivanovitch keeps himself; Gapka is a healthy girl, with ruddy cheeks and calves, and goes about in coarse cloth garments.

And what a pious man is Ivan Ivanovitch! Every Sunday he dons his pelisse and goes to church. On entering, he bows on all sides, generally stations himself in the choir, and sings a very good bass. When the service is over, Ivan Ivanovitch cannot refrain from passing the poor people in review. He probably would not have cared to undertake this tiresome work if his natural goodness had not urged him to it. "Good-day, beggar!" he generally said, selecting the most crippled old woman, in the most patched and threadbare garments. "Whence come you, my poor woman?"

"I come from the farm, sir. 'Tis two days since I have eaten or drunk: my own children drove me out."

"Poor soul! why did you come hither?"

"To beg alms, sir, to see whether some one will not give me at least enough for bread."

"Hm! so you want bread?" Ivan Ivanovitch generally inquired.

"How should it be otherwise? I am as hungry as a dog."

"Hm!" replied Ivan Ivanovitch usually, "and perhaps you would like butter too?"

"Yes; everything which your kindness will give; I will be content with all."

"Hm! Is butter better than bread?"

"How is a hungry person to choose? Anything you please, all is good." Thereupon the old woman generally extended her hand.

"Well, go with God's blessing," said Ivan Ivanovitch. "Why do you stand there? I'm not beating you." And turning to a second and a third with the same questions, he finally returns home, or goes to drink a little glass of vodka with his neighbour, Ivan Nikiforovitch, or the judge, or the chief of police.

Ivan Ivanovitch is very fond of receiving presents. They please him greatly.

A very fine man too is Ivan Nikiforovitch. They are such friends as the world never saw. Anton Prokofievitch Pupopuz, who goes about to this hour in his cinnamon-coloured surtout with blue sleeves and dines every Sunday with the judge, was in the habit of saying that the Devil himself had bound Ivan Ivanovitch and Ivan Nikiforovitch together with a rope: where one went, the other followed.

Ivan Nikiforovitch has never married. Although it was reported that he was married it was completely false. I know Ivan Nikiforovitch very well, and am able to state that he never even had any intention of marrying. Where do all these scandals originate? In the same way it was rumoured that Ivan Nikiforovitch was born with a tail! But this invention is so clumsy and at the same time so horrible and indecent that I do not even consider it necessary to refute it for the benefit of civilised readers, to whom it is doubtless known that only witches, and very few even of these, have tails. Witches, moreover, belong more to the feminine than to the masculine gender.

In spite of their great friendship, these rare friends are not always agreed between themselves. Their characters can best be judged by comparing them. Ivan Ivanovitch has the usual gift of speaking in an extremely pleasant manner. Heavens! How he does speak! The feeling can best be described by comparing it to that which you experience when some one combs your head or draws his finger softly across your heel. You listen and listen until you drop your head. Pleasant, exceedingly pleasant! like the sleep after a bath. Ivan Nikiforovitch, on the contrary, is more reticent; but if he once takes up his parable, look out for yourself! He can talk your head off.

Ivan Ivanovitch is tall and thin: Ivan Nikiforovitch is rather shorter in stature, but he makes it up in thickness. Ivan Ivanovitch's head is like a radish, tail down; Ivan Nikiforovitch's like a radish with the tail up. Ivan Ivanovitch lolls on the balcony in his shirt sleeves after dinner only: in the evening he dons his pelisse and goes out somewhere, either to the village shop, where he supplies flour, or into the fields to catch quail. Ivan Nikiforovitch lies all day at his porch: if the day is not too hot he generally turns his back to the sun and will not go anywhere. If it happens to occur to him in the morning he walks through the yard, inspects the domestic affairs, and retires again to his room. In early days he used to call on Ivan Ivanovitch. Ivan Ivanovitch is a very refined man, and never utters an impolite word. Ivan Nikiforovitch is not always on his guard. On such occasions Ivan Ivanovitch usually rises from his seat, and says, "Enough, enough, Ivan Nikiforovitch! It's better to go out at once than to utter such godless words."

Ivan Ivanovitch gets into a terrible rage if a fly falls into his beet-soup. Then he is fairly beside himself; he flings away his plate and the housekeeper catches it. Ivan Nikiforovitch is very fond of bathing; and when he gets up to the neck in water, orders a table and a samovar, or tea urn, to be placed on the water, for he is very fond of drinking tea in that cool position. Ivan Ivanovitch shaves twice a week; Ivan Nikiforovitch once. Ivan Ivanovitch is extremely curious. God preserve you if you begin to tell him anything and do not finish it! If he is displeased with anything he lets it be seen at once. It is very hard to tell from Ivan Nikiforovitch's countenance whether he is pleased or angry; even if he is rejoiced at anything, he will not show it. Ivan Ivanovitch is of a rather timid character: Ivan Nikiforovitch, on the contrary, has, as the saying is, such full folds in his trousers that if you were to inflate them you might put the courtyard, with its storehouses and buildings, inside them.

Ivan Ivanovitch has large, expressive eyes, of a snuff colour, and a mouth shaped something like the letter V; Ivan Nikiforovitch has small, yellowish eyes, quite concealed between heavy brows and fat cheeks; and his nose is the shape of a ripe plum. If Ivanovitch treats you to snuff, he always licks the cover of his box first with his tongue, then taps on it with his finger and says, as he raises it, if you are an acquaintance, "Dare I beg you, sir, to give me the pleasure?" if a stranger, "Dare I beg you, sir, though I have not the honour of knowing your rank, name, and family, to do me the favour?" but Ivan Nikiforovitch puts his box straight into your hand and merely adds, "Do me the favour." Neither Ivan Ivanovitch nor Ivan Nikiforovitch loves fleas; and therefore, neither Ivan Ivanovitch nor Ivan Nikiforovitch will, on no account, admit a Jew with his wares, without purchasing of him remedies against these insects, after having first rated him well for belonging to the Hebrew faith.

But in spite of numerous dissimilarities, Ivan Ivanovitch and Ivan Nikiforovitch are both very fine fellows.

CHAPTER II

FROM WHICH MAY BE SEEN WHENCE AROSE THE DISCUSSION BETWEEN IVAN IVANOVITCH AND IVAN NIKIFOROVITCH

One morning--it was in July--Ivan Ivanovitch was lying on his balcony. The day was warm; the air was dry, and came in gusts. Ivan Ivanovitch had been to town, to the mower's, and at the farm, and had succeeded in asking all the muzhiks and women whom he met all manner of questions. He was fearfully tired and had laid down to rest. As he lay there, he looked at the storehouse, the courtyard, the sheds, the chickens running about, and thought to himself, "Heavens! What a well-to-do man I am! What is there that I have not? Birds, buildings, granaries, everything I take a fancy to;

genuine distilled vodka; pears and plums in the orchard; poppies, cabbages, peas in the garden; what is there that I have not? I should like to know what there is that I have not?"

 As he put this question to himself, Ivan Ivanovitch reflected; and meantime his eyes, in their search after fresh objects, crossed the fence into Ivan Nikiforovitch's yard and involuntarily took note of a curious sight. A fat woman was bringing out clothes, which had been packed away, and spreading them out on the line to air. Presently an old uniform with worn trimmings was swinging its sleeves in the air and embracing a brocade gown; from behind it peeped a court-coat, with buttons stamped with coats-of-arms, and moth-eaten collar; and white kersymere pantaloons with spots, which had once upon a time clothed Ivan Nikiforovitch's legs, and might now possibly fit his fingers. Behind them were speedily hung some more in the shape of the letter pi. Then came a blue Cossack jacket, which Ivan Nikiforovitch had had made twenty years before, when he was preparing to enter the militia, and allowed his moustache to grow. And one after another appeared a sword, projecting into the air like a spit, and the skirts of a grass-green caftan-like garment, with copper buttons the size of a five-kopek piece, unfolded themselves. From among the folds peeped a vest bound with gold, with a wide opening in front. The vest was soon concealed by an old petticoat belonging to his dead grandmother, with pockets which would have held a water-melon.

 All these things piled together formed a very interesting spectacle for Ivan Ivanovitch; while the sun's rays, falling upon a blue or green sleeve, a red binding, or a scrap of gold brocade, or playing in the point of a sword, formed an unusual sight, similar to the representations of the Nativity given at farmhouses by wandering bands; particularly that part where the throng of people, pressing close together, gaze at King Herod in his golden crown or at Anthony leading his goat.

 Presently the old woman crawled, grunting, from the storeroom, dragging after her an old-fashioned saddle with broken stirrups, worn leather holsters, and saddle-cloth, once red, with gilt embroidery and copper disks.

 "Here's a stupid woman," thought Ivan Ivanovitch. "She'll be dragging Ivan Nikiforovitch out and airing him next."

 Ivan Ivanovitch was not so far wrong in his surmise. Five minutes later, Ivan Nikiforovitch's nankeen trousers appeared, and took nearly half the yard to themselves. After that she fetched out a hat and a gun. "What's the meaning of this?" thought Ivan Ivanovitch. "I never knew Ivan Nikiforovitch had a gun. What does he want with it? Whether he shoots, or not, he keeps a gun! Of what use is it to him? But it's a splendid thing. I have long wanted just such a one. I should like that gun very much: I like to amuse myself with a gun. Hello, there, woman, woman!" shouted Ivan Ivanovitch, beckoning to her.

The old woman approached the fence.

"What's that you have there, my good woman?"

"A gun, as you see."

"What sort of a gun?"

"Who knows what sort of a gun? If it were mine, perhaps I should know what it is made of; but it is my master's, therefore I know nothing of it."

Ivan Ivanovitch rose, and began to examine the gun on all sides, and forgot to reprove the old woman for hanging it and the sword out to air.

"It must be iron," went on the old woman.

"Hm, iron! why iron?" said Ivan Ivanovitch. "Has your master had it long?"

"Yes; long, perhaps."

"It's a nice gun!" continued Ivan Ivanovitch. "I will ask him for it. What can he want with it? I'll make an exchange with him for it. Is your master at home, my good woman?"

"Yes."

"What is he doing? lying down?"

"Yes, lying down."

"Very well, I will come to him."

Ivan Ivanovitch dressed himself, took his well-seasoned stick for the benefit of the dogs, for, in Mirgorod, there are more dogs than people to be met in the street, and went out.

Although Ivan Nikiforovitch's house was next door to Ivan Ivanovitch's, so that you could have got from one to the other by climbing the fence, yet Ivan Ivanovitch went by way of the street. From the street it was necessary to turn into an alley which was so narrow that if two one-horse carts chanced to meet they could not get out, and were forced to remain there until the drivers, seizing the hind-wheels, dragged them back in opposite directions into the street, whilst pedestrians drew aside like flowers growing by the fence on either hand. Ivan Ivanovitch's waggon-shed adjoined this alley on one side; and on the other were Ivan Nikiforovitch's granary, gate, and pigeon-house.

Ivan Ivanovitch went up to the gate and rattled the latch. Within arose the barking of dogs; but the motley-haired pack ran back, wagging their tails when they saw the well-known face. Ivan Ivanovitch traversed the courtyard, in which were collected Indian doves, fed by Ivan Nikiforovitch's own hand, melon-rinds, vegetables, broken wheels, barrel-hoops, and a small boy wallowing with dirty blouse--a picture such as painters love. The shadows of the fluttering clothes covered nearly the whole of the yard and lent it a degree of coolness. The woman greeted him with a bend of her head and stood, gaping, in one spot. The front of the house was adorned with a small porch, with its roof supported on two oak pillars--a welcome protection from the sun, which at that season in Little Russia loves not to jest, and bathes the pedestrian from head to foot in perspiration. It may be judged how powerful Ivan Ivanovitch's desire to obtain the coveted article was when he made up his mind, at such an hour, to depart from his usual custom, which was to walk abroad only in the evening.

The room which Ivan Ivanovitch entered was quite dark, for the shutters were closed; and the ray of sunlight passing through a hole made in one of them took on the colours of the rainbow, and, striking the opposite wall, sketched upon it a parti-coloured picture of the outlines of roofs, trees, and the clothes suspended in the yard, only upside down. This gave the room a peculiar half-light.

"God assist you!" said Ivan Ivanovitch.

"Ah! how do you do, Ivan Ivanovitch?" replied a voice from the corner of the room. Then only did Ivan Ivanovitch perceive Ivan Nikiforovitch lying upon a rug which was spread on the floor. "Excuse me for appearing before you in a state of nature."

"Not at all. You have been asleep, Ivan Nikiforovitch?"

"I have been asleep. Have you been asleep, Ivan Ivanovitch?"

"I have."

"And now you have risen?"

"Now I have risen. Christ be with you, Ivan Nikiforovitch! How can you sleep until this time? I have just come from the farm. There's very fine barley on the road, charming! and the hay is tall and soft and golden!"

"Gorpina!" shouted Ivan Nikiforovitch, "fetch Ivan Ivanovitch some vodka, and some pastry and sour cream!"

"Fine weather we're having to-day."

"Don't praise it, Ivan Ivanovitch! Devil take it! You can't get away from the heat."

"Now, why need you mention the devil! Ah, Ivan Nikiforovitch! you will recall my words when it's too late. You will suffer in the next world for such godless words."

"How have I offended you, Ivan Ivanovitch? I have not attacked your father nor your mother. I don't know how I have insulted you."

"Enough, enough, Ivan Nikiforovitch!"

"By Heavens, Ivan Ivanovitch, I did not insult you!"

"It's strange that the quails haven't come yet to the whistle."

"Think what you please, but I have not insulted you in any way."

"I don't know why they don't come," said Ivan Ivanovitch, as if he did not hear Ivan Nikiforovitch; "it is more than time for them already; but they seem to need more time for some reason."

"You say that the barley is good?"

"Splendid barley, splendid!"

A silence ensued.

"So you are having your clothes aired, Ivan Nikiforovitch?" said Ivan Ivanovitch at length.

"Yes; those cursed women have ruined some beautiful clothes; almost new they were too. Now I'm having them aired; the cloth is fine and good. They only need turning to make them fit to wear again."

"One thing among them pleased me extremely, Ivan Nikiforovitch."

"What was that?"

"Tell me, please, what use do you make of the gun that has been put to air with the clothes?" Here Ivan Ivanovitch offered his snuff. "May I ask you to do me the favour?"

"By no means! take it yourself; I will use my own." Thereupon Ivan Nikiforovitch felt about him, and got hold of his snuff-box. "That stupid woman! So she hung the gun out to air. That Jew at Sorotchintzi makes good snuff. I don't know what he puts in it, but it is so very fragrant. It is a little like tansy. Here, take a little and chew it; isn't it like tansy?"

"Ivan Nikiforovitch, I want to talk about that gun; what are you going to do with it? You don't need it."

"Why don't I need it? I might want to go shooting."

"God be with you, Ivan Nikiforovitch! When will you go shooting? At the millennium, perhaps? So far as I know, or any one can recollect, you never killed even a duck; yes, and you are not built to go shooting. You have a dignified bearing and figure; how are you to drag yourself about the marshes, especially when your garment, which it is not polite to mention in conversation by name, is being aired at this very moment? No; you require rest, repose." Ivan Ivanovitch as has been hinted at above, employed uncommonly picturesque language when it was necessary to persuade any one. How he talked! Heavens, how he could talk! "Yes, and you require polite actions. See here, give it to me!"

"The idea! The gun is valuable; you can't find such guns anywhere nowadays. I bought it of a Turk when I joined the militia; and now, to give it away all of a sudden! Impossible! It is an indispensable article."

"Indispensable for what?"

"For what? What if robbers should attack the house? . . . Indispensable indeed! Glory to God! I know that a gun stands in my storehouse."

"A fine gun that! Why, Ivan Nikiforovitch, the lock is ruined."

"What do you mean by ruined? It can be set right; all that needs to be done is to rub it with hemp-oil, so that it may not rust."

"I see in your words, Ivan Nikiforovitch, anything but a friendly disposition towards me. You will do nothing for me in token of friendship."

"How can you say, Ivan Ivanovitch, that I show you no friendship? You ought to be ashamed of yourself. Your oxen pasture on my steppes and I have never interfered with them. When you go to Poltava, you always ask for my waggon, and what then? Have I ever refused? Your children climb over the fence into my yard and play with my dogs--I never say anything; let them play, so long as they touch nothing; let them play!"

"If you won't give it to me, then let us make some exchange."

"What will you give me for it?" Thereupon Ivan Nikiforovitch raised himself on his elbow, and looked at Ivan Ivanovitch.

"I will give you my dark-brown sow, the one I have fed in the sty. A magnificent sow. You'll see, she'll bring you a litter of pigs next year."

"I do not see, Ivan Ivanovitch, how you can talk so. What could I do with your sow? Make a funeral dinner for the devil?"

"Again! You can't get along without the devil! It's a sin! by Heaven, it's a sin, Ivan Nikiforovitch!"

"What do you mean, Ivan Ivanovitch, by offering the deuce knows what kind of a sow for my gun?"

"Why is she 'the deuce knows what,' Ivan Nikiforovitch?"

"Why? You can judge for yourself perfectly well; here's the gun, a known thing; but the deuce knows what that sow is like! If it had not been you who said it, Ivan Ivanovitch, I might have put an insulting construction on it."

"What defect have you observed in the sow?"

"For what do you take me--for a sow?"

"Sit down, sit down! I won't-- No matter about your gun; let it rot and rust where it stands in the corner of the storeroom. I don't want to say anything more about it!"

After this a pause ensued.

"They say," began Ivan Ivanovitch, "that three kings have declared war against our Tzar."

"Yes, Peter Feodorovitch told me so. What sort of war is this, and why is it?"

"I cannot say exactly, Ivan Nikiforovitch, what the cause is. I suppose the kings want us to adopt the Turkish faith."

"Fools! They would have it," said Ivan Nikiforovitch, raising his head.

"So, you see, our Tzar has declared war on them in consequence. 'No,' says he, 'do you adopt the faith of Christ!'"

"Oh, our people will beat them, Ivan Ivanovitch!"

"They will. So you won't exchange the gun, Ivan Nikiforovitch?"

"It's a strange thing to me, Ivan Ivanovitch, that you, who seem to be a man distinguished for sense, should talk such nonsense. What a fool I should be!"

"Sit down, sit down. God be with it! let it burst! I won't mention it again."

At this moment lunch was brought in.

Ivan Ivanovitch drank a glass and ate a pie with sour cream. "Listen, Ivan Nikiforovitch: I will give you, besides the sow, two sacks of oats. You did not sow any oats. You'll have to buy some this year in any case."

"By Heaven, Ivan Ivanovitch, I must tell you you are very foolish! Who ever heard of swapping a gun for two sacks of oats? Never fear, you don't offer your coat."

"But you forget, Ivan Nikiforovitch, that I am to give you the sow too."

"What! two sacks of oats and a sow for a gun?"

"Why, is it too little?"

"For a gun?"

"Of course, for a gun."

"Two sacks for a gun?"

"Two sacks, not empty, but filled with oats; and you've forgotten the sow."

"Kiss your sow; and if you don't like that, then go to the Evil One!"

"Oh, get angry now, do! See here; they'll stick your tongue full of red-hot needles in the other world for such godless words. After a conversation with you, one has to wash one's face and hands and fumigate one's self."

"Excuse me, Ivan Ivanovitch; my gun is a choice thing, a most curious thing; and besides, it is a very agreeable decoration in a room."

"You go on like a fool about that gun of yours, Ivan Nikiforovitch," said Ivan Ivanovitch with vexation; for he was beginning to be really angry.

"And you, Ivan Ivanovitch, are a regular goose!"

If Ivan Nikiforovitch had not uttered that word they would not have quarrelled, but would have parted friends as usual; but now things took quite another turn. Ivan Ivanovitch flew into a rage.

"What was that you said, Ivan Nikiforovitch?" he said, raising his voice.

"I said you were like a goose, Ivan Ivanovitch!"

"How dare you, sir, forgetful of decency and the respect due to a man's rank and family, insult him with such a disgraceful name!"

"What is there disgraceful about it? And why are you flourishing your hands so, Ivan Ivanovitch?"

"How dared you, I repeat, in disregard of all decency, call me a goose?"

"I spit on your head, Ivan Ivanovitch! What are you screeching about?"

Ivan Ivanovitch could no longer control himself. His lips quivered; his mouth lost its usual V shape, and became like the letter O; he glared so that he was terrible to look at. This very rarely happened with Ivan Ivanovitch: it was necessary that he should be extremely angry at first.

"Then, I declare to you," exclaimed Ivan Ivanovitch, "that I will no longer know you!"

"A great pity! By Heaven, I shall never weep on that account!" retorted Ivan Nikiforovitch. He lied, by Heaven, he lied! for it was very annoying to him.

"I will never put my foot inside your house gain!"

"Oho, ho!" said Ivan Nikiforovitch, vexed, yet not knowing himself what to do, and rising to his feet, contrary to his custom. "Hey, there, woman, boy!" Thereupon there appeared at the door the same fat woman and the small boy, now enveloped in a long and wide coat. "Take Ivan Ivanovitch by the arms and lead him to the door!"

"What! a nobleman?" shouted Ivan Ivanovitch with a feeling of vexation and dignity. "Just do it if you dare! Come on! I'll annihilate you and your stupid master. The crows won't be able to find your bones." Ivan Ivanovitch spoke with uncommon force when his spirit was up.

The group presented a striking picture: Ivan Nikiforovitch standing in the middle of the room; the woman with her mouth wide open and a senseless, terrified look on her face, and Ivan Ivanovitch with uplifted hand, as the Roman tribunes are depicted. This was a magnificent spectacle: and yet there was but one spectator; the boy in the ample coat, who stood quite quietly and picked his nose with his finger.

Finally Ivan Ivanovitch took his hat. "You have behaved well, Ivan Nikiforovitch, extremely well! I shall remember it."

"Go, Ivan Ivanovitch, go! and see that you don't come in my way: if you do, I'll beat your ugly face to a jelly, Ivan Ivanovitch!"

"Take that, Ivan Nikiforovitch!" retorted Ivan Ivanovitch, making an insulting gesture and banged the door, which squeaked and flew open again behind him.

Ivan Nikiforovitch appeared at it and wanted to add something more; but Ivan Ivanovitch did not glance back and hastened from the yard.

CHAPTER III

WHAT TOOK PLACE AFTER IVAN IVANOVITCH'S QUARREL WITH IVAN NIKIFOROVITCH

And thus two respectable men, the pride and honour of Mirgorod, had quarrelled, and about what? About a bit of nonsense--a goose. They would not see each other, broke off all connection, though hitherto they had been known as the most inseparable friends. Every day Ivan Ivanovitch and Ivan Nikiforovitch had sent to inquire about each other's health, and often conversed together from their balconies and said such charming things as did the heart good to listen to. On Sundays, Ivan Ivanovitch, in his lambskin pelisse, and Ivan Nikiforovitch, in his cinnamon-coloured nankeen spencer, used to set out for church almost arm in arm; and if Ivan Ivanovitch, who had remarkably sharp eyes, was the first to catch sight of a puddle or any dirt in the street, which sometimes happened in Mirgorod, he always said to Ivan Nikiforovitch, "Look out! don't put your foot there, it's dirty." Ivan Nikiforovitch, on his side, exhibited the same touching tokens of friendship; and whenever he chanced to be standing, always held out his hand to Ivan Ivanovitch with his snuff-box, saying: "Do me the favour!" And what fine managers both were!-- And these two friends!-- When I heard of it, it struck me like a flash of lightning. For a long time I would not believe it. Ivan Ivanovitch quarrelling with Ivan Nikiforovitch! Such worthy people! What is to be depended upon, then, in this world?

When Ivan Ivanovitch reached home, he remained for some time in a state of strong excitement. He usually went, first of all, to the stable to see whether his mare was eating her hay; for he had a bay mare with a white star on her forehead, and a very pretty little mare she was too; then to feed the turkeys and the little pigs with his own hand, and then to his room, where he either made wooden dishes, for he could make various vessels of wood very tastefully, quite as well as any turner, or read a book printed by Liubia, Garia, and Popoff (Ivan Ivanovitch could never remember the name, because the serving-maid had long before torn off the top part of the title-page while amusing the children), or rested on the balcony. But now he did not betake himself to any of his ordinary occupations. Instead, on encountering Gapka, he at once began to scold her for loitering about without any occupation, though she was carrying groats to the kitchen; flung a stick at a cock which came upon the balcony for his customary treat; and when the dirty little boy, in his little torn blouse, ran up to him and shouted: "Papa, papa! give me a honey-cake," he threatened him and stamped at him so fiercely that the frightened child fled, God knows whither.

But at last he bethought himself, and began to busy himself about his every-day duties. He dined late, and it was almost night when he lay down to rest on the balcony. A good beet-soup with pigeons, which Gapka had cooked for him, quite drove from his mind the occurrences of the morning. Again Ivan Ivanovitch began to gaze at his belongings with satisfaction. At length his eye rested on the neighbouring yard; and he said to himself, "I have not been to Ivan Nikiforovitch's to-day: I'll go there now." So saying, Ivan Ivanovitch took his stick and his hat, and directed his steps to the street; but scarcely had he passed through the gate than he recollected the quarrel, spit, and turned back. Almost the same thing happened at Ivan Nikiforovitch's house. Ivan Ivanovitch saw the woman put her foot on the fence, with the intention of climbing over into his yard, when suddenly Ivan Nikiforovitch's voice was heard crying: "Come back! it won't do!" But Ivan Ivanovitch found it very tiresome. It is quite possible that these worthy men would have made their peace next day if a certain occurrence in Ivan Nikiforovitch's house had not destroyed all hopes and poured oil upon the fire of enmity which was ready to die out.

*

On the evening of that very day, Agafya Fedosyevna arrived at Ivan Nikiforovitch's. Agafya Fedosyevna was not Ivan Nikiforovitch's relative, nor his sister-in-law, nor even his fellow-godparent. There seemed to be no reason why she should come to him, and he was not particularly glad of her company; still, she came, and lived on him for weeks at a time, and even longer. Then she took possession of the keys and took the management of the whole house into her own hands. This was extremely displeasing to Ivan Nikiforovitch; but he, to his amazement, obeyed her like a child; and although he occasionally attempted to dispute, yet Agafya Fedosyevna always got the better of him.

I must confess that I do not understand why things are so arranged, that women should seize us by the nose as deftly as they do the handle of a teapot. Either their hands are so constructed or else our noses are good for nothing else. And notwithstanding the fact that Ivan Nikiforovitch's nose somewhat resembled a plum, she grasped that nose and led him about after her like a dog. He even, in her presence, involuntarily altered his ordinary manner of life.

Agafya Fedosyevna wore a cap on her head, and a coffee-coloured cloak with yellow flowers and had three warts on her nose. Her figure was like a cask, and it would have been as hard to tell where to look for her waist as for her to see her nose without a mirror. Her feet were small and shaped like two cushions. She talked scandal, ate boiled beet-soup in the morning, and swore extremely; and amidst all these various occupations her countenance never for one instant changed its expression, which phenomenon, as a rule, women alone are capable of displaying.

As soon as she arrived, everything went wrong.

"Ivan Nikiforovitch, don't you make peace with him, nor ask his forgiveness; he wants to ruin you; that's the kind of man he is! you don't know him yet!" That cursed woman whispered and whispered, and managed so that Ivan Nikiforovitch would not even hear Ivan Ivanovitch mentioned.

Everything assumed another aspect. If his neighbour's dog ran into the yard, it was beaten within an inch of its life; the children, who climbed over the fence, were sent back with howls, their little shirts stripped up, and marks of a switch behind. Even the old woman, when Ivan Ivanovitch ventured to ask her about something, did something so insulting that Ivan Ivanovitch, being an extremely delicate man, only spit, and muttered, "What a nasty woman! even worse than her master!"

Finally, as a climax to all the insults, his hated neighbour built a goose-shed right against his fence at the spot where they usually climbed over, as if with the express intention of redoubling the insult. This shed, so hateful to Ivan Ivanovitch, was constructed with diabolical swiftness--in one day.

This aroused wrath and a desire for revenge in Ivan Ivanovitch. He showed no signs of bitterness, in spite of the fact that the shed encroached on his land; but his heart beat so violently that it was extremely difficult for him to preserve his calm appearance.

He passed the day in this manner. Night came-- Oh, if I were a painter, how magnificently I would depict the night's charms! I would describe how all Mirgorod sleeps; how steadily the myriads of stars gaze down upon it; how the apparent quiet is filled far and near with the barking of dogs; how the love-sick sacristan steals past them, and scales the fence with knightly fearlessness; how the white walls of the houses, bathed in the moonlight, grow whiter still, the overhanging trees darker; how the shadows of the trees fall blacker, the flowers and the silent grass become more fragrant, and the crickets, unharmonious cavaliers of the night, strike up their rattling song in friendly fashion on all sides. I would describe how, in one of the little, low-roofed, clay houses, the black-browed village maid, tossing on her lonely couch, dreams with heaving bosom of some hussar's spurs and moustache, and how the moonlight smiles upon her cheeks. I would describe how the black shadows of the bats flit along the white road before they alight upon the white chimneys of the cottages.

But it would hardly be within my power to depict Ivan Ivanovitch as he crept out that night, saw in hand; or the various emotions written on his countenance! Quietly, most quietly, he crawled along and climbed upon the goose-shed. Ivan Nikiforovitch's dogs knew nothing, as yet, of the quarrel between them; and so they permitted him, as an old friend, to enter the shed, which rested upon four oaken posts. Creeping up to the nearest post he applied his saw and began to cut. The noise produced by the saw caused him to glance about him every moment, but the recollection of the insult restored his courage. The first post was sawed through. Ivan Ivanovitch began upon the next. His eyes burned and he saw nothing for terror.

All at once he uttered an exclamation and became petrified with fear. A ghost appeared to him; but he speedily recovered himself on perceiving that it was a goose, thrusting its neck out at him. Ivan Ivanovitch spit with vexation and proceeded with his work. The second post was sawed through; the building trembled. His heart beat so violently when he began on the third, that he had to stop several times. The post was more than half sawed through when the frail building quivered violently.

Ivan Ivanovitch had barely time to spring back when it came down with a crash. Seizing his saw, he ran home in the greatest terror and flung himself upon his bed, without having sufficient courage to peep from the window at the consequences of his terrible deed. It seemed to him as though Ivan Nikiforovitch's entire household--the old woman, Ivan Nikiforovitch, the boy in the endless coat, all with sticks, and led by Agafya Fedosyevna-- were coming to tear down and destroy his house.

Ivan Ivanovitch passed the whole of the following day in a perfect fever. It seemed to him that his detested neighbour would set fire to his house at least in revenge for this; and so he gave orders to Gapka to keep a constant lookout, everywhere, and see whether dry straw were laid against it anywhere. Finally, in order to forestall Ivan Nikiforovitch, he determined to enter a complaint against him before the district judge of Mirgorod. In what it consisted can be learned from the following chapter.

CHAPTER IV

WHAT TOOK PLACE BEFORE THE DISTRICT JUDGE OF MIRGOROD

A wonderful town is Mirgorod! How many buildings are there with straw, rush, and even wooden roofs! On the right is a street, on the left a street, and fine fences everywhere. Over them twine hop-vines, upon them hang pots; from behind them the sunflowers show their sun-like heads, poppies blush, fat pumpkins peep; all is luxury itself! The fence is invariably garnished with articles which render it still more picturesque: woman's widespread undergarments of checked woollen stuff, shirts, or trousers. There is no such thing as theft or rascality in Mirgorod, so everybody hangs upon his fence whatever strikes his fancy. If you go on to the square, you will surely stop and admire the view: such a wonderful pool is there! The finest you ever saw. It occupies nearly the whole of the square. A truly magnificent pool! The houses and cottages, which at a distance might be mistaken for hayricks, stand around it, lost in admiration of its beauty.

But I agree with those who think that there is no better house than that of the district judge. Whether it is of oak or birch is nothing to the point; but it has, my dear sirs, eight windows! eight windows in a row, looking directly on the square and upon that watery expanse which I have just mentioned, and which the chief of police calls a lake. It alone is painted the colour of granite. All the other houses in Mirgorod are merely whitewashed. Its roof is of wood, and would have been even painted red, had not the government clerks eaten the oil which had been prepared for that purpose, as it happened during a fast; and so the roof remained unpainted. Towards the square projects a porch, which the chickens frequently visit, because that porch is nearly always strewn with grain or something edible, not intentionally, but through the carelessness of visitors.

The house is divided into two parts: one of which is the court-room; the other the jail. In the half which contains the court-room are two neat, whitewashed rooms, the front one for clients, the other having a table adorned with ink-spots, and with a looking-glass upon it, and four oak chairs with tall backs; whilst along the wall stand iron-bound chests, in which are preserved bundles of papers relating to district law-suits. Upon one of the chests stood at that time a pair of boots, polished with wax.

The court had been open since morning. The judge, a rather stout man, though thinner than Ivan Nikiforovitch, with a good-natured face, a greasy dressing-gown, a pipe, and a cup of tea, was conversing with the clerk of the court.

The judge's lips were directly under his nose, so that he could snuff his upper lip as much as he liked. It served him instead of a snuff-box, for the snuff intended for his nose almost always lodged upon it. So the judge was talking with the assistant. A barefooted girl stood holding a tray with cups at once side of them. At the end of the table, the secretary was reading the decision in some case, but in such a mournful and monotonous voice that the condemned man himself would have fallen asleep while listening to it. The judge, no doubt, would have been the first to do so had he not entered into an engrossing conversation while it was going on.

"I expressly tried to find out," said the judge, sipping his already cold tea from the cup, "how they manage to sing so well. I had a splendid thrush two years ago. Well, all of a sudden he was completely done for, and began to sing, God knows what! He got worse and worse and worse and worse as time went on; he began to rattle and get hoarse--just good for nothing! And this is how it happened: a little lump, not so big as a pea, had come under his throat. It was only necessary to prick that little swelling with a needle-- Zachar Prokofievitch taught me that; and, if you like, I'll just tell you how it was. I went to him--"

"Shall I read another, Demyan Demyanovitch?" broke in the secretary, who had not been reading for several minutes.

"Have you finished already? Only think how quickly! And I did not hear a word of it! Where is it? Give it me and I'll sign it. What else have you there?"

"The case of Cossack Bokitok for stealing a cow."

"Very good; read it!-- Yes, so I went to him--I can even tell you in detail how he entertained me. There was vodka, and dried sturgeon, excellent! Yes, not our sturgeon," there the judge smacked his tongue and smiled, upon which his nose took a sniff at its usual snuff-box, "such as our Mirgorod shops sell us. I ate no herrings, for, as you know, they give me heart-burn; but I tasted the caviare--very fine caviare, too! There's no doubt it, excellent! Then I drank some peach-brandy, real gentian. There was saffron-brandy also; but, as you know, I never take that. You see, it was all very good. In the first place, to whet your appetite, as they say, and then to satisfy it-- Ah! speak of an angel," exclaimed the judge, all at once, catching sight of Ivan Ivanovitch as he entered.

"God be with us! I wish you a good-morning," said Ivan Ivanovitch, bowing all round with his usual politeness. How well he understood the art of fascinating everybody in his manner! I never beheld such refinement. He knew his own worth quite well, and therefore looked for universal respect as his due. The judge himself handed Ivan Ivanovitch a chair; and his nose inhaled all the snuff resting on his upper lip, which, with him, was always a sign of great pleasure.

"What will you take, Ivan Ivanovitch?" he inquired: "will you have a cup of tea?"

"No, much obliged," replied Ivan Ivanovitch, as he bowed and seated himself.

"Do me the favour--one little cup," repeated the judge.

"No, thank you; much obliged for your hospitality," replied Ivan Ivanovitch, and rose, bowed, and sat down again.

"Just one little cup," repeated the judge.

"No, do not trouble yourself, Demyan Demyanovitch." Whereupon Ivan Ivanovitch again rose, bowed, and sat down.

"A little cup!"

"Very well, then, just a little cup," said Ivan Ivanovitch, and reached out his hand to the tray. Heavens! What a height of refinement there was in that man! It is impossible to describe what a pleasant impression such manners produce!

"Will you not have another cup?"

"I thank you sincerely," answered Ivan Ivanovitch, turning his cup upside down upon the tray and bowing.

"Do me the favour, Ivan Ivanovitch."

"I cannot; much obliged." Thereupon Ivan Ivanovitch bowed and sat down.

"Ivan Ivanovitch, for the sake of our friendship, just one little cup!"

"No: I am extremely indebted for your hospitality." So saying, Ivan Ivanovitch bowed and seated himself.

"Only a cup, one little cup!"

Ivan Ivanovitch put his hand out to the tray and took a cup. Oh, the deuce! How can a man contrive to support his dignity!

"Demyan Demyanovitch," said Ivan Ivanovitch, swallowing the last drain, "I have pressing business with you; I want to enter a complaint."

Then Ivan Ivanovitch set down his cup, and drew from his pocket a sheet of stamped paper, written over. "A complaint against my enemy, my declared enemy."

"And who is that?"

"Ivan Nikiforovitch Dovgotchkun."

At these words, the judge nearly fell off his chair. "What do you say?" he exclaimed, clasping his hands; "Ivan Ivanovitch, is this you?"

"You see yourself that it is I."

"The Lord and all the saints be with you! What! You! Ivan Ivanovitch! you have fallen out with Ivan Nikiforovitch! Is it your mouth which says that? Repeat it! Is not some one hid behind you who is speaking instead of you?"

"What is there incredible about it? I can't endure the sight of him: he has done me a deadly injury--he has insulted my honour."

"Holy Trinity! How am I to believe my mother now? Why, every day, when I quarrel with my sister, the old woman says, 'Children, you live together like dogs. If you would only take pattern by Ivan Ivanovitch and Ivan Nikiforovitch, they are friends indeed! such friends! such worthy people!' There you are with your friend! Tell me what this is about. How is it?"

"It is a delicate business, Demyan Demyanovitch; it is impossible to relate it in words: be pleased rather to read my plaint. Here, take it by this side; it is more convenient."

"Read it, Taras Tikhonovitch," said the judge, turning to the secretary.

Taras Tikhonovitch took the plaint; and blowing his nose, as all district judges' secretaries blow their noses, with the assistance of two fingers, he began to read:--

"From the nobleman and landed proprietor of the Mirgorod District, Ivan Pererepenko, son of Ivan, a plaint: concerning which the following points are to be noted:--

"1. Ivan Dovgotchkun, son of Nikifor, nobleman, known to all the world for his godless acts, which inspire disgust, and in lawlessness exceed all bounds, on the seventh day of July of this year 1810, inflicted upon me a deadly insult, touching my personal honour, and likewise tending to the humiliation and confusion of my rank and family. The said nobleman, of repulsive aspect, has also a pugnacious disposition, and is full to overflowing with blasphemy and quarrelsome words."

Here the reader paused for an instant to blow his nose again; but the judge folded his hands in approbation and murmured to himself, "What a ready pen! Lord! how this man does write!"

Ivan Ivanovitch requested that the reading might proceed, and Taras Tikhonovitch went on:--

"The said Ivan Dovgotchkun, son of Nikifor, when I went to him with a friendly proposition, called me publicly by an epithet insulting and injurious to my honour, namely, a goose, whereas it is known to the whole district of Mirgorod, that I never was named after that disgusting creature, and have no intention of ever being named after it. The proof of my noble extraction is that, in the baptismal register to be found in the Church of the Three Bishops, the day of my birth, and likewise the fact of my baptism, are inscribed. But a goose, as is well known to every one who has any knowledge of science, cannot be inscribed in the baptismal register; for a goose is not a man but a fowl; which, likewise, is sufficiently well known even to persons who have not been to college. But the said evil-minded nobleman, being privy to all these facts, affronted me with the aforesaid foul word, for no other purpose than to offer a deadly insult to my rank and station.

"2. And the same impolite and indecent nobleman, moreover, attempted injury to my property, inherited by me from my father, a member of the clerical profession, Ivan Pererepenko, son of Onisieff, of blessed memory, inasmuch that he, contrary to all law, transported directly opposite my porch a goose-shed, which was done with no other intention that to emphasise the insult offered me; for the said shed had, up to that time, stood in a very suitable situation, and was still sufficiently strong. But the loathsome intention of the aforesaid nobleman consisted simply in this: viz., in making me a witness of unpleasant occurrences; for it is well known that no man goes into a shed, much less into a goose-shed, for polite purposes. In the execution of his lawless deed, the two front posts trespassed on my land, received by me during the lifetime of my father, Ivan Pererepenko, son of Onisieff, of blessed memory, beginning at the granary, thence in a straight line to the spot where the women wash the pots.

"3. The above-described nobleman, whose very name and surname inspire thorough disgust, cherishes in his mind a malicious design to burn me in my own house. Which the infallible signs, hereinafter mentioned, fully demonstrate; in the first place, the said wicked nobleman has begun to emerge frequently from his apartments, which he never did formerly on account of his laziness and the disgusting corpulence of his body; in the second place, in his servants' apartments, adjoining the fence, surrounding my own land, received by me from my father of blessed memory, Ivan Pererepenko, son of Onisieff, a light burns every day, and for a remarkably long period of time, which is also a clear proof of the fact. For hitherto, owing to his repulsive niggardliness, not only the tallow-candle but also the grease-lamp has been extinguished.

"And therefore I pray that the said nobleman, Ivan Dovgotchkun, son of Nikifor, being plainly guilty of incendiarism, of insult to my rank, name, and family, and of illegal appropriation of my property, and, worse than all else, of malicious and deliberate addition to my surname, of the nickname of goose, be condemned by the court, to fine, satisfaction, costs, and damages, and, being chained, be removed to the town jail, and that judgment be rendered upon this, my plaint, immediately and without delay.

"Written and composed by Ivan Pererepenko, son of Ivan, nobleman, and landed proprietor of Mirgorod."

After the reading of the plaint was concluded, the judge approached Ivanovitch, took him by the button, and began to talk to him after this fashion: "What are you doing, Ivan Ivanovitch? Fear God! throw away that plaint, let it go! may Satan carry it off! Better take Ivan Nikiforovitch by the hand and kiss him, buy some Santurinski or Nikopolski liquor, make a punch, and call me in. We will drink it up together and forget all unpleasantness."

"No, Demyan Demyanovitch! it's not that sort of an affair," said Ivan Ivanovitch, with the dignity which always became him so well; "it is not an affair which can be arranged by a friendly agreement. Farewell! Good-day to you, too, gentlemen," he continued with the same dignity, turning to them all. "I hope that my plaint will lead to proper action being taken;" and out he went, leaving all present in a state of stupefaction.

The judge sat down without uttering a word; the secretary took a pinch of snuff; the clerks upset some broken fragments of bottles which served for inkstands; and the judge himself, in absence of mind, spread out a puddle of ink upon the table with his finger.

"What do you say to this, Dorofei Trofimovitch?" said the judge, turning to the assistant after a pause.

"I've nothing to say," replied the clerk.

"What things do happen!" continued the judge. He had not finished saying this before the door creaked and the front half of Ivan Nikiforovitch presented itself in the court-room; the rest of him remaining in the ante-room. The appearance of Ivan Nikiforovitch, and in court too, seemed so extraordinary that the judge screamed; the secretary stopped reading; one clerk, in his frieze imitation of a dress-coat, took his pen in his lips; and the other swallowed a fly. Even the constable on duty and the watchman, a discharged soldier who up to that moment had stood by the door scratching about his dirty tunic, with chevrons on its arm, dropped his jaw and trod on some one's foot.

"What chance brings you here? How is your health, Ivan Nikiforovitch?"

But Ivan Nikiforovitch was neither dead nor alive; for he was stuck fast in the door, and could not take a step either forwards or backwards. In vain did the judge shout into the ante-room that some one there should push Ivan Nikiforovitch forward into the court-room. In the ante-room there was only one old woman with a petition, who, in spite of all the efforts of her bony hands, could accomplish nothing. Then one of the clerks, with thick lips, a thick nose, eyes which looked askance and intoxicated, broad shoulders, and ragged elbows, approached the front half of Ivan Nikiforovitch, crossed his hands for him as though he had been a child, and winked at the old soldier, who braced his knee against Ivan Nikiforovitch's belly, so, in spite of the latter's piteous moans, he was squeezed out into the ante-room. Then they pulled the bolts, and opened the other half of the door. Meanwhile the clerk and his assistant, breathing hard with their friendly exertions, exhaled such a strong odour that the court-room seemed temporarily turned into a drinking-room.

"Are you hurt, Ivan Nikiforovitch? I will tell my mother to send you a decoction of brandy, with which you need but to rub your back and stomach and all your pains will disappear."

But Ivan Nikiforovitch dropped into a chair, and could utter no word beyond prolonged oh's. Finally, in a faint and barely audible voice from fatigue, he exclaimed, "Wouldn't you like some?" and drawing his snuff-box from his pocket, added, "Help yourself, if you please."

"Very glad to see you," replied the judge; "but I cannot conceive what made you put yourself to so much trouble, and favour us with so unexpected an honour."

"A plaint!" Ivan Nikiforovitch managed to ejaculate.

"A plaint? What plaint?"

"A complaint . . ." here his asthma entailed a prolonged pause--"Oh! a complaint against that rascal--Ivan Ivanovitch Pererepenko!"

"And you too! Such particular friends! A complaint against such a benevolent man?"

"He's Satan himself!" ejaculated Ivan Nikiforovitch abruptly.

The judge crossed himself.

"Take my plaint, and read it."

"There is nothing to be done. Read it, Taras Tikhonovitch," said the judge, turning to the secretary with an expression of displeasure, which caused his nose to sniff at his upper lip, which generally occurred only as a sign of great enjoyment. This independence on the part of his nose caused the judge still greater vexation. He pulled out his handkerchief, and rubbed off all the snuff from his upper lip in order to punish it for its daring.

The secretary, having gone through the usual performance, which he always indulged in before he began to read, that is to say, blowing his nose without the aid of a pocket-handkerchief, began in his ordinary voice, in the following manner:--

"Ivan Dovgotchkun, son of Nikifor, nobleman of the Mirgorod District, presents a plaint, and begs to call attention to the following points:--

"1. Through his hateful malice and plainly manifested ill-will, the person calling himself a nobleman, Ivan Pererepenko, son of Ivan, perpetrates against me every manner of injury, damage, and like spiteful deeds, which inspire me with terror. Yesterday afternoon, like a brigand and thief, with axes, saws, chisels, and various locksmith's tools, he came by night into my yard and into my own goose-shed located within it, and with his own hand, and in outrageous manner, destroyed it; for which very illegal and burglarious deed on my side I gave no manner of cause.

"2. The same nobleman Pererepenko has designs upon my life; and on the 7th of last month, cherishing this design in secret, he came to me, and began, in a friendly and insidious manner, to ask of me a gun which was in my chamber, and offered me for it, with the miserliness peculiar to him, many worthless objects, such as a brown sow and two sacks of oats. Divining at that time his criminal intentions, I endeavoured in every way to dissuade him from it: but the said rascal and scoundrel, Ivan Pererepenko, son of Ivan, abused me like a muzhik, and since that time has cherished against me an irreconcilable enmity. His sister was well known to every one as a loose character, and went off with a regiment of chasseurs which was stationed at Mirgorod five years ago; but she inscribed her husband as a peasant. His father and mother too were not law-abiding people, and both were inconceivable drunkards. The afore-mentioned nobleman and robber, Pererepenko, in his beastly and blameworthy actions, goes beyond all his family, and under the guise of piety does the most immoral things. He does not observe the fasts; for on the eve of St. Philip's this atheist bought a sheep, and next day ordered his mistress, Gapka, to kill it, alleging that he needed tallow for lamps and candles at once.

"Therefore I pray that the said nobleman, a manifest robber, church-thief, and rascal, convicted of plundering and stealing, may be put in irons, and confined in the jail or the government prison, and there, under supervision, deprived of his rank and nobility, well flogged, and banished to forced labour in Siberia, and that he may be commanded to pay damages and costs, and that judgment may be rendered on this my petition.

"To this plaint, Ivan Dovgotchkun, son of Nikifor, noble of the Mirgorod district, has set his hand."

As soon as the secretary had finished reading, Ivan Nikiforovitch seized his hat and bowed, with the intention of departing.

"Where are you going, Ivan Nikiforovitch?" the judge called after him. "Sit down a little while. Have some tea. Orishko, why are you standing there, you stupid girl, winking at the clerks? Go, bring tea."

But Ivan Nikiforovitch, in terror at having got so far from home, and at having undergone such a fearful quarantine, made haste to crawl through the door, saying, "Don't trouble yourself. It is with pleasure that I--" and closed it after him, leaving all present stupefied.

There was nothing to be done. Both plaints were entered; and the affair promised to assume a sufficiently serious aspect when an unforeseen occurrence lent an added interest to it. As the judge was leaving the court in company with the clerk and secretary, and the employees were thrusting into sacks the fowls, eggs, loaves, pies, cracknels, and other odds and ends brought by the plaintiffs--just at that moment a brown sow rushed into the room and snatched, to the amazement of the spectators, neither a pie nor a crust of bread but Ivan Nikiforovitch's plaint, which lay at the end of the table with its leaves hanging over. Having seized the document, mistress sow ran off so briskly that not one of the clerks or officials could catch her, in spite of the rulers and ink-bottles they hurled after her.

This extraordinary occurrence produced a terrible muddle, for there had not even been a copy taken of the plaint. The judge, that is to say, his secretary and the assistant debated for a long time upon such an unheard-of affair. Finally it was decided to write a report of the matter to the governor, as the investigation of the matter pertained more to the department of the city police. Report No. 389 was despatched to him that same day; and also upon that day there came to light a sufficiently curious explanation, which the reader may learn from the following chapter.

CHAPTER V

IN WHICH ARE DETAILED THE DELIBERATIONS OF TWO IMPORTANT PERSONAGES OF MIRGOROD

As soon as Ivan Ivanovitch had arranged his domestic affairs and stepped out upon the balcony, according to his custom, to lie down, he saw, to his indescribable amazement, something red at the gate. This was the red facings of the chief of police's coat, which were polished equally with his collar, and resembled varnished leather on the edges.

Ivan Ivanovitch thought to himself, "It's not bad that Peter Feodorovitch has come to talk it over with me." But he was very much surprised to see that the chief was walking remarkably fast and flourishing his hands, which was very rarely the case with him. There were eight buttons on the chief of police's uniform: the ninth, torn off in some manner during the procession at the consecration of the church two years before, the police had not been able to find up to this time: although the chief, on the occasion of the daily reports made to him by the sergeants, always asked, "Has that button been found?" These eight buttons were strewn about him as women sow beans--one to the right and one to the left. His left foot had been struck by a ball in the last campaign, and so he limped and threw it out so far to one side as to almost counteract the efforts of the right foot. The more briskly the chief of police worked his walking apparatus the less progress he made in advance. So while he was getting to the balcony, Ivan Ivanovitch had plenty of time to lose himself in surmises as to why the chief was flourishing his hands so vigorously. This interested him the more, as the matter seemed one of unusual importance; for the chief had on a new dagger.

"Good morning, Peter Feodorovitch!" cried Ivan Ivanovitch, who was, as has already been stated, exceedingly curious, and could not restrain his impatience as the chief of police began to ascend to the balcony, yet never raised his eyes, and kept grumbling at his foot, which could not be persuaded to mount the step at the first attempt.

"I wish my good friend and benefactor, Ivan Ivanovitch, a good-day," replied the chief.

"Pray sit down. I see that you are weary, as your lame foot hinders--"

"My foot!" screamed the chief, bestowing upon Ivan Ivanovitch a glance such as a giant might cast upon a pigmy, a pedant upon a dancing-master: and he stretched out his foot and stamped upon the floor with it. This boldness cost him dear; for his whole body wavered and his nose struck the railing; but the brave preserver of order, with the purpose of making light of it, righted himself immediately, and began to feel in his pocket as if to get his snuff-box. "I must report to you, my dear friend and benefactor, Ivan Ivanovitch, that never in all my days have I made such a march. Yes, seriously. For instance, during the campaign of 1807-- Ah! I will tell to you how I crawled through the enclosure to see a pretty little German." Here the chief closed one eye and executed a diabolically sly smile.

"Where have you been to-day?" asked Ivan Ivanovitch, wishing to cut the chief short and bring him more speedily to the object of his visit. He would have very much liked to inquire what the chief meant to tell him, but his extensive knowledge of the world showed him the impropriety of such a question; and so he had to keep himself well in hand and await a solution, his heart, meanwhile, beating with unusual force.

"Ah, excuse me! I was going to tell you--where was I?" answered the chief of police. "In the first place, I report that the weather is fine to-day."

At these last words, Ivan Ivanovitch nearly died.

"But permit me," went on the chief. "I have come to you to-day about a very important affair." Here the chief's face and bearing assumed the same careworn aspect with which he had ascended to the balcony.

Ivan Ivanovitch breathed again, and shook as if in a fever, omitting not, as was his habit, to put a question. "What is the important matter? Is it important?"

"Pray judge for yourself; in the first place I venture to report to you, dear friend and benefactor, Ivan Ivanovitch, that you-- I beg you to observe that, for my own part, I should have nothing to say; but the rules of government require it--that you have transgressed the rules of propriety."

"What do you mean, Peter Feodorovitch? I don't understand at all."

"Pardon me, Ivan Ivanovitch! how can it be that you do not understand? Your own beast has destroyed an important government document; and you can still say, after that, that you do not understand!"

"What beast?"

"Your own brown sow, with your permission, be it said."

"How can I be responsible? Why did the door-keeper of the court open the door?"

"But, Ivan Ivanovitch, your own brown sow. You must be responsible."

"I am extremely obliged to you for comparing me to a sow."

"But I did not say that, Ivan Ivanovitch! By Heaven! I did not say so! Pray judge from your own clear conscience. It is known to you without doubt, that in accordance with the views of the government, unclean animals are forbidden to roam about the town, particularly in the principal streets. Admit, now, that it is prohibited."

"God knows what you are talking about! A mighty important business that a sow got into the street!"

"Permit me to inform you, Ivan Ivanovitch, permit me, permit me, that this is utterly inadvisable. What is to be done? The authorities command, we must obey. I don't deny that sometimes chickens and geese run about the street, and even about the square, pray observe, chickens and geese; but only last year, I gave orders that pigs and goats were not to be admitted to the public squares, which regulations I directed to be read aloud at the time before all the people."

"No, Peter Feodorovitch, I see nothing here except that you are doing your best to insult me."

"But you cannot say that, my dearest friend and benefactor, that I have tried to insult you. Bethink yourself: I never said a word to you last year when you built a roof a whole foot higher than is allowed by law. On the contrary, I pretended not to have observed it. Believe me, my dearest friend, even now, I would, so to speak--but my duty--in a word, my duty demands that I should have an eye to cleanliness. Just judge for yourself, when suddenly in the principal street--"

"Fine principal streets yours are! Every woman goes there and throws down any rubbish she chooses."

"Permit me to inform you, Ivan Ivanovitch, that it is you who are insulting me. That does sometimes happen, but, as a rule, only besides fences, sheds, or storehouses; but that a filthy sow should intrude herself in the main street, in the square, now is a matter--"

"What sort of a matter? Peter Feodorovitch! surely a sow is one of God's creatures!"

"Agreed. Everybody knows that you are a learned man, that you are acquainted with sciences and various other subjects. I never studied the sciences: I began to learn to write in my thirteenth year. Of course you know that I was a soldier in the ranks."

"Hm!" said Ivan Ivanovitch.

"Yes," continued the chief of police, "in 1801 I was in the Forty-second Regiment of chasseurs, lieutenant in the fourth company. The commander of our company was, if I may be permitted to mention it, Captain Eremeeff." Thereupon the chief of police thrust his fingers into the snuff-box which Ivan Ivanovitch was holding open, and stirred up the snuff.

Ivan Ivanovitch answered, "Hm!"

"But my duty," went on the chief of police, "is to obey the commands of the authorities. Do you know, Ivan Ivanovitch, that a person who purloins a government document in the court-room incurs capital punishment equally with other criminals?"

"I know it; and, if you like, I can give you lessons. It is so decreed with regard to people, as if you, for instance, were to steal a document; but a sow is an animal, one of God's creatures."

"Certainly; but the law reads, 'Those guilty of theft'--I beg of you to listen most attentively--'Those guilty!' Here is indicated neither race nor sex nor rank: of course an animal can be guilty. You may say what you please; but the animal, until the sentence is pronounced by the court, should be committed to the charge of the police as a transgressor of the law."

"No, Peter Feodorovitch," retorted Ivan Ivanovitch coolly, "that shall not be."

"As you like: only I must carry out the orders of the authorities."

"What are you threatening me with? Probably you want to send that one-armed soldier after her. I shall order the woman who tends the door to drive him off with the poker: he'll get his last arm broken."

"I dare not dispute with you. In case you will not commit the sow to the charge of the police, then do what you please with her: kill her for Christmas, if you like, and make hams of her, or eat her as she is. Only I should like to ask you, in case you make sausages, to send me a couple, such as your Gapka makes so well, of blood and lard. My Agrafena Trofimovna is extremely fond of them."

"I will send you a couple of sausages if you permit."

"I shall be extremely obliged to you, dear friend and benefactor. Now permit me to say one word more. I am commissioned by the judge, as well as by all our acquaintances, so to speak, to effect a reconciliation between you and your friend, Ivan Nikiforovitch."

"What! with that brute! I to be reconciled to that clown! Never! It shall not be, it shall not be!" Ivan Ivanovitch was in a remarkably determined frame of mind.

"As you like," replied the chief of police, treating both nostrils to snuff. "I will not venture to advise you; but permit me to mention--here you live at enmity, and if you make peace. . ."

But Ivan Ivanovitch began to talk about catching quail, as he usually did when he wanted to put an end to a conversation. So the chief of police was obliged to retire without having achieved any success whatever.

CHAPTER VI

FROM WHICH THE READER CAN EASILY DISCOVER WHAT IS CONTAINED IN IT

In spite of all the judge's efforts to keep the matter secret, all Mirgorod knew by the next day that Ivan Ivanovitch's sow had stolen Ivan Nikiforovitch's petition. The chief of police himself, in a moment of forgetfulness, was the first to betray himself. When Ivan Nikiforovitch was informed of it he said nothing: he merely inquired, "Was it the brown one?"

But Agafya Fedosyevna, who was present, began again to urge on Ivan Nikiforovitch. "What's the matter with you, Ivan Nikiforovitch? People will laugh at you as at a fool if you let it pass. How can you remain a nobleman after that? You will be worse than the old woman who sells the honeycakes with hemp-seed oil you are so fond of."

And the mischief-maker persuaded him. She hunted up somewhere a middle-aged man with dark complexion, spots all over his face, and a dark-blue surtout patched on the elbows, a regular official scribbler. He blacked his boots with tar, wore three pens behind his ear, and a glass vial tied to his buttonhole with a string instead of an ink-bottle: ate as many as nine pies at once, and put the tenth in his pocket, and wrote so many slanders of all sorts on a single sheet of stamped paper that no reader could get through all at one time without interspersing coughs and sneezes. This man laboured, toiled, and wrote, and finally concocted the following document:-

"To the District Judge of Mirgorod, from the noble, Ivan Dovgotchkun, son of Nikifor.

"In pursuance of my plaint which was presented by me, Ivan Dovgotchkun, son of Nikifor, against the nobleman, Ivan Pererepenko, son of Ivan, to which the judge of the Mirgorod district court has exhibited indifference; and the shameless, high-handed deed of the brown sow being kept secret, and coming to my ears from outside parties.

"And the said neglect, plainly malicious, lies incontestably at the judge's door; for the sow is a stupid animal, and therefore unfitted for the theft of papers. From which it plainly appears that the said frequently mentioned sow was not otherwise than instigated to the same by the opponent, Ivan Pererepenko, son of Ivan, calling himself a nobleman, and already convicted of theft, conspiracy against life, and desecration of a church. But the said Mirgorod judge, with the partisanship peculiar to him, gave his private consent to this individual; for without such consent the said sow could by no possible means have been admitted to carry off the document; for the judge of the district court of Mirgorod is well provided with servants: it was only necessary to summon a soldier, who is always on duty in the reception-room, and who, although he has but one eye and one somewhat damaged arm, has powers quite adequate to driving out a sow, and to beating it with a stick, from which is credibly evident the criminal neglect of the said Mirgorod judge and the incontestable sharing of the Jew-like spoils therefrom resulting from these mutual conspirators. And the aforesaid robber and nobleman, Ivan Pererepenko, son of Ivan, having disgraced himself, finished his turning on his lathe. Wherefore, I, the noble Ivan Dovgotchkun, son of Nikifor, declare to the said district judge in proper form that if the said brown sow, or the man Pererepenko, be not summoned to the court, and judgment in accordance with justice and my advantage pronounced upon her, then I, Ivan Dovgotchkun, son of Nikifor, shall present a plaint, with observance of all due formalities, against the said district judge for his illegal partisanship to the superior courts.

"Ivan Dovgotchkun, son of Nikifor, noble of the Mirgorod District."

This petition produced its effect. The judge was a man of timid disposition, as all good people generally are. He betook himself to the secretary. But the secretary emitted from his lips a thick "Hm," and exhibited on his countenance that indifferent and diabolically equivocal expression which Satan alone assumes when he sees his victim hastening to his feet. One resource remained to him, to reconcile the two friends. But how to set about it, when all attempts up to that time had been so unsuccessful? Nevertheless, it was decided to make another effort; but Ivan Ivanovitch declared outright that he would not hear of it, and even flew into a violent passion; whilst Ivan Nikiforovitch, in lieu of an answer, turned his back and would not utter a word.

Then the case went on with the unusual promptness upon which courts usually pride themselves. Documents were dated, labelled, numbered, sewed together, registered all in one day, and the matter laid on the shelf, where it continued to lie, for one, two, or three years. Many brides were married; a new street was laid out in Mirgorod; one of the judge's double teeth fell out and two of his eye-teeth; more children than ever ran about Ivan Ivanovitch's yard; Ivan Nikiforovitch, as a reproof to Ivan Ivanovitch, constructed a new goose-shed, although a little farther back than the first, and built himself completely off from his neighbour, so that these worthy people hardly ever beheld each other's faces; but still the case lay in the cabinet, which had become marbled with ink-pots.

In the meantime a very important event for all Mirgorod had taken place. The chief of police had given a reception. Whence shall I obtain the brush and colours to depict this varied gathering and magnificent feast? Take your watch, open it, and look what is going on inside. A fearful confusion, is it not? Now, imagine almost the same, if not a greater, number of wheels standing in the chief of police's courtyard. How many carriages and waggons were there! One was wide behind and narrow in front; another narrow behind and wide in front. One was a carriage and a waggon combined; another neither a carriage nor a waggon. One resembled a huge hayrick or a fat merchant's wife; another a dilapidated Jew or a skeleton not quite freed from the skin. One was a perfect pipe with long stem in profile; another, resembling nothing whatever, suggested some strange, shapeless, fantastic object. In the midst of this chaos of wheels rose coaches with windows like those of a room. The drivers, in grey Cossack coats, gaberdines, and white hare-skin coats, sheepskin hats and caps of various patterns, and with pipes in their hands, drove the unharnessed horses through the yard.

What a reception the chief of police gave! Permit me to run through the list of those who were there: Taras Tarasovitch, Evpl Akinfovitch, Evtikhiy

Evtikhievitch, Ivan Ivanovitch--not that Ivan Ivanovitch but another--Gabba Bavrilonovitch, our Ivan Ivanovitch, Elevferiy Elevferievitch, Makar Nazarevitch, Thoma Grigorovitch--I can say no more: my powers fail me, my hand stops writing. And how many ladies were there! dark and fair, tall and short, some fat like Ivan Nikiforovitch, and some so thin that it seemed as though each one might hide herself in the scabbard of the chief's sword. What head-dresses! what costumes! red, yellow, coffee-colour, green, blue, new, turned, re-made dresses, ribbons, reticules. Farewell, poor eyes! you will never be good for anything any more after such a spectacle. And how long the table was drawn out! and how all talked! and what a noise they made! What is a mill with its driving-wheel, stones, beams, hammers, wheels, in comparison with this? I cannot tell you exactly what they talked about, but presumably of many agreeable and useful things, such as the weather, dogs, wheat, caps, and dice. At length Ivan Ivanovitch--not our Ivan Ivanovitch, but the other, who had but one eye--said, "It strikes me as strange that my right eye," this one-eyed Ivan Ivanovitch always spoke sarcastically about himself, "does not see Ivan Nikiforovitch, Gospodin Dovgotchkun."

"He would not come," said the chief of police.

"Why not?"

"It's two years now, glory to God! since they quarrelled; that is, Ivan Ivanovitch and Ivan Nikiforovitch; and where one goes, the other will not go."

"You don't say so!" Thereupon one-eyed Ivan Ivanovitch raised his eye and clasped his hands. "Well, if people with good eyes cannot live in peace, how am I to live amicably, with my bad one?"

At these words they all laughed at the tops of their voices. Every one liked one-eyed Ivan Ivanovitch, because he cracked jokes in that style. A tall, thin man in a frieze coat, with a plaster on his nose, who up to this time had sat in the corner, and never once altered the expression of his face, even when a fly lighted on his nose, rose from his seat, and approached nearer to the crowd which surrounded one-eyed Ivan Ivanovitch. "Listen," said Ivan Ivanovitch, when he perceived that quite a throng had collected about him; "suppose we make peace between our friends. Ivan Ivanovitch is talking with the women and girls; let us send quietly for Ivan Nikiforovitch and bring them together."

Ivan Ivanovitch's proposal was unanimously agreed to; and it was decided to send at once to Ivan Nikiforovitch's house, and beg him, at any rate, to come to the chief of police's for dinner. But the difficult question as to who was to be intrusted with this weighty commission rendered all thoughtful. They debated long as to who was the most expert in diplomatic matters. At length it was unanimously agreed to depute Anton Prokofievitch to do this business.

But it is necessary, first of all, to make the reader somewhat acquainted with this noteworthy person. Anton Prokofievitch was a truly good man, in the fullest meaning of the term. If any one in Mirgorod gave him a neckerchief or underclothes, he returned thanks; if any one gave him a fillip on the nose, he returned thanks too. If he was asked, "Why, Anton Prokofievitch, do you wear a light brown coat with blue sleeves?" he generally replied, "Ah, you haven't one like it! Wait a bit, it will soon fade and will be alike all over." And, in point of fact, the blue cloth, from the effects of the sun, began to turn cinnamon colour, and became of the same tint as the rest of the coat. But the strange part of it was that Anton Prokofievitch had a habit of wearing woollen clothing in summer and nankeen in winter.

Anton Prokofievitch had no house of his own. He used to have one on the outskirts of the town; but he sold it, and with the purchase-money bought a team of brown horses and a little carriage in which he drove about to stay with the squires. But as the horses were a deal of trouble and money was required for oats, Anton Prokofievitch bartered them for a violin and a housemaid, with twenty-five paper rubles to boot. Afterwards Anton Prokofievitch sold the violin, and exchanged the girl for a morocco and gold tobacco-pouch; now he has such a tobacco-pouch as no one else has. As a result of this luxury, he can no longer go about among the country houses, but has to remain in the town and pass the night at different houses, especially of those gentlemen who take pleasure in tapping him on the nose. Anton Prokofievitch is very fond of good eating, and plays a good game at cards. Obeying orders always was his forte; so, taking his hat and cane, he set out at once on his errand.

But, as he walked along, he began to ponder in what manner he should contrive to induce Ivan Nikiforovitch to come to the assembly. The unbending character of the latter, who was otherwise a worthy man, rendered the undertaking almost hopeless. How, indeed, was he to persuade him to come, when even rising from his bed cost him so great an effort? But supposing that he did rise, how could he get him to come, where, as he doubtless knew, his irreconcilable enemy already was? The more Anton Prokofievitch reflected, the more difficulties he perceived. The day was sultry, the sun beat down, the perspiration poured from him in streams. Anton Prokofievitch was a tolerably sharp man in many respects though they did tap him on the nose. In bartering, however, he was not fortunate. He knew very well when to play the fool, and sometimes contrived to turn things to his own profit amid circumstances and surroundings from which a wise man could rarely escape without loss.

His ingenious mind had contrived a means of persuading Ivan Nikiforovitch; and he was proceeding bravely to face everything when an unexpected occurrence somewhat disturbed his equanimity. There is no harm, at this point, in admitting to the reader that, among other things, Anton Prokofievitch was the owner of a pair of trousers of such singular properties that whenever he put them on the dogs always bit his calves. Unfortunately, he had donned this particular pair of trousers; and he had hardly given himself up to meditation before a fearful barking on all sides saluted his ears. Anton Prokofievitch raised such a yell, no one could scream louder than he, that not only did the well-known woman and the occupant of the endless coat rush out to meet him, but even the small boys from Ivan Ivanovitch's yard. But although the dogs succeeded in tasting only one of his calves, this sensibility diminished his courage, and he entered the porch with a certain amount of timidity.

CHAPTER VII

HOW A RECONCILIATION WAS SOUGHT TO BE EFFECTED AND A LAW SUIT ENSUED

"Ah! how do you do? Why do you irritate the dogs?" said Ivan Nikiforovitch, on perceiving Anton Prokofievitch; for no one spoke otherwise than jestingly with Anton Prokofievitch.

"Hang them! who's been irritating them?" retorted Anton Prokofievitch.

"You have!"

"By Heavens, no! You are invited to dinner by Peter Feodorovitch."

"Hm!"

"He invited you in a more pressing manner than I can tell you. 'Why,' says he, 'does Ivan Nikiforovitch shun me like an enemy? He never comes round to have a chat, or make a call.'"

Ivan Nikiforovitch stroked his beard.

"'If,' says he, 'Ivan Nikiforovitch does not come now, I shall not know what to think: surely, he must have some design against me. Pray, Anton Prokofievitch, persuade Ivan Nikiforovitch!' Come, Ivan Nikiforovitch, let us go! a very choice company is already met there."

Ivan Nikiforovitch began to look at a cock, which was perched on the roof, crowing with all its might.

"If you only knew, Ivan Nikiforovitch," pursued the zealous ambassador, "what fresh sturgeon and caviare Peter Feodorovitch has had sent to him!" Whereupon Ivan Nikiforovitch turned his head and began to listen attentively. This encouraged the messenger. "Come quickly: Thoma Grigorovitch is there too. Why don't you come?" he added, seeing that Ivan Nikiforovitch still lay in the same position. "Shall we go, or not?"

"I won't!"

This "I won't" startled Anton Prokofievitch. He had fancied that his alluring representations had quite moved this very worthy man; but instead, he heard that decisive "I won't."

"Why won't you?" he asked, with a vexation which he very rarely exhibited, even when they put burning paper on his head, a trick which the judge and the chief of police were particularly fond of indulging in.

Ivan Nikiforovitch took a pinch of snuff.

"Just as you like, Ivan Nikiforovitch. I do not know what detains you."

"Why don't I go?" said Ivan Nikiforovitch at length: "because that brigand will be there!" This was his ordinary way of alluding to Ivan Ivanovitch. "Just God! and is it long?"

"He will not be there, he will not be there! May the lightning kill me on the spot!" returned Anton Prokofievitch, who was ready to perjure himself ten times in an hour. "Come along, Ivan Nikiforovitch!"

"You lie, Anton Prokofievitch! he is there!"

"By Heaven, by Heaven, he's not! May I never stir from this place if he's there! Now, just think for yourself, what object have I in lying? May my hands and feet wither!-- What, don't you believe me now? May I perish right here in your presence! Don't you believe me yet?"

Ivan Nikiforovitch was entirely reassured by these asseverations, and ordered his valet, in the boundless coat, to fetch his trousers and nankeen spencer.

To describe how Ivan Nikiforovitch put on his trousers, how they wound his neckerchief about his neck, and finally dragged on his spencer, which burst under the left sleeve, would be quite superfluous. Suffice it to say, that during the whole of the time he preserved a becoming calmness of demeanour, and answered not a word to Anton Prokofievitch's proposition to exchange something for his Turkish tobacco-pouch.

Meanwhile, the assembly awaited with impatience the decisive moment when Ivan Nikiforovitch should make his appearance and at length comply with the general desire that these worthy people should be reconciled to each other. Many were almost convinced that Ivan Nikiforovitch would not come. Even the chief of police offered to bet with one-eyed Ivan Ivanovitch that he would not come; and only desisted when one-eyed Ivan Ivanovitch demanded that he should wager his lame foot against his own bad eye, at which the chief of police was greatly offended, and the company enjoyed a quiet laugh. No one had yet sat down to the table, although it was long past two o'clock, an hour before which in Mirgorod, even on ceremonial occasions, every one had already dined.

No sooner did Anton Prokofievitch show himself in the doorway, then he was instantly surrounded. Anton Prokofievitch, in answer to all inquiries, shouted the all-decisive words, "He will not come!" No sooner had he uttered them than a hailstorm of reproaches, scoldings, and, possibly, even fillips were about to descend upon his head for the ill success of his mission, when all at once the door opened, and--Ivan Nikiforovitch entered.

If Satan himself or a corpse had appeared, it would not have caused such consternation amongst the company as Ivan Nikiforovitch's unexpected arrival created. But Anton Prokofievitch only went off into a fit of laughter, and held his sides with delight at having played such a joke upon the company.

At all events, it was almost past the belief of all that Ivan Nikiforovitch could, in so brief a space of time, have attired himself like a respectable gentleman. Ivan Ivanovitch was not there at the moment: he had stepped out somewhere. Recovering from their amazement, the guests expressed an interest in Ivan Nikiforovitch's health, and their pleasure at his increase in breadth. Ivan Nikiforovitch kissed every one, and said, "Very much obliged!"

Meantime, the fragrance of the beet-soup was wafted through the apartment, and tickled the nostrils of the hungry guests very agreeably. All rushed headlong to table. The line of ladies, loquacious and silent, thin and stout, swept on, and the long table soon glittered with all the hues of the rainbow. I will not describe the courses: I will make no mention of the curd dumplings with sour cream, nor of the dish of pig's fry that was served with the soup, nor of the turkey with plums and raisins, nor of the dish which greatly resembled in appearance a boot soaked in kvas, nor of the sauce, which is the swan's song of the old-fashioned cook, nor of that other dish which was brought in all enveloped in the flames of spirit, and amused as well as frightened the ladies extremely. I will say nothing of these dishes, because I like to eat them better than to spend many words in discussing them.

Ivan Ivanovitch was exceedingly pleased with the fish dressed with horse-radish. He devoted himself especially to this useful and nourishing preparation. Picking out all the fine bones from the fish, he laid them on his plate; and happening to glance across the table--Heavenly Creator; but this was strange! Opposite him sat Ivan Nikiforovitch.

At the very same instant Ivan Nikiforovitch glanced up also-- No, I can do no more-- Give me a fresh pen with a fine point for this picture! mine is flabby. Their faces seemed to turn to stone whilst still retaining their defiant expression. Each beheld a long familiar face, to which it should have seemed the most natural of things to step up, involuntarily, as to an unexpected friend, and offer a snuff-box, with the words, "Do me the favour," or "Dare I beg you to do me the favour?" Instead of this, that face was terrible as a forerunner of evil. The perspiration poured in streams from Ivan Ivanovitch and Ivan Nikiforovitch.

All the guests at the table grew dumb with attention, and never once took their eyes off the former friends. The ladies, who had been busy up to that time on a sufficiently interesting discussion as to the preparation of capons, suddenly cut their conversation short. All was silence. It was a picture worthy of the brush of a great artist.

At length Ivan Ivanovitch pulled out his handkerchief and began to blow his nose; whilst Ivan Nikiforovitch glanced about and his eye rested on the open door. The chief of police at once perceived this movement, and ordered the door to be fastened. Then both of the friends began to eat, and never once glanced at each other again.

As soon as dinner was over, the two former friends both rose from their seats, and began to look for their hats, with a view to departure. Then the chief beckoned; and Ivan Ivanovitch--not our Ivan Ivanovitch, but the other with the one eye--got behind Ivan Nikiforovitch, and the chief stepped behind Ivan Ivanovitch, and the two began to drag them backwards, in order to bring them together, and not release them till they had shaken hands with each other. Ivan Ivanovitch, the one-eyed, pushed Ivan Nikiforovitch, with tolerable success, towards the spot where stood Ivan Ivanovitch. But the chief of police directed his course too much to one side, because he could not steer himself with his refractory leg, which obeyed no orders whatever on this occasion, and, as if with malice and aforethought, swung itself uncommonly far, and in quite the contrary direction, possibly from the fact that there had been an unusual amount of fruit wine after dinner, so that Ivan Ivanovitch fell over a lady in a red gown, who had thrust herself into the very midst, out of curiosity.

Such an omen forboded no good. Nevertheless, the judge, in order to set things to rights, took the chief of police's place, and, sweeping all the snuff from his upper lip with his nose, pushed Ivan Ivanovitch in the opposite direction. In Mirgorod this is the usual manner of effecting a reconciliation: it somewhat resembles a game of ball. As soon as the judge pushed Ivan Ivanovitch, Ivan Ivanovitch with the one eye exerted all his strength, and pushed Ivan Nikiforovitch, from whom the perspiration streamed like rain-water from a roof. In spite of the fact that the friends resisted to the best of their ability, they were nevertheless brought together, for the two chief movers received reinforcements from the ranks of their guests.

Then they were closely surrounded on all sides, not to be released until they had decided to give one another their hands. "God be with you, Ivan Nikiforovitch and Ivan Ivanovitch! declare upon your honour now, that what you quarrelled about were mere trifles, were they not? Are you not ashamed of yourselves before people and before God?"

"I do not know," said Ivan Nikiforovitch, panting with fatigue, though it is to be observed that he was not at all disinclined to a reconciliation, "I do not know what I did to Ivan Ivanovitch; but why did he destroy my coop and plot against my life?"

"I am innocent of any evil designs!" said Ivan Ivanovitch, never looking at Ivan Nikiforovitch. "I swear before God and before you, honourable noblemen, I did nothing to my enemy! Why does he calumniate me and insult my rank and family?"

"How have I insulted you, Ivan Ivanovitch?" said Ivan Nikiforovitch. One moment more of explanation, and the long enmity would have been extinguished. Ivan Nikiforovitch was already feeling in his pocket for his snuff-box, and was about to say, "Do me the favour."

"Is it not an insult," answered Ivan Ivanovitch, without raising his eyes, "when you, my dear sir, insulted my honour and my family with a word which it is improper to repeat here?"

"Permit me to observe, in a friendly manner, Ivan Ivanovitch," here Ivan Nikiforovitch touched Ivan Ivanovitch's button with his finger, which clearly indicated the disposition of his mind, "that you took offence, the deuce only knows at what, because I called you a 'goose'--"

It occurred to Ivan Nikiforovitch that he had made a mistake in uttering that word; but it was too late: the word was said. Everything went to the winds. It, on the utterance of this word without witnesses, Ivan Ivanovitch lost control of himself and flew into such a passion as God preserve us from beholding any man in, what was to be expected now? I put it to you, dear readers, what was to be expected now, when the fatal word was uttered in an assemblage of persons among whom were ladies, in whose presence Ivan Ivanovitch liked to be particularly polite? If Ivan Nikiforovitch had set to work in any other manner, if he had only said bird and not goose, it might still have been arranged, but all was at an end.

He gave one look at Ivan Nikiforovitch, but such a look! If that look had possessed active power, then it would have turned Ivan Nikiforovitch into dust. The guests understood the look and hastened to separate them. And this man, the very model of gentleness, who never let a single poor woman go by without interrogating her, rushed out in a fearful rage. Such violent storms do passions produce!

For a whole month nothing was heard of Ivan Ivanovitch. He shut himself up at home. His ancestral chest was opened, and from it were taken silver rubles, his grandfather's old silver rubles! And these rubles passed into the ink-stained hands of legal advisers. The case was sent up to the higher court; and when Ivan Ivanovitch received the joyful news that it would be decided on the morrow, then only did he look out upon the world and resolve to emerge from his house. Alas! from that time forth the council gave notice day by day that the case would be finished on the morrow, for the space of ten years.

Five years ago, I passed through the town of Mirgorod. I came at a bad time. It was autumn, with its damp, melancholy weather, mud and mists. An unnatural verdure, the result of incessant rains, covered with a watery network the fields and meadows, to which it is as well suited as youthful pranks to an old man, or roses to an old woman. The weather made a deep impression on me at the time: when it was dull, I was dull; but in spite of this, when I came to pass through Mirgorod, my heart beat violently. God, what reminiscences! I had not seen Mirgorod for twenty years. Here had lived, in touching friendship, two inseparable friends. And how many prominent people had died! Judge Demyan Demyanovitch was already gone: Ivan Ivanovitch, with the one eye, had long ceased to live.

I entered the main street. All about stood poles with bundles of straw on top: some alterations were in progress. Several dwellings had been removed. The remnants of board and wattled fences projected sadly here and there. It was a festival day. I ordered my basket chaise to stop in front of the church, and entered softly that no one might turn round. To tell the truth, there was no need of this: the church was almost empty; there were very few people; it was evident that even the most pious feared the mud. The candles seemed strangely unpleasant in that gloomy, or rather sickly, light. The dim vestibule was melancholy; the long windows, with their circular panes, were bedewed with tears of rain. I retired into the vestibule, and addressing a respectable old man, with greyish hair, said, "May I inquire if Ivan Nikiforovitch is still living?"

At that moment the lamp before the holy picture burned up more brightly and the light fell directly upon the face of my companion. What was my surprise, on looking more closely, to behold features with which I was acquainted! It was Ivan Nikiforovitch himself! But how he had changed!

"Are you well, Ivan Nikiforovitch? How old you have grown!"

"Yes, I have grown old. I have just come from Poltava to-day," answered Ivan Nikiforovitch.

"You don't say so! you have been to Poltava in such bad weather?"

"What was to be done? that lawsuit--"

At this I sighed involuntarily.

Ivan Nikiforovitch observed my sigh, and said, "Do not be troubled: I have reliable information that the case will be decided next week, and in my favour."

I shrugged my shoulders, and went to seek news of Ivan Ivanovitch.

"Ivan Ivanovitch is here," some one said to me, "in the choir."

I saw a gaunt form. Was that Ivan Ivanovitch? His face was covered with wrinkles, his hair was perfectly white; but the pelisse was the same as ever. After the first greetings were over, Ivan Ivanovitch, turning to me with a joyful smile which always became his funnel-shaped face, said, "Have you been told the good news?"

"What news?" I inquired.

"My case is to be decided to-morrow without fail: the court has announced it decisively."

I sighed more deeply than before, made haste to take my leave, for I was bound on very important business, and seated myself in my kibitka.

The lean nags known in Mirgorod as post-horses started, producing with their hoofs, which were buried in a grey mass of mud, a sound very displeasing to the ear. The rain poured in torrents upon the Jew seated on the box, covered with a rug. The dampness penetrated through and through me. The gloomy barrier with a sentry-box, in which an old soldier was repairing his weapons, was passed slowly. Again the same fields, in some places black where they had been dug up, in others of a greenish hue; wet daws and crows; monotonous rain; a tearful sky, without one gleam of light! . . . It is gloomy in this world, gentlemen!

THE MYSTERIOUS PORTRAIT

PART I

Nowhere did so many people pause as before the little picture-shop in the Shtchukinui Dvor. This little shop contained, indeed, the most varied collection of curiosities. The pictures were chiefly oil-paintings covered with dark varnish, in frames of dingy yellow. Winter scenes with white trees; very red sunsets, like raging conflagrations, a Flemish boor, more like a turkey-cock in cuffs than a human being, were the prevailing subjects. To these must be added a few engravings, such as a portrait of Khozreff-Mirza in a sheepskin cap, and some generals with three-cornered hats and hooked noses. Moreover, the doors of such shops are usually festooned with bundles of those publications, printed on large sheets of bark, and then coloured by hand, which bear witness to the native talent of the Russian.

On one was the Tzarevna Miliktrisa Kirbitievna; on another the city of Jerusalem. There are usually but few purchasers of these productions, but gazers are many. Some truant lackey probably yawns in front of them, holding in his hand the dishes containing dinner from the cook-shop for his master, who will not get his soup very hot. Before them, too, will most likely be standing a soldier wrapped in his cloak, a dealer from the old-clothes mart, with a couple of penknives for sale, and a huckstress, with a basketful of shoes. Each expresses admiration in his own way. The muzhiks generally touch them with their fingers; the dealers gaze seriously at them; serving boys and apprentices laugh, and tease each other with the coloured caricatures; old lackeys in frieze cloaks look at them merely for the sake of yawning away their time somewhere; and the hucksters, young Russian women, halt by instinct to hear what people are gossiping about, and to see what they are looking at.

At the time our story opens, the young painter, Tchartkoff, paused involuntarily as he passed the shop. His old cloak and plain attire showed him to be a man who was devoted to his art with self-denying zeal, and who had no time to trouble himself about his clothes. He halted in front of the little shop, and at first enjoyed an inward laugh over the monstrosities in the shape of pictures.

At length he sank unconsciously into a reverie, and began to ponder as to what sort of people wanted these productions? It did not seem remarkable to him that the Russian populace should gaze with rapture upon "Eruslanoff Lazarevitch," on "The Glutton" and "The Carouser," on "Thoma and Erema." The delineations of these subjects were easily intelligible to the masses. But where were there purchases for those streaky, dirty oil-paintings? Who needed those Flemish boors, those red and blue landscapes, which put forth some claims to a higher stage of art, but which really expressed the depths of its degradation? They did not appear the works of a self-taught child. In that case, in spite of the caricature of drawing, a sharp distinction would have manifested itself. But here were visible only simple dullness, steady-going incapacity, which stood, through self-will, in the ranks of art, while its true place was among the lowest trades. The same colours, the same manner, the same practised hand, belonging rather to a manufacturing automaton than to a man!

He stood before the dirty pictures for some time, his thoughts at length wandering to other matters. Meanwhile the proprietor of the shop, a little grey man, in a frieze cloak, with a beard which had not been shaved since Sunday, had been urging him to buy for some time, naming prices, without even knowing what pleased him or what he wanted. "Here, I'll take a silver piece for these peasants and this little landscape. What painting! it fairly dazzles one; only just received from the factory; the varnish isn't dry yet. Or here is a winter scene--take the winter scene; fifteen rubles; the frame alone is worth it. What a winter scene!" Here the merchant gave a slight fillip to the canvas, as if to demonstrate all the merits of the winter scene. "Pray have them put up and sent to your house. Where do you live? Here, boy, give me some string!"

"Hold, not so fast!" said the painter, coming to himself, and perceiving that the brisk dealer was beginning in earnest to pack some pictures up. He was rather ashamed not to take anything after standing so long in front of the shop; so saying, "Here, stop! I will see if there is anything I want here!" he stooped and began to pick up from the floor, where they were thrown in a heap, some worn, dusty old paintings. There were old family portraits, whose descendants, probably could not be found on earth; with torn canvas and frames minus their gilding; in short, trash. But the painter began his search, thinking to himself, "Perhaps I may come across something." He had heard stories about pictures of the great masters having been found among the rubbish in cheap print-sellers' shops.

The dealer, perceiving what he was about, ceased his importunities, and took up his post again at the door, hailing the passers-by with, "Hither, friends, here are pictures; step in, step in; just received from the makers!" He shouted his fill, and generally in vain, had a long talk with a rag-merchant, standing opposite, at the door of his shop; and finally, recollecting that he had a customer in his shop, turned his back on the public and went inside. "Well, friend, have you chosen anything?" said he. But the painter had already been standing motionless for some time before a portrait in a large and originally magnificent frame, upon which, however, hardly a trace of gilding now remained.

It represented an old man, with a thin, bronzed face and high cheek-bones; the features seemingly depicted in a moment of convulsive agitation. He wore a flowing Asiatic costume. Dusty and defaced as the portrait was, Tchartkoff saw, when he had succeeded in removing the dirt from the face, traces of the work of a great artist. The portrait appeared to be unfinished, but the power of the handling was striking. The eyes were the most remarkable picture of all: it seemed as though the full power of the artist's brush had been lavished upon them. They fairly gazed out of the portrait, destroying its harmony with their strange liveliness. When he carried the portrait to the door, the eyes gleamed even more penetratingly. They produced nearly the same impression on the public. A woman standing behind him exclaimed, "He is looking, he is looking!" and jumped back. Tchartkoff experienced an unpleasant feeling, inexplicable even to himself, and placed the portrait on the floor.

"Well, will you take the portrait?" said the dealer.

"How much is it?" said the painter.

"Why chaffer over it? give me seventy-five kopeks."

"No."

"Well, how much will you give?"

"Twenty kopeks," said the painter, preparing to go.

"What a price! Why, you couldn't buy the frame for that! Perhaps you will decide to purchase to-morrow. Sir, sir, turn back! Add ten kopeks. Take it, take it! give me twenty kopeks. To tell the truth, you are my only customer to-day, and that's the only reason."

Thus Tchartkoff quite unexpectedly became the purchaser of the old portrait, and at the same time reflected, "Why have I bought it? What is it to me?" But there was nothing to be done. He pulled a twenty-kopek piece from his pocket, gave it to the merchant, took the portrait under his arm, and carried it home. On the way thither, he remembered that the twenty-kopek piece he had given for it was his last. His thoughts at once became gloomy. Vexation and careless indifference took possession of him at one and the same moment. The red light of sunset still lingered in one half the sky; the houses facing that way still gleamed with its warm light; and meanwhile the cold blue light of the moon grew brighter. Light, half-transparent shadows fell in bands upon the ground. The painter began by degrees to glance up at the sky, flushed with a transparent light; and at the same moment from his mouth fell the words, "What a delicate tone! What a nuisance! Deuce take it!" Re-adjusting the portrait, which kept slipping from under his arm, he quickened his pace.

Weary and bathed in perspiration, he dragged himself to Vasilievsky Ostroff. With difficulty and much panting he made his way up the stairs flooded with soap-suds, and adorned with the tracks of dogs and cats. To his knock there was no answer: there was no one at home. He leaned against the window, and disposed himself to wait patiently, until at last there resounded behind him the footsteps of a boy in a blue blouse, his servant, model, and colour-grinder. This boy was called Nikita, and spent all his time in the streets when his master was not at home. Nikita tried for a long time to get the key into the lock, which was quite invisible, by reason of the darkness.

Finally the door was opened. Tchartkoff entered his ante-room, which was intolerably cold, as painters' rooms always are, which fact, however, they do not notice. Without giving Nikita his coat, he went on into his studio, a large room, but low, fitted up with all sorts of artistic rubbish--plaster hands, canvases, sketches begun and discarded, and draperies thrown over chairs. Feeling very tired, he took off his cloak, placed the portrait abstractedly between two small canvasses, and threw himself on the narrow divan. Having stretched himself out, he finally called for a light.

"There are no candles," said Nikita.

"What, none?"

"And there were none last night," said Nikita. The artist recollected that, in fact, there had been no candles the previous evening, and became silent. He let Nikita take his coat off, and put on his old worn dressing-gown.

"There has been a gentleman here," said Nikita.

"Yes, he came for money, I know," said the painter, waving his hand.

"He was not alone," said Nikita.

"Who else was with him?"

"I don't know, some police officer or other."

"But why a police officer?"

"I don't know why, but he says because your rent is not paid."

"Well, what will come of it?"

"I don't know what will come of it: he said, 'If he won't pay, why, let him leave the rooms.' They are both coming again to-morrow."

"Let them come," said Tchartkoff, with indifference; and a gloomy mood took full possession of him.

Young Tchartkoff was an artist of talent, which promised great things: his work gave evidence of observation, thought, and a strong inclination to approach nearer to nature.

"Look here, my friend," his professor said to him more than once, "you have talent; it will be a shame if you waste it: but you are impatient; you have but to be attracted by anything, to fall in love with it, you become engrossed with it, and all else goes for nothing, and you won't even look at it. See to it that you do not become a fashionable artist. At present your colouring begins to assert itself too loudly; and your drawing is at times quite weak; you are already striving after the fashionable style, because it strikes the eye at once. Have a care! society already begins to have its attraction for you: I have seen you with a shiny hat, a foppish neckerchief. . . .

It is seductive to paint fashionable little pictures and portraits for money; but talent is ruined, not developed, by that means. Be patient; think out every piece of work, discard your foppishness; let others amass money, your own will not fail you."

The professor was partly right. Our artist sometimes wanted to enjoy himself, to play the fop, in short, to give vent to his youthful impulses in some way or other; but he could control himself withal. At times he would forget everything, when he had once taken his brush in his hand, and could not tear himself from it except as from a delightful dream. His taste perceptibly developed. He did not as yet understand all the depths of Raphael, but he was attracted by Guido's broad and rapid handling, he paused before Titian's portraits, he delighted in the Flemish masters. The dark veil enshrouding the ancient pictures had not yet wholly passed away from before them; but he already saw something in them, though in private he did not agree with the professor that the secrets of the old masters are irremediably lost to us. It seemed to him that the nineteenth century had improved upon them considerably, that the delineation of nature was more clear, more vivid, more close. It sometimes vexed him when he saw how a strange artist, French or German, sometimes not even a painter by profession, but only a skilful dauber, produced, by the celerity of his brush and the vividness of his colouring, a universal commotion, and amassed in a twinkling a funded capital. This did not occur to him when fully occupied with his own work, for then he forgot food and drink and all the world. But when dire want arrived, when he had no money wherewith to buy brushes and colours, when his implacable landlord came ten times a day to demand the rent for his rooms, then did the luck of the wealthy artists recur to his hungry imagination; then did the thought which so often traverses Russian minds, to give up altogether, and go down hill, utterly to the bad, traverse his. And now he was almost in this frame of mind.

"Yes, it is all very well, to be patient, be patient!" he exclaimed, with vexation; "but there is an end to patience at last. Be patient! but what money have I to buy a dinner with to-morrow? No one will lend me any. If I did bring myself to sell all my pictures and sketches, they would not give me twenty kopeks for the whole of them. They are useful; I feel that not one of them has been undertaken in vain; I have learned something from each one. Yes, but of what use is it? Studies, sketches, all will be studies, trial-sketches to the end. And who will buy, not even knowing me by name? Who wants drawings from the antique, or the life class, or my unfinished love of a Psyche, or the interior of my room, or the portrait of Nikita, though it is better, to tell the truth, than the portraits by any of the fashionable artists? Why do I worry, and toil like a learner over the alphabet, when I might shine as brightly as the rest, and have money, too, like them?"

Thus speaking, the artist suddenly shuddered, and turned pale. A convulsively distorted face gazed at him, peeping forth from the surrounding canvas; two terrible eyes were fixed straight upon him; on the mouth was written a menacing command of silence. Alarmed, he tried to scream and summon Nikita, who already was snoring in the ante-room; but he suddenly paused and laughed. The sensation of fear died away in a moment; it was the portrait he had bought, and which he had quite forgotten. The light of the moon illuminating the chamber had fallen upon it, and lent it a strange likeness to life.

He began to examine it. He moistened a sponge with water, passed it over the picture several times, washed off nearly all the accumulated and incrusted dust and dirt, hung it on the wall before him, wondering yet more at the remarkable workmanship. The whole face had gained new life, and the eyes gazed at him so that he shuddered; and, springing back, he exclaimed in a voice of surprise: "It looks with human eyes!" Then suddenly there occurred to him a story he had heard long before from his professor, of a certain portrait by the renowned Leonardo da Vinci, upon which the great master laboured several years, and still regarded as incomplete, but which, according to Vasari, was nevertheless deemed by all the most complete and finished product of his art. The most finished thing about it was the eyes, which amazed his contemporaries; the very smallest, barely visible veins in them being reproduced on the canvas.

But in the portrait now before him there was something singular. It was no longer art; it even destroyed the harmony of the portrait; they were living, human eyes! It seemed as though they had been cut from a living man and inserted. Here was none of that high enjoyment which takes possession of the soul at the sight of an artist's production, no matter how terrible the subject he may have chosen.

Again he approached the portrait, in order to observe those wondrous eyes, and perceived, with terror, that they were gazing at him. This was no copy from Nature; it was life, the strange life which might have lighted up the face of a dead man, risen from the grave. Whether it was the effect of the moonlight, which brought with it fantastic thoughts, and transformed things into strange likenesses, opposed to those of matter-of-fact day, or from some other cause, but it suddenly became terrible to him, he knew not why, to sit alone in the room. He draw back from the portrait, turned aside, and tried not to look at it; but his eye involuntarily, of its own accord, kept glancing sideways towards it. Finally, he became afraid to walk about the room. It seemed as though some one were on the point of stepping up behind him; and every time he turned, he glanced timidly back. He had never been a coward; but his imagination and nerves were sensitive, and that evening he could not explain his involuntary fear. He seated himself in one corner, but even then it seemed to him that some one was peeping over his shoulder into his face. Even Nikita's snores, resounding from the ante-room, did not chase away his fear. At length he rose from the seat, without raising his eyes, went behind a screen, and lay down on his bed. Through the cracks of the screen he saw his room lit up by the moon, and the portrait hanging stiffly on the wall. The eyes were fixed upon him in a yet more terrible and significant manner, and it seemed as if they would not look at anything but himself. Overpowered with a feeling of oppression, he decided to rise from his bed, seized a sheet, and, approaching the portrait, covered it up completely.

 Having done this, he lay done more at ease on his bed, and began to meditate upon the poverty and pitiful lot of the artist, and the thorny path lying before him in the world. But meanwhile his eye glanced involuntarily through the joint of the screen at the portrait muffled in the sheet. The light of the moon heightened the whiteness of the sheet, and it seemed to him as though those terrible eyes shone through the cloth. With terror he fixed his eyes more steadfastly on the spot, as if wishing to convince himself that it was all nonsense. But at length he saw--saw clearly; there was no longer a sheet--the portrait was quite uncovered, and was gazing beyond everything around it, straight at him; gazing as it seemed fairly into his heart. His heart grew cold. He watched anxiously; the old man moved, and suddenly, supporting himself on the frame with both arms, raised himself by his hands, and, putting forth both feet, leapt out of the frame. Through the crack of the screen, the empty frame alone was now visible. Footsteps resounded through the room, and approached nearer and nearer to the screen. The poor artist's heart began beating fast. He expected every moment, his breath failing for fear, that the old man would look round the screen at him. And lo! he did look from behind the screen, with the very same bronzed face, and with his big eyes roving about.

 Tchartkoff tried to scream, and felt that his voice was gone; he tried to move; his limbs refused their office. With open mouth, and failing breath, he gazed at the tall phantom, draped in some kind of a flowing Asiatic robe, and waited for what it would do. The old man sat down almost on his very feet, and then pulled out something from among the folds of his wide garment. It was a purse. The old man untied it, took it by the end, and shook it. Heavy rolls of coin fell out with a dull thud upon the floor. Each was wrapped in blue paper, and on each was marked, "1000 ducats." The old man protruded his long, bony hand from his wide sleeves, and began to undo the rolls. The gold glittered. Great as was the artist's unreasoning fear, he concentrated all his attention upon the gold, gazing motionless, as it made its appearance in the bony hands, gleamed, rang lightly or dully, and was wrapped up again. Then he perceived one packet which had rolled farther than the rest, to the very leg of his bedstead, near his pillow. He grasped it almost convulsively, and glanced in fear at the old man to see whether he noticed it.

 But the old man appeared very much occupied: he collected all his rolls, replaced them in the purse, and went outside the screen without looking at him. Tchartkoff's heart beat wildly as he heard the rustle of the retreating footsteps sounding through the room. He clasped the roll of coin more closely in his hand, quivering in every limb. Suddenly he heard the footsteps approaching the screen again. Apparently the old man had recollected that one roll was missing. Lo! again he looked round the screen at him. The artist in despair grasped the roll with all his strength, tried with all his power to make a movement, shrieked--and awoke.

 He was bathed in a cold perspiration; his heart beat as hard as it was possible for it to beat; his chest was oppressed, as though his last breath was about to issue from it. "Was it a dream?" he said, seizing his head with both hands. But the terrible reality of the apparition did not resemble a dream. As he woke, he saw the old man step into the frame: the skirts of the flowing garment even fluttered, and his hand felt plainly that a moment before it had held something heavy. The moonlight lit up the room, bringing out from the dark corners here a canvas, there the model of a hand: a drapery thrown over a chair; trousers and dirty boots. Then he perceived that he was not lying in his bed, but standing upright in front of the portrait. How he had come there, he could not in the least comprehend. Still more surprised was he to find the portrait uncovered, and with actually no sheet over it. Motionless with terror, he gazed at it, and perceived that the living, human eyes were fastened upon him. A cold perspiration broke out upon his forehead. He wanted to move away, but felt that his feet had in some way become rooted to the earth. And he felt that this was not a dream. The old man's features moved, and his lips began to project towards him, as though he wanted to suck him in. With a yell of despair he jumped back-- and awoke.

"Was it a dream?" With his heart throbbing to bursting, he felt about him with both hands. Yes, he was lying in bed, and in precisely the position in which he had fallen asleep. Before him stood the screen. The moonlight flooded the room. Through the crack of the screen, the portrait was visible, covered with the sheet, as it should be, just as he had covered it. And so that, too, was a dream? But his clenched fist still felt as though something had been held in it. The throbbing of his heart was violent, almost terrible; the weight upon his breast intolerable. He fixed his eyes upon the crack, and stared steadfastly at the sheet. And lo! he saw plainly the sheet begin to open, as though hands were pushing from underneath, and trying to throw it off. "Lord God, what is it!" he shrieked, crossing himself in despair--and awoke.

And was this, too, a dream? He sprang from his bed, half-mad, and could not comprehend what had happened to him. Was it the oppression of a nightmare, the raving of fever, or an actual apparition? Striving to calm, as far as possible, his mental tumult, and stay the wildly rushing blood, which beat with straining pulses in every vein, he went to the window and opened it. The cool breeze revived him. The moonlight lay on the roofs and the white walls of the houses, though small clouds passed frequently across the sky. All was still: from time to time there struck the ear the distant rumble of a carriage. He put his head out of the window, and gazed for some time. Already the signs of approaching dawn were spreading over the sky. At last he felt drowsy, shut to the window, stepped back, lay down in bed, and quickly fell, like one exhausted, into a deep sleep.

He awoke late, and with the disagreeable feeling of a man who has been half-suffocated with coal-gas: his head ached painfully. The room was dim: an unpleasant moisture pervaded the air, and penetrated the cracks of his windows. Dissatisfied and depressed as a wet cock, he seated himself on his dilapidated divan, not knowing what to do, what to set about, and at length remembered the whole of his dream. As he recalled it, the dream presented itself to his mind as so oppressively real that he even began to wonder whether it were a dream, whether there were not something more here, whether it were not really an apparition. Removing the sheet, he looked at the terrible portrait by the light of day. The eyes were really striking in their liveliness, but he found nothing particularly terrible about them, though an indescribably unpleasant feeling lingered in his mind. Nevertheless, he could not quite convince himself that it was a dream. It struck him that there must have been some terrible fragment of reality in the vision. It seemed as though there were something in the old man's very glance and expression which said that he had been with him that night: his hand still felt the weight which had so recently lain in it as if some one had but just snatched it from him. It seemed to him that, if he had only grasped the roll more firmly, it would have remained in his hand, even after his awakening.

"My God, if I only had a portion of that money!" he said, breathing heavily; and in his fancy, all the rolls of coin, with their fascinating inscription, "1000 ducats," began to pour out of the purse. The rolls opened, the gold glittered, and was wrapped up again; and he sat motionless, with his eyes fixed on the empty air, as if he were incapable of tearing himself from such a sight, like a child who sits before a plate of sweets, and beholds, with watering mouth, other people devouring them.

At last there came a knock on the door, which recalled him unpleasantly to himself. The landlord entered with the constable of the district, whose presence is even more disagreeable to poor people than is the presence of a beggar to the rich. The landlord of the little house in which Tchartkoff lived resembled the other individuals who own houses anywhere in the Vasilievsky Ostroff, on the St. Petersburg side, or in the distant regions of Kolomna--individuals whose character is as difficult to define as the colour of a threadbare surtout. In his youth he had been a captain and a braggart, a master in the art of flogging, skilful, foppish, and stupid; but in his old age he combined all these various qualities into a kind of dim indefiniteness. He was a widower, already on the retired list, no longer boasted, nor was dandified, nor quarrelled, but only cared to drink tea and talk all sorts of nonsense over it. He walked about his room, and arranged the ends of the tallow candles; called punctually at the end of each month upon his lodgers for money; went out into the street, with the key in his hand, to look at the roof of his house, and sometimes chased the porter out of his den, where he had hidden himself to sleep. In short, he was a man on the retired list, who, after the turmoils and wildness of his life, had only his old-fashioned habits left.

"Please to see for yourself, Varukh Kusmitch," said the landlord, turning to the officer, and throwing out his hands, "this man does not pay his rent, he does not pay."

"How can I when I have no money? Wait, and I will pay."

"I can't wait, my good fellow," said the landlord angrily, making a gesture with the key which he held in his hand. "Lieutenant-Colonel Potogonkin has lived with me seven years, seven years already; Anna Petrovna Buchmisteroff rents the coach-house and stable, with the exception of two stalls, and has three household servants: that is the kind of lodgers I have. I say to you frankly, that this is not an establishment where people do not pay their rent. Pay your money at once, please, or else clear out."

"Yes, if you rented the rooms, please to pay," said the constable, with a slight shake of the head, as he laid his finger on one of the buttons of his uniform.

"Well, what am I to pay with? that's the question. I haven't a groschen just at present."

"In that case, satisfy the claims of Ivan Ivanovitch with the fruits of your profession," said the officer: "perhaps he will consent to take pictures."

"No, thank you, my good fellow, no pictures. Pictures of holy subjects, such as one could hang upon the walls, would be well enough; or some general with a star, or Prince Kutusoff's portrait. But this fellow has painted that muzhik, that muzhik in his blouse, his servant who grinds his colours! The idea of painting his portrait, the hog! I'll thrash him well: he took all the nails out of my bolts, the scoundrel! Just see what subjects! Here he has drawn his room. It would have been well enough had he taken a clean, well-furnished room; but he has gone and drawn this one, with all the dirt and rubbish he has collected. Just see how he has defaced my room! Look for yourself. Yes, and my lodgers have been with me seven years, the lieutenant-colonel, Anna Petrovna Buchmisteroff. No, I tell you, there is no worse lodger than a painter: he lives like a pig--God have mercy!"

The poor artist had to listen patiently to all this. Meanwhile the officer had occupied himself with examining the pictures and studies, and showed that his mind was more advanced than the landlord's, and that he was not insensible to artistic impressions.

"Heh!" said he, tapping one canvas, on which was depicted a naked woman, "this subject is--lively. But why so much black under her nose? did she take snuff?"

"Shadow," answered Tchartkoff gruffly, without looking at him.

"But it might have been put in some other place: it is too conspicuous under the nose," observed the officer. "And whose likeness is this?" he continued, approaching the old man's portrait. "It is too terrible. Was he really so dreadful? Ah! why, he actually looks at one! What a thunder-cloud! From whom did you paint it?"

"Ah! it is from a--" said Tchartkoff, but did not finish his sentence: he heard a crack. It seems that the officer had pressed too hard on the frame of the portrait, thanks to the weight of his constable's hands. The small boards at the side caved in, one fell on the floor, and with it fell, with a heavy crash, a roll of blue paper. The inscription caught Tchartkoff's eye--"1000 ducats." Like a madman, he sprang to pick it up, grasped the roll, and gripped it convulsively in his hand, which sank with the weight.

"Wasn't there a sound of money?" inquired the officer, hearing the noise of something falling on the floor, and not catching sight of it, owing to the rapidity with which Tchartkoff had hastened to pick it up.

"What business is it of yours what is in my room?"

"It's my business because you ought to pay your rent to the landlord at once; because you have money, and won't pay, that's why it's my business."

"Well, I will pay him to-day."

"Well, and why wouldn't you pay before, instead of giving trouble to your landlord, and bothering the police to boot?"

"Because I did not want to touch this money. I will pay him in full this evening, and leave the rooms to-morrow. I will not stay with such a landlord."

"Well, Ivan Ivanovitch, he will pay you," said the constable, turning to the landlord. "But in case you are not satisfied in every respect this evening, then you must excuse me, Mr. Painter." So saying, he put on his three-cornered hat, and went into the ante-room, followed by the landlord hanging his head, and apparently engaged in meditation.

"Thank God, Satan has carried them off!" said Tchartkoff, as he heard the outer door of the ante-room close. He looked out into the ante-room, sent Nikita off on some errand, in order to be quite alone, fastened the door behind him, and, returning to his room, began with wildly beating heart to undo the roll.

In it were ducats, all new, and bright as fire. Almost beside himself, he sat down beside the pile of gold, still asking himself, "Is not this all a dream?" There were just a thousand in the roll, the exterior of which was precisely like what he had seen in his dream. He turned them over, and looked at them for some minutes. His imagination recalled up all the tales he had heard of hidden hoards, cabinets with secret drawers, left by ancestors for their spendthrift descendants, with firm belief in the extravagance of their life. He pondered this: "Did not some grandfather, in the present instance, leave a gift for his grandchild, shut up in the frame of a family portrait?" Filled with romantic fancies, he began to think whether this had not some secret connection with his fate? whether the existence of the portrait was not bound up with his own, and whether his acquisition of it was not due to a kind of predestination?

He began to examine the frame with curiosity. On one side a cavity was hollowed out, but concealed so skilfully and neatly by a little board, that, if the massive hand of the constable had not effected a breach, the ducats might have remained hidden to the end of time. On examining the portrait, he marvelled again at the exquisite workmanship, the extraordinary treatment of the eyes. They no longer appeared terrible to him; but, nevertheless, each time he looked at them a disagreeable feeling involuntarily lingered in his mind.

"No," he said to himself, "no matter whose grandfather you were, I'll put a glass over you, and get you a gilt frame." Then he laid his hand on the golden pile before him, and his heart beat faster at the touch. "What shall I do with them?" he said, fixing his eyes on them. "Now I am independent for at least three years: I can shut myself up in my room and work. I have money for colours now; for food and lodging--no one will annoy and disturb me now. I will buy myself a first-class lay figure, I will order a plaster torso, and some model feet, I will have a Venus. I will buy engravings of the best pictures. And if I work three years to satisfy myself, without haste or with the idea of selling, I shall surpass all, and may become a distinguished artist."

Thus he spoke in solitude, with his good judgment prompting him; but louder and more distinct sounded another voice within him. As he glanced once more at the gold, it was not thus that his twenty-two years and fiery youth reasoned. Now everything was within his power on which he had hitherto gazed with envious eyes, had viewed from afar with longing. How his heart beat when he thought of it! To wear a fashionable coat, to feast after long abstinence, to hire handsome apartments, to go at once to the theatre, to the confectioner's, to . . . other places; and seizing his money, he was in the street in a moment.

First of all he went to the tailor, was clothed anew from head to foot, and began to look at himself like a child. He purchased perfumes and pomades; hired the first elegant suite of apartments with mirrors and plateglass windows which he came across in the Nevsky Prospect, without haggling about the price; bought, on the impulse of the moment, a costly eye-glass; bought, also on the impulse, a number of neckties of every description, many more than he needed; had his hair curled at the hairdresser's; rode through the city twice without any object whatever; ate an immense quantity of sweetmeats at the confectioner's; and went to the French Restaurant, of which he had heard rumours as indistinct as though they had concerned the Empire of China. There he dined, casting proud glances at the other visitors, and continually arranging his curls in the glass. There he drank a bottle of champagne, which had been known to him hitherto only by hearsay. The wine rather affected his head; and he emerged into the street, lively, pugnacious, and ready to raise the Devil, according to the Russian expression. He strutted along the pavement, levelling his eye-glass at everybody. On the bridge he caught sight of his former professor, and slipped past him neatly, as if he did not see him, so that the astounded professor stood stock-still on the bridge for a long time, with a face suggestive of a note of interrogation.

All his goods and chattels, everything he owned, easels, canvas, pictures, were transported that same evening to his elegant quarters. He arranged the best of them in conspicuous places, threw the worst into a corner, and promenaded up and down the handsome rooms, glancing constantly in the mirrors. An unconquerable desire to take the bull by the horns, and show himself to the world at once, had arisen in his mind. He already heard the shouts, "Tchartkoff! Tchartkoff! Tchartkoff paints! What talent Tchartkoff has!" He paced the room in a state of rapture.

The next day he took ten ducats, and went to the editor of a popular journal asking his charitable assistance. He was joyfully received by the journalist, who called him on the spot, "Most respected sir," squeezed both his hands, and made minute inquiries as to his name, birthplace, residence. The next day there appeared in the journal, below a notice of some newly invented tallow candles, an article with the following heading:--

"TCHARTKOFF'S IMMENSE TALENT

"We hasten to delight the cultivated inhabitants of the capital with a discovery which we may call splendid in every respect. All are agreed that there are among us many very handsome faces, but hitherto there has been no means of committing them to canvas for transmission to posterity. This want has now been supplied: an artist has been found who unites in himself all desirable qualities. The beauty can now feel assured that she will be depicted with all the grace of her charms, airy, fascinating, butterfly-like, flitting among the flowers of spring. The stately father of a family can see himself surrounded by his family. Merchant, warrior, citizen, statesman-- hasten one and all, wherever you may be. The artist's magnificent establishment [Nevsky Prospect, such and such a number] is hung with portraits from his brush, worthy of Van Dyck or Titian. We do not know which to admire most, their truth and likeness to the originals, or the wonderful brilliancy and freshness of the colouring. Hail to you, artist! you have drawn a lucky number in the lottery. Long live Andrei Petrovitch!" (The journalist evidently liked familiarity.) "Glorify yourself and us. We know how to prize you. Universal popularity, and with it wealth, will be your meed, though some of our brother journalists may rise against you."

The artist read this article with secret satisfaction; his face beamed. He was mentioned in print; it was a novelty to him: he read the lines over several times. The comparison with Van Dyck and Titian flattered him extremely. The praise, "Long live Andrei Petrovitch," also pleased him greatly: to be spoken of by his Christian name and patronymic in print was an honour hitherto totally unknown to him. He began to pace the chamber briskly, now he sat down in an armchair, now he sprang up, and seated himself on the sofa, planning each moment how he would receive visitors, male and female; he went to his canvas and made a rapid sweep of the brush, endeavouring to impart a graceful movement to his hand.

The next day, the bell at his door rang. He hastened to open it. A lady entered, accompanied by a girl of eighteen, her daughter, and followed by a lackey in a furred livery-coat.

"You are the painter Tchartkoff?"

The artist bowed.

"A great deal is written about you: your portraits, it is said, are the height of perfection." So saying, the lady raised her glass to her eyes and glanced rapidly over the walls, upon which nothing was hanging. "But where are your portraits?"

"They have been taken away" replied the artist, somewhat confusedly: "I have but just moved into these apartments; so they are still on the road, they have not arrived."

"You have been in Italy?" asked the lady, levelling her glass at him, as she found nothing else to point it at.

"No, I have not been there; but I wish to go, and I have deferred it for a while. Here is an arm-chair, madame: you are fatigued?"

"Thank you: I have been sitting a long time in the carriage. Ah, at last I behold your work!" said the lady, running to the opposite wall, and bringing her glass to bear upon his studies, sketches, views and portraits which were standing there on the floor. "It is charming. Lise! Lise, come here. Rooms in the style of Teniers. Do you see? Disorder, disorder, a table with a bust upon it, a hand, a palette; dust, see how the dust is painted! It is charming. And here on this canvas is a woman washing her face. What a pretty face! Ah! a little muzhik! So you do not devote yourself exclusively to portraits?"

"Oh! that is mere rubbish. I was trying experiments, studies."

"Tell me your opinion of the portrait painters of the present day. Is it not true that there are none now like Titian? There is not that strength of colour, that--that-- What a pity that I cannot express myself in Russian." The lady was fond of paintings, and had gone through all the galleries in Italy with her eye-glass. "But Monsieur Nohl--ah, how well he paints! what remarkable work! I think his faces have been more expression than Titian's. You do not know Monsieur Nohl?"

"Who is Nohl?" inquired the artist.

"Monsieur Nohl. Ah, what talent! He painted her portrait when she was only twelve years old. You must certainly come to see us. Lise, you shall show him your album. You know, we came expressly that you might begin her portrait immediately."

"What? I am ready this very moment." And in a trice he pulled forward an easel with a canvas already prepared, grasped his palette, and fixed his eyes on the daughter's pretty little face. If he had been acquainted with human nature, he might have read in it the dawning of a childish passion for balls, the dawning of sorrow and misery at the length of time before dinner and after dinner, the heavy traces of uninterested application to various arts, insisted upon by her mother for the elevation of her mind. But the artist saw only the tender little face, a seductive subject for his brush, the body almost as transparent as porcelain, the delicate white neck, and the aristocratically slender form. And he prepared beforehand to triumph, to display the delicacy of his brush, which had hitherto had to deal only with the harsh features of coarse models, and severe antiques and copies of classic masters. He already saw in fancy how this delicate little face would turn out.

"Do you know," said the lady with a positively touching expression of countenance, "I should like her to be painted simply attired, and seated among green shadows, like meadows, with a flock or a grove in the distance, so that it could not be seen that she goes to balls or fashionable entertainments. Our balls, I must confess, murder the intellect, deaden all remnants of feeling. Simplicity! would there were more simplicity!" Alas, it was stamped on the faces of mother and daughter that they had so overdanced themselves at balls that they had become almost wax figures.

Tchartkoff set to work, posed his model, reflected a bit, fixed upon the idea, waved his brush in the air, settling the points mentally, and then began and finished the sketching in within an hour. Satisfied with it, he began to paint. The task fascinated him; he forgot everything, forgot the very existence of the aristocratic ladies, began even to display some artistic tricks, uttering various odd sounds and humming to himself now and then as artists do when immersed heart and soul in their work. Without the slightest ceremony, he made the sitter lift her head, which finally began to express utter weariness.

"Enough for the first time," said the lady.

"A little more," said the artist, forgetting himself.

"No, it is time to stop. Lise, three o'clock!" said the lady, taking out a tiny watch which hung by a gold chain from her girdle. "How late it is!"

"Only a minute," said Tchartkoff innocently, with the pleading voice of a child.

But the lady appeared to be not at all inclined to yield to his artistic demands on this occasion; she promised, however, to sit longer the next time.

"It is vexatious, all the same," thought Tchartkoff to himself: "I had just got my hand in;" and he remembered no one had interrupted him or stopped him when he was at work in his studio on Vasilievsky Ostroff. Nikita sat motionless in one place. You might even paint him as long as you pleased; he even went to sleep in the attitude prescribed him. Feeling dissatisfied, he laid his brush and palette on a chair, and paused in irritation before the picture.

The woman of the world's compliments awoke him from his reverie. He flew to the door to show them out: on the stairs he received an invitation to dine with them the following week, and returned with a cheerful face to his apartments. The aristocratic lady had completely charmed him. Up to that time he had looked upon such beings as unapproachable, born solely to ride in magnificent carriages, with liveried footmen and stylish coachmen, and to cast indifferent glances on the poor man travelling on foot in a cheap cloak. And now, all of a sudden, one of these very beings had entered his room; he was painting her portrait, was invited to dinner at an aristocratic house. An unusual feeling of pleasure took possession of him: he was completely intoxicated, and rewarded himself with a splendid dinner, an evening at the theatre, and a drive through the city in a carriage, without any necessity whatever.

But meanwhile his ordinary work did not fall in with his mood at all. He did nothing but wait for the moment when the bell should ring. At last the aristocratic lady arrived with her pale daughter. He seated them, drew forward the canvas with skill, and some efforts of fashionable airs, and began to paint. The sunny day and bright light aided him not a little: he saw in his dainty sitter much which, caught and committed to canvas, would give great value to the portrait. He perceived that he might accomplish something good if he could reproduce, with accuracy, all that nature then offered to his eyes. His heart began to beat faster as he felt that he was expressing something which others had not even seen as yet. His work engrossed him completely: he was wholly taken up with it, and again forgot the aristocratic origin of the sitter. With heaving breast he saw the delicate features and the almost transparent body of the fair maiden grow beneath his hand. He had caught every shade, the slight sallowness, the almost imperceptible blue tinge under the eyes--and was already preparing to put in the tiny mole on the brow, when he suddenly heard the mother's voice behind him.

"Ah! why do you paint that? it is not necessary: and you have made it here, in several places, rather yellow; and here, quite so, like dark spots."

The artist undertook to explain that the spots and yellow tinge would turn out well, that they brought out the delicate and pleasing tones of the face. He was informed that they did not bring out tones, and would not turn out well at all. It was explained to him that just to-day Lise did not feel quite well; that she never was sallow, and that her face was distinguished for its fresh colouring.

Sadly he began to erase what his brush had put upon the canvas. Many a nearly imperceptible feature disappeared, and with it vanished too a portion of the resemblance. He began indifferently to impart to the picture that commonplace colouring which can be painted mechanically, and which lends to a face, even when taken from nature, the sort of cold ideality observable on school programmes. But the lady was satisfied when the objectionable tone was quite banished. She merely expressed surprise that the work lasted so long, and added that she had heard that he finished a portrait completely in two sittings. The artist could not think of any answer to this. The ladies rose, and prepared to depart. He laid aside his brush, escorted them to the door, and then stood disconsolate for a long while in one spot before the portrait.

He gazed stupidly at it; and meanwhile there floated before his mind's eye those delicate features, those shades, and airy tints which he had copied, and which his brush had annihilated. Engrossed with them, he put the portrait on one side and hunted up a head of Psyche which he had some time before thrown on canvas in a sketchy manner. It was a pretty little face, well painted, but entirely ideal, and having cold, regular features not lit up by life. For lack of occupation, he now began to tone it up, imparting to it all he had taken note of in his aristocratic sitter. Those features, shadows, tints, which he had noted, made their appearance here in the purified form in which they appear when the painter, after closely observing nature, subordinates himself to her, and produces a creation equal to her own.

Psyche began to live: and the scarcely dawning thought began, little by little, to clothe itself in a visible form. The type of face of the fashionable young lady was unconsciously transferred to Psyche, yet nevertheless she had an expression of her own which gave the picture claims to be considered in truth an original creation. Tchartkoff gave himself up entirely to his work. For several days he was engrossed by it alone, and the ladies surprised him at it on their arrival. He had not time to remove the picture from the easel. Both ladies uttered a cry of amazement, and clasped their hands.

"Lise, Lise! Ah, how like! Superb, superb! What a happy thought, too, to drape her in a Greek costume! Ah, what a surprise!"

The artist could not see his way to disabuse the ladies of their error. Shamefacedly, with drooping head, he murmured, "This is Psyche."

"In the character of Psyche? Charming!" said the mother, smiling, upon which the daughter smiled too. "Confess, Lise, it pleases you to be painted in the character of Psyche better than any other way? What a sweet idea! But what treatment! It is Correggio himself. I must say that, although I had read and heard about you, I did not know you had so much talent. You positively must paint me too." Evidently the lady wanted to be portrayed as some kind of Psyche too.

"What am I to do with them?" thought the artist. "If they will have it so, why, let Psyche pass for what they choose;" and added aloud, "Pray sit a little: I will touch it up here and there."

"Ah! I am afraid you will . . . it is such a capital likeness now!"

But the artist understood that the difficulty was with respect to the sallowness, and so he reassured them by saying that he only wished to give more brilliancy and expression to the eyes. In truth, he was ashamed, and wanted to impart a little more likeness to the original, lest any one should accuse him of actual barefaced flattery. And the features of the pale young girl at length appeared more closely in Psyche's countenance.

"Enough," said the mother, beginning to fear that the likeness might become too decided. The artist was remunerated in every way, with smiles, money, compliments, cordial pressures of the hand, invitations to dinner: in short, he received a thousand flattering rewards.

The portrait created a furore in the city. The lady exhibited it to her friends, and all admired the skill with which the artist had preserved the likeness, and at the same time conferred more beauty on the original. The last remark, of course, was prompted by a slight tinge of envy. The artist was suddenly overwhelmed with work. It seemed as if the whole city wanted to be painted by him. The door-bell rang incessantly. From one point of view, this might be considered advantageous, as presenting to him endless practice in variety and number of faces. But, unfortunately, they were all people who were hard to get along with, either busy, hurried people, or else belonging to the fashionable world, and consequently more occupied than any one else, and therefore impatient to the last degree. In all quarters, the demand was merely that the likeness should be good and quickly executed. The artist perceived that it was a simple impossibility to finish his work; that it was necessary to exchange power of treatment for lightness and rapidity, to catch only the general expression, and not waste labour on delicate details.

Moreover, nearly all of his sitters made stipulations on various points. The ladies required that mind and character should be represented in their portraits; that all angles should be rounded, all unevenness smoothed away, and even removed entirely if possible; in short, that their faces should be such as to cause every one to stare at them with admiration, if not fall in love with them outright. When they sat to him, they sometimes assumed expressions which greatly amazed the artist; one tried to express melancholy; another, meditation; a third wanted to make her mouth appear small on any terms, and puckered it up to such an extent that it finally looked like a spot about as big as a pinhead. And in spite of all this, they demanded of him good likenesses and unconstrained naturalness. The men were no better: one insisted on being painted with an energetic, muscular turn to his head; another, with upturned, inspired eyes; a lieutenant of the guard demanded that Mars should be visible in his eyes; an official in the civil service drew himself up to his full height in order to have his uprightness expressed in his face, and that his hand might rest on a book bearing the words in plain characters, "He always stood up for the right."

At first such demands threw the artist into a cold perspiration. Finally he acquired the knack of it, and never troubled himself at all about it. He understood at a word how each wanted himself portrayed. If a man wanted Mars in his face, he put in Mars: he gave a Byronic turn and attitude to those who aimed at Byron. If the ladies wanted to be Corinne, Undine, or Aspasia, he agreed with great readiness, and threw in a sufficient measure of good looks from his own imagination, which does no harm, and for the sake of which an artist is even forgiven a lack of resemblance. He soon began to wonder himself at the rapidity and dash of his brush. And of course those who sat to him were in ecstasies, and proclaimed him a genius.

Tchartkoff became a fashionable artist in every sense of the word. He began to dine out, to escort ladies to picture galleries, to dress foppishly, and to assert audibly that an artist should belong to society, that he must uphold his profession, that artists mostly dress like showmakers, do not know how to behave themselves, do not maintain the highest tone, and are lacking in all polish. At home, in his studio, he carried cleanliness and spotlessness to the last extreme, set up two superb footmen, took fashionable pupils, dressed several times a day, curled his hair, practised various manners of receiving his callers, and busied himself in adorning his person in every conceivable way, in order to produce a pleasing impression on the ladies. In short, it would soon have been impossible for any one to have recognised in him the modest artist who had formerly toiled unknown in his miserable quarters in the Vasilievsky Ostroff.

He now expressed himself decidedly concerning artists and art; declared that too much credit had been given to the old masters; that even Raphael did not always paint well, and that fame attached to many of his works simply by force of tradition: that Michael Angelo was a braggart because he could boast only a knowledge of anatomy; that there was no grace about him, and that real brilliancy and power of treatment and colouring were to be looked for in the present century. And there, naturally, the question touched him personally. "I do not understand," said he, "how others toil and work with difficulty: a man who labours for months over a picture is a dauber, and no artist in my opinion; I don't believe he has any talent: genius works boldly, rapidly. Here is this portrait which I painted in two days, this head in one day, this in a few hours, this in little more than an hour. No, I confess I do not recognise as art that which adds line to line; that is a handicraft, not art." In this manner did he lecture his visitors; and the visitors admired the strength and boldness of his works, uttered exclamations on hearing how fast they had been produced, and said to each other, "This is talent, real talent! see how he speaks, how his eyes gleam! There is something really extraordinary in his face!"

It flattered the artist to hear such reports about himself. When printed praise appeared in the papers, he rejoiced like a child, although this praise was purchased with his money. He carried the printed slips about with him everywhere, and showed them to friends and acquaintances as if by accident. His fame increased, his works and orders multiplied. Already the same portraits over and over again wearied him, by the same attitudes and turns, which he had learned by heart. He painted them now without any great interest in his work, brushing in some sort of a head, and giving them to his pupil's to finish. At first he had sought to devise a new attitude each time. Now this had grown wearisome to him. His brain was tired with planning and thinking. It was out of his power; his fashionable life bore him far away from labour and thought. His work grew cold and colourless; and he betook himself with indifference to the reproduction of monotonous, well-worn forms. The eternally spick-and-span uniforms, and the so-to-speak buttoned-up faces of the government officials, soldiers, and statesmen, did not offer a wide field for his brush: it forgot how to render superb draperies and powerful emotion and passion. Of grouping, dramatic effect and its lofty connections, there was nothing. In face of him was only a uniform, a corsage, a dress-coat, and before which the artist feels cold and all imagination vanishes. Even his own peculiar merits were no longer visible in his works, yet they continued to enjoy renown; although genuine connoisseurs and artists merely shrugged their shoulders when they saw his latest productions. But some who had known Tchartkoff in his earlier days could not understand how the talent of which he had given such clear indications in the outset could so have vanished; and strove in vain to divine by what means genius could be extinguished in a man just when he had attained to the full development of his powers.

 But the intoxicated artist did not hear these criticisms. He began to attain to the age of dignity, both in mind and years: to grow stout, and increase visibly in flesh. He often read in the papers such phrases as, "Our most respected Andrei Petrovitch; our worthy Andrei Petrovitch." He began to receive offers of distinguished posts in the service, invitations to examinations and committees. He began, as is usually the case in maturer years, to advocate Raphael and the old masters, not because he had become thoroughly convinced of their transcendent merits, but in order to snub the younger artists. His life was already approaching the period when everything which suggests impulse contracts within a man; when a powerful chord appeals more feebly to the spirit; when the touch of beauty no longer converts virgin strength into fire and flame, but when all the burnt-out sentiments become more vulnerable to the sound of gold, hearken more attentively to its seductive music, and little by little permit themselves to be completely lulled to sleep by it. Fame can give no pleasure to him who has stolen it, not won it; so all his feelings and impulses turned towards wealth. Gold was his passion, his ideal, his fear, his delight, his aim. The bundles of bank-notes increased in his coffers; and, like all to whose lot falls this fearful gift, he began to grow inaccessible to every sentiment except the love of gold. But something occurred which gave him a powerful shock, and disturbed the whole tenor of his life.

One day he found upon his table a note, in which the Academy of Painting begged him, as a worthy member of its body, to come and give his opinion upon a new work which had been sent from Italy by a Russian artist who was perfecting himself there. The painter was one of his former comrades, who had been possessed with a passion for art from his earliest years, had given himself up to it with his whole soul, estranged himself from his friends and relatives, and had hastened to that wonderful Rome, at whose very name the artist's heart beats wildly and hotly. There he buried himself in his work from which he permitted nothing to entice him. He visited the galleries unweariedly, he stood for hours at a time before the works of the great masters, seizing and studying their marvellous methods. He never finished anything without revising his impressions several times before these great teachers, and reading in their works silent but eloquent counsels. He gave each impartially his due, appropriating from all only that which was most beautiful, and finally became the pupil of the divine Raphael alone, as a great poet, after reading many works, at last made Homer's "Iliad" his only breviary, having discovered that it contains all one wants, and that there is nothing which is not expressed in it in perfection. And so he brought away from his school the grand conception of creation, the mighty beauty of thought, the high charm of that heavenly brush.

When Tchartkoff entered the room, he found a crowd of visitors already collected before the picture. The most profound silence, such as rarely settles upon a throng of critics, reigned over all. He hastened to assume the significant expression of a connoisseur, and approached the picture; but, O God! what did he behold!

Pure, faultless, beautiful as a bride, stood the picture before him. The critics regarded this new hitherto unknown work with a feeling of involuntary wonder. All seemed united in it: the art of Raphael, reflected in the lofty grace of the grouping; the art of Correggio, breathing from the finished perfection of the workmanship. But more striking than all else was the evident creative power in the artist's mind. The very minutest object in the picture revealed it; he had caught that melting roundness of outline which is visible in nature only to the artist creator, and which comes out as angles with a copyist. It was plainly visible how the artist, having imbibed it all from the external world, had first stored it in his mind, and then drawn it thence, as from a spiritual source, into one harmonious, triumphant song. And it was evident, even to the uninitiated, how vast a gulf there was fixed between creation and a mere copy from nature. Involuntary tears stood ready to fall in the eyes of those who surrounded the picture. It seemed as though all joined in a silent hymn to the divine work.

Motionless, with open mouth, Tchartkoff stood before the picture. At length, when by degrees the visitors and critics began to murmur and comment upon the merits of the work, and turning to him, begged him to express an opinion, he came to himself once more. He tried to assume an indifferent, everyday expression; strove to utter some such commonplace remark as; "Yes, to tell the truth, it is impossible to deny the artist's talent; there is something in it;" but the speech died upon his lips, tears and sobs burst forth uncontrollably, and he rushed from the room like one beside himself.

In a moment he stood in his magnificent studio. All his being, all his life, had been aroused in one instant, as if youth had returned to him, as if the dying sparks of his talent had blazed forth afresh. The bandage suddenly fell from his eyes. Heavens! to think of having mercilessly wasted the best years of his youth, of having extinguished, trodden out perhaps, that spark of fire which, cherished in his breast, might perhaps have been developed into magnificence and beauty, and have extorted too, its meed of tears and admiration! It seemed as though those impulses which he had known in other days re-awoke suddenly in his soul.

He seized a brush and approached his canvas. One thought possessed him wholly, one desire consumed him; he strove to depict a fallen angel. This idea was most in harmony with his frame of mind. The perspiration started out upon his face with his efforts; but, alas! his figures, attitudes, groups, thoughts, arranged themselves stiffly, disconnectedly. His hand and his imagination had been too long confined to one groove; and the fruitless effort to escape from the bonds and fetters which he had imposed upon himself, showed itself in irregularities and errors. He had despised the long, wearisome ladder to knowledge, and the first fundamental law of the future great man, hard work. He gave vent to his vexation. He ordered all his later productions to be taken out of his studio, all the fashionable, lifeless pictures, all the portraits of hussars, ladies, and councillors of state.

He shut himself up alone in his room, would order no food, and devoted himself entirely to his work. He sat toiling like a scholar. But how pitifully wretched was all which proceeded from his hand! He was stopped at every step by his ignorance of the very first principles: simple ignorance of the mechanical part of his art chilled all inspiration and formed an impassable barrier to his imagination. His brush returned involuntarily to hackneyed forms: hands folded themselves in a set attitude; heads dared not make any unusual turn; the very garments turned out commonplace, and would not drape themselves to any unaccustomed posture of the body. And he felt and saw this all himself.

"But had I really any talent?" he said at length: "did not I deceive myself?" Uttering these words, he turned to the early works which he had painted so purely, so unselfishly, in former days, in his wretched cabin yonder in lonely Vasilievsky Ostroff. He began attentively to examine them all; and all the misery of his former life came back to him. "Yes," he cried despairingly, "I had talent: the signs and traces of it are everywhere visible--"

He paused suddenly, and shivered all over. His eyes encountered other eyes fixed immovably upon him. It was that remarkable portrait which he had bought in the Shtchukinui Dvor. All this time it had been covered up, concealed by other pictures, and had utterly gone out of his mind. Now, as if by design, when all the fashionable portraits and paintings had been removed from the studio, it looked forth, together with the productions of his early youth. As he recalled all the strange events connected with it; as he remembered that this singular portrait had been, in a manner, the cause of his errors; that the hoard of money which he had obtained in such peculiar fashion had given birth in his mind to all the wild caprices which had destroyed his talent--madness was on the point of taking possession of him. At once he ordered the hateful portrait to be removed.

But his mental excitement was not thereby diminished. His whole being was shaken to its foundation; and he suffered that fearful torture which is sometimes exhibited when a feeble talent strives to display itself on a scale too great for it and cannot do so. A horrible envy took possession of him-- an envy which bordered on madness. The gall flew to his heart when he beheld a work which bore the stamp of talent. He gnashed his teeth, and devoured it with the glare of a basilisk. He conceived the most devilish plan which ever entered into the mind of man, and he hastened with the strength of madness to carry it into execution. He began to purchase the best that art produced of every kind. Having bought a picture at a great price, he transported it to his room, flung himself upon it with the ferocity of a tiger, cut it, tore it, chopped it into bits, and stamped upon it with a grin of delight.

The vast wealth he had amassed enabled him to gratify this devilish desire. He opened his bags of gold and unlocked his coffers. No monster of ignorance ever destroyed so many superb productions of art as did this raging avenger. At any auction where he made his appearance, every one despaired at once of obtaining any work of art. It seemed as if an angry heaven had sent this fearful scourge into the world expressly to destroy all harmony. Scorn of the world was expressed in his countenance. His tongue uttered nothing save biting and censorious words. He swooped down like a harpy into the street: and his acquaintances, catching sight of him in the distance, sought to turn aside and avoid a meeting with him, saying that it poisoned all the rest of the day.

Fortunately for the world and art, such a life could not last long: his passions were too overpowering for his feeble strength. Attacks of madness began to recur more frequently, and ended at last in the most frightful illness. A violent fever, combined with galloping consumption, seized upon him with such violence, that in three days there remained only a shadow of his former self. To this was added indications of hopeless insanity. Sometimes several men were unable to hold him. The long-forgotten, living eyes of the portrait began to torment him, and then his madness became dreadful. All the people who surrounded his bed seemed to him horrible portraits. The portrait doubled and quadrupled itself; all the walls seemed hung with portraits, which fastened their living eyes upon him; portraits glared at him from the ceiling, from the floor; the room widened and lengthened endlessly, in order to make room for more of the motionless eyes. The doctor who had undertaken to attend him, having learned something of his strange history, strove with all his might to fathom the secret connection between the visions of his fancy and the occurrences of his life, but without the slightest success. The sick man understood nothing, felt nothing, save his own tortures, and gave utterance only to frightful yells and unintelligible gibberish. At last his life ended in a final attack of unutterable suffering. Nothing could be found of all his great wealth; but when they beheld the mutilated fragments of grand works of art, the value of which exceeded a million, they understood the terrible use which had been made of it.

PART II

A THRONG of carriages and other vehicles stood at the entrance of a house in which an auction was going on of the effects of one of those wealthy art-lovers who have innocently passed for Maecenases, and in a simple-minded fashion expended, to that end, the millions amassed by their thrifty fathers, and frequently even by their own early labours. The long saloon was filled with the most motley throng of visitors, collected like birds of prey swooping down upon an unburied corpse. There was a whole squadron of Russian shop-keepers from the Gostinnui Dvor, and from the old-clothes mart, in blue coats of foreign make. Their faces and expressions were a little more natural here, and did not display that fictitious desire to be subservient which is so marked in the Russian shop-keeper when he stands before a customer in his shop. Here they stood upon no ceremony, although the saloons were full of those very aristocrats before whom, in any other place, they would have been ready to sweep, with reverence, the dust brought in by their feet. They were quite at their ease, handling pictures and books without ceremony, when desirous of ascertaining the value of the goods, and boldly upsetting bargains mentally secured in advance by noble connoisseurs. There were many of those infallible attendants of auctions who make it a point to go to one every day as regularly as to take their breakfast; aristocratic connoisseurs who look upon it as their duty not to miss any opportunity of adding to their collections, and who have no other occupation between twelve o'clock and one; and noble gentlemen, with garments very threadbare, who make their daily appearance without any selfish object in view, but merely to see how it all goes off.

A quantity of pictures were lying about in disorder: with them were mingled furniture, and books with the cipher of the former owner, who never was moved by any laudable desire to glance into them. Chinese vases, marble slabs for tables, old and new furniture with curving lines, with griffins, sphinxes, and lions' paws, gilded and ungilded, chandeliers, sconces, all were heaped together in a perfect chaos of art.

The auction appeared to be at its height.

The surging throng was competing for a portrait which could not but arrest the attention of all who possessed any knowledge of art. The skilled hand of an artist was plainly visible in it. The portrait, which had apparently been several times restored and renovated, represented the dark features of an Asiatic in flowing garments, and with a strange and remarkable expression of countenance; but what struck the buyers more than anything else was the peculiar liveliness of the eyes. The more they were looked at, the more did they seem to penetrate into the gazer's heart. This peculiarity, this strange illusion achieved by the artist, attracted the attention of nearly all. Many who had been bidding gradually withdrew, for the price offered had risen to an incredible sum. There remained only two well-known aristocrats, amateurs of painting, who were unwilling to forego such an acquisition. They grew warm, and would probably have run the bidding up to an impossible sum, had not one of the onlookers suddenly exclaimed, "Permit me to interrupt your competition for a while: I, perhaps, more than any other, have a right to this portrait."

These words at once drew the attention of all to him. He was a tall man of thirty-five, with long black curls. His pleasant face, full of a certain bright nonchalance, indicated a mind free from all wearisome, worldly excitement; his garments had no pretence to fashion: all about him indicated the artist. He was, in fact, B. the painter, a man personally well known to many of those present.

"However strange my words may seem to you," he continued, perceiving that the general attention was directed to him, "if you will listen to a short story, you may possibly see that I was right in uttering them. Everything assures me that this is the portrait which I am looking for."

A natural curiosity illuminated the faces of nearly all present; and even the auctioneer paused as he was opening his mouth, and with hammer uplifted in the air, prepared to listen. At the beginning of the story, many glanced involuntarily towards the portrait; but later on, all bent their attention solely on the narrator, as his tale grew gradually more absorbing.

"You know that portion of the city which is called Kolomna," he began. "There everything is unlike anything else in St. Petersburg. Retired officials remove thither to live; widows; people not very well off, who have acquaintances in the senate, and therefore condemn themselves to this for nearly the whole of their lives; and, in short, that whole list of people who can be described by the words ash-coloured--people whose garments, faces, hair, eyes, have a sort of ashy surface, like a day when there is in the sky neither cloud nor sun. Among them may be retired actors, retired titular councillors, retired sons of Mars, with ruined eyes and swollen lips.

"Life in Kolomna is terribly dull: rarely does a carriage appear, except, perhaps, one containing an actor, which disturbs the universal stillness by its rumble, noise, and jingling. You can get lodgings for five rubles a month, coffee in the morning included. Widows with pensions are the most aristocratic families there; they conduct themselves well, sweep their rooms often, chatter with their friends about the dearness of beef and cabbage, and frequently have a young daughter, a taciturn, quiet, sometimes pretty creature; an ugly dog, and wall-clocks which strike in a melancholy fashion. Then come the actors whose salaries do not permit them to desert Kolomna, an independent folk, living, like all artists, for pleasure. They sit in their dressing-gowns, cleaning their pistols, gluing together all sorts of things out of cardboard, playing draughts and cards with any friend who chances to drop in, and so pass away the morning, doing pretty nearly the same in the evening, with the addition of punch now and then. After these great people and aristocracy of Kolomna, come the rank and file. It is as difficult to put a name to them as to remember the multitude of insects which breed in stale vinegar. There are old women who get drunk, who make a living by incomprehensible means, like ants, dragging old clothes and rags from the Kalinkin Bridge to the old clothes-mart, in order to sell them for fifteen kopeks--in short, the very dregs of mankind, whose conditions no beneficent, political economist has devised any means of ameliorating.

"I have mentioned them in order to point out how often such people find themselves under the necessity of seeking immediate temporary assistance and having recourse to borrowing. Hence there settles among them a peculiar race of money-lenders who lend small sums on security at an enormous percentage. Among these usurers was a certain . . . but I must not omit to mention that the occurrence which I have undertaken to relate occurred the last century, in the reign of our late Empress Catherine the Second. So, among the usurers, at that epoch, was a certain person--an extraordinary being in every respect, who had settled in that quarter of the city long before. He went about in flowing Asiatic garb; his dark complexion indicated a Southern origin, but to what particular nation he belonged, India, Greece, or Persia, no one could say with certainty. Of tall, almost colossal stature, with dark, thin, ardent face, heavy overhanging brows, and an indescribably strange colour in his large eyes of unwonted fire, he differed sharply and strongly from all the ash-coloured denizens of the capital.

"His very dwelling was unlike the other little wooden houses. It was of stone, in the style of those formerly much affected by Genoese merchants, with irregular windows of various sizes, secured with iron shutters and bars. This usurer differed from other usurers also in that he could furnish any required sum, from that desired by the poor old beggar-woman to that demanded by the extravagant grandee of the court. The most gorgeous equipages often halted in front of his house, and from their windows sometimes peeped forth the head of an elegant high-born lady. Rumour, as usual, reported that his iron coffers were full of untold gold, treasures, diamonds, and all sorts of pledges, but that, nevertheless, he was not the slave of that avarice which is characteristic of other usurers. He lent money willingly, and on very favourable terms of payment apparently, but, by some curious method of reckoning, made them mount to an incredible percentage. So said rumour, at any rate. But what was strangest of all was the peculiar fate of those who received money from him: they all ended their lives in some unhappy way. Whether this was simply the popular superstition, or the result of reports circulated with an object, is not known. But several instances which happened within a brief space of time before the eyes of every one were vivid and striking.

"Among the aristocracy of that day, one who speedily drew attention to himself was a young man of one of the best families who had made a figure in his early years in court circles, a warm admirer of everything true and noble, zealous in his love for art, and giving promise of becoming a Maecenas. He was soon deservedly distinguished by the Empress, who conferred upon him an important post, fully proportioned to his deserts--a post in which he could accomplish much for science and the general welfare. The youthful dignitary surrounded himself with artists, poets, and learned men. He wished to give work to all, to encourage all. He undertook, at his own expense, a number of useful publications; gave numerous orders to artists; offered prizes for the encouragement of different arts; spent a great deal of money, and finally ruined himself. But, full of noble impulses, he did not wish to relinquish his work, sought to raise a loan, and finally betook himself to the well-known usurer. Having borrowed a considerable sum from him, the man in a short time changed completely. He became a persecutor and oppressor of budding talent and intellect. He saw the bad side in everything produced, and every word he uttered was false.

"Then, unfortunately, came the French Revolution. This furnished him with an excuse for every kind of suspicion. He began to discover a revolutionary tendency in everything; to concoct terrible and unjust accusations, which made scores of people unhappy. Of course, such conduct could not fail in time to reach the throne. The kind-hearted Empress was shocked; and, full of the noble spirit which adorns crowned heads, she uttered words still engraven on many hearts. The Empress remarked that not under a monarchical government were high and noble impulses persecuted; not there were the creations of intellect, poetry, and art contemned and oppressed. On the other hand, monarchs alone were their protectors. Shakespeare and Moliere flourished under their magnanimous protection, while Dante could not find a corner in his republican birthplace. She said that true geniuses arise at the epoch of brilliancy and power in emperors and empires, but not in the time of monstrous political apparitions and republican terrorism, which, up to that time, had never given to the world a single poet; that poet-artists should be marked out for favour, since peace and divine quiet alone compose their minds, not excitement and tumult; that learned men, poets, and all producers of art are the pearls and diamonds in the imperial crown: by them is the epoch of the great ruler adorned, and from them it receives yet greater brilliancy.

"As the Empress uttered these words she was divinely beautiful for the moment, and I remember old men who could not speak of the occurrence without tears. All were interested in the affair. It must be remarked, to the honour of our national pride, that in the Russian's heart there always beats a fine feeling that he must adopt the part of the persecuted. The dignitary who had betrayed his trust was punished in an exemplary manner and degraded from his post. But he read a more dreadful punishment in the faces of his fellow-countrymen: universal scorn. It is impossible to describe what he suffered, and he died in a terrible attack of raving madness.

"Another striking example also occurred. Among the beautiful women in which our northern capital assuredly is not poor, one decidedly surpassed the rest. Her loveliness was a combination of our Northern charms with those of the South, a gem such as rarely makes its appearance on earth. My father said that he had never beheld anything like it in the whole course of his life. Everything seemed to be united in her, wealth, intellect, and wit. She had throngs of admirers, the most distinguished of them being Prince R., the most noble-minded of all young men, the finest in face, and an ideal of romance in his magnanimous and knightly sentiments. Prince R. was passionately in love, and was requited by a like ardent passion.

"But the match seemed unequal to the parents. The prince's family estates had not been in his possession for a long time, his family was out of favour, and the sad state of his affairs was well known to all. Of a sudden the prince quitted the capital, as if for the purpose of arranging his affairs, and after a short interval reappeared, surrounded with luxury and splendour. Brilliant balls and parties made him known at court. The lady's father began to relent, and the wedding took place. Whence this change in circumstances, this unheard-of-wealth, came, no one could fully explain; but it was whispered that he had entered into a compact with the mysterious usurer, and had borrowed money of him. However that may have been, the wedding was a source of interest to the whole city, and the bride and bridegroom were objects of general envy. Every one knew of their warm and faithful love, the long persecution they had had to endure from every quarter, the great personal worth of both. Ardent women at once sketched out the heavenly bliss which the young couple would enjoy. But it turned out very differently.

"In the course of a year a frightful change came over the husband. His character, up to that time so noble, became poisoned with jealous suspicions, irritability, and inexhaustible caprices. He became a tyrant to his wife, a thing which no one could have foreseen, and indulged in the most inhuman deeds, and even in blows. In a year's time no one would have recognised the woman who, such a little while before, had dazzled and drawn about her throngs of submissive adorers. Finally, no longer able to endure her lot, she proposed a divorce. Her husband flew into a rage at the very suggestion. In the first outburst of passion, he chased her about the room with a knife, and would doubtless have murdered her then and there, if they had not seized him and prevented him. In a fit of madness and despair he turned the knife against himself, and ended his life amid the most horrible sufferings.

"Besides these two instances which occurred before the eyes of all the world, stories circulated of many more among the lower classes, nearly all of which had tragic endings. Here an honest sober man became a drunkard; there a shopkeeper's clerk robbed his master; again, a driver who had conducted himself properly for a number of years cut his passenger's throat for a groschen. It was impossible that such occurrences, related, not without embellishments, should not inspire a sort of involuntary horror amongst the sedate inhabitants of Kolomna. No one entertained any doubt as to the presence of an evil power in the usurer. They said that he imposed conditions which made the hair rise on one's head, and which the miserable wretch never afterward dared reveal to any other being; that his money possessed a strange power of attraction; that it grew hot of itself, and that it bore strange marks. And it is worthy of remark, that all the colony of Kolomna, all these poor old women, small officials, petty artists, and insignificant people whom we have just recapitulated, agreed that it was better to endure anything, and to suffer the extreme of misery, rather than to have recourse to the terrible usurer. Old women were even found dying of hunger, who preferred to kill their bodies rather than lose their soul. Those who met him in the street experienced an involuntary sense of fear. Pedestrians took care to turn aside from his path, and gazed long after his tall, receding figure. In his face alone there was sufficient that was uncommon to cause any one to ascribe to him a supernatural nature. The strong features, so deeply chiselled; the glowing bronze of his complexion; the incredible thickness of his brows; the intolerable, terrible eyes-- everything seemed to indicate that the passions of other men were pale compared to those raging within him. My father stopped short every time he met him, and could not refrain each time from saying, 'A devil, a perfect devil!' But I must introduce you as speedily as possible to my father, the chief character of this story.

"My father was a remarkable man in many respects. He was an artist of rare ability, a self-taught artist, without teachers or schools, principles and rules, carried away only by the thirst for perfection, and treading a path indicated by his own instincts, for reasons unknown, perchance, even to himself. Through some lofty and secret instinct he perceived the presence of a soul in every object. And this secret instinct and personal conviction turned his brush to Christian subjects, grand and lofty to the last degree. His was a strong character: he was an honourable, upright, even rough man, covered with a sort of hard rind without, not entirely lacking in pride, and given to expressing himself both sharply and scornfully about people. He worked for very small results; that is to say, for just enough to support his family and obtain the materials he needed; he never, under any circumstances, refused to aid any one, or to lend a helping hand to a poor artist; and he believed with the simple, reverent faith of his ancestors. At length, by his unintermitting labour and perseverance in the path he had marked out for himself, he began to win the approbation of those who honoured his self-taught talent. They gave him constant orders for churches, and he never lacked employment.

"One of his paintings possessed a strong interest for him. I no longer recollect the exact subject: I only know that he needed to represent the Spirit of Darkness in it. He pondered long what form to give him: he wished to concentrate in his face all that weighs down and oppresses a man. In the midst of his meditations there suddenly occurred to his mind the image of the mysterious usurer; and he thought involuntarily, 'That's how I ought to paint the Devil!' Imagine his amazement when one day, as he was at work in his studio, he heard a knock at the door, and directly after there entered that same terrible usurer.

"'You are an artist?' he said to my father abruptly.

"'I am,' answered my father in surprise, waiting for what should come next.

"'Good! Paint my portrait. I may possibly die soon. I have no children; but I do not wish to die completely, I wish to live. Can you paint a portrait that shall appear as though it were alive?'

"My father reflected, 'What could be better! he offers himself for the Devil in my picture.' He promised. They agreed upon a time and price; and the next day my father took palette and brushes and went to the usurer's house. The lofty court-yard, dogs, iron doors and locks, arched windows, coffers, draped with strange covers, and, last of all, the remarkable owner himself, seated motionless before him, all produced a strange impression on him. The windows seemed intentionally so encumbered below that they admitted the light only from the top. 'Devil take him, how well his face is lighted!' he said to himself, and began to paint assiduously, as though afraid that the favourable light would disappear. 'What power!' he repeated to himself. 'If I only accomplish half a likeness of him, as he is now, it will surpass all my other works: he will simply start from the canvas if I am only partly true to nature. What remarkable features!' He redoubled his energy; and began himself to notice how some of his sitter's traits were making their appearance on the canvas.

"But the more closely he approached resemblance, the more conscious he became of an aggressive, uneasy feeling which he could not explain to himself. Notwithstanding this, he set himself to copy with literal accuracy every trait and expression. First of all, however, he busied himself with the eyes. There was so much force in those eyes, that it seemed impossible to reproduce them exactly as they were in nature. But he resolved, at any price, to seek in them the most minute characteristics and shades, to penetrate their secret. As soon, however, as he approached them in resemblance, and began to redouble his exertions, there sprang up in his mind such a terrible feeling of repulsion, of inexplicable expression, that he was forced to lay aside his brush for a while and begin anew. At last he could bear it no longer: he felt as if these eyes were piercing into his soul, and causing intolerable emotion. On the second and third days this grew still stronger. It became horrible to him. He threw down his brush, and declared abruptly that he could paint the stranger no longer. You should have seen how the terrible usurer changed countenance at these words. He threw himself at his feet, and besought him to finish the portrait, saying that his fate and his existence depended on it; that he had already caught his prominent features; that if he could reproduce them accurately, his life would be preserved in his portrait in a supernatural manner; that by that means he would not die completely; that it was necessary for him to continue to exist in the world.

"My father was frightened by these words: they seemed to him strange and terrible to such a degree, that he threw down his brushes and palette and rushed headlong from the room.

"The thought of it troubled him all day and all night; but the next morning he received the portrait from the usurer, by a woman who was the only creature in his service, and who announced that her master did not want the portrait, and would pay nothing for it, and had sent it back. On the evening of the same day he learned that the usurer was dead, and that preparations were in progress to bury him according to the rites of his religion. All this seemed to him inexplicably strange. But from that day a marked change showed itself in his character. He was possessed by a troubled, uneasy feeling, of which he was unable to explain the cause; and he soon committed a deed which no one could have expected of him. For some time the works of one of his pupils had been attracting the attention of a small circle of connoisseurs and amateurs. My father had perceived his talent, and manifested a particular liking for him in consequence. Suddenly the general interest in him and talk about him became unendurable to my father who grew envious of him. Finally, to complete his vexation, he learned that his pupil had been asked to paint a picture for a recently built and wealthy church. This enraged him. 'No, I will not permit that fledgling to triumph!' said he: 'it is early, friend, to think of consigning old men to the gutters. I still have powers, God be praised! We'll soon see which will put down the other.'

"And this straightforward, honourable man employed intrigues which he had hitherto abhorred. He finally contrived that there should be a competition for the picture which other artists were permitted to enter into. Then he shut himself up in his room, and grasped his brush with zeal. It seemed as if he were striving to summon all his strength up for this occasion. And, in fact, the result turned out to be one of his best works. No one doubted that he would bear off the palm. The pictures were placed on exhibition, and all the others seemed to his as night to day. But of a sudden, one of the members present, an ecclesiastical personage if I mistake not, made a remark which surprised every one. 'There is certainly much talent in this artist's picture,' said he, 'but no holiness in the faces: there is even, on the contrary, a demoniacal look in the eyes, as though some evil feeling had guided the artist's hand.' All looked, and could not but acknowledge the truth of these words. My father rushed forward to his picture, as though to verify for himself this offensive remark, and perceived with horror that he had bestowed the usurer's eyes upon nearly all the figures. They had such a diabolical gaze that he involuntarily shuddered. The picture was rejected; and he was forced to hear, to his indescribable vexation, that the palm was awarded to his pupil.

"It is impossible to describe the state of rage in which he returned home. He almost killed my mother, he drove the children away, broke his brushes and easels, tore down the usurer's portrait from the wall, demanded a knife, and ordered a fire to be built in the chimney, intending to cut it in pieces and burn it. A friend, an artist, caught him in the act as he entered the room--a jolly fellow, always satisfied with himself, inflated by unattainable wishes, doing daily anything that came to hand, and taking still more gaily to his dinner and little carouses.

"'What are you doing? What are you preparing to burn?' he asked, and stepped up to the portrait. 'Why, this is one of your very best works. It is the usurer who died a short time ago: yes, it is a most perfect likeness. You did not stop until you had got into his very eyes. Never did eyes look as these do now.'

"'Well, I'll see how they look in the fire!' said my father, making a movement to fling the portrait into the grate.

"'Stop, for Heaven's sake!' exclaimed his friend, restraining him: 'give it to me, rather, if it offends your eyes to such a degree.' My father resisted, but yielded at length; and the jolly fellow, well pleased with his acquisition, carried the portrait home with him.

"When he was gone, my father felt more calm. The burden seemed to have disappeared from his soul in company with the portrait. He was surprised himself at his evil feelings, his envy, and the evident change in his character. Reviewing his acts, he became sad at heart; and not without inward sorrow did he exclaim, 'No, it was God who punished me! my picture, in fact, was meant to ruin my brother-man. A devilish feeling of envy guided my brush, and that devilish feeling must have made itself visible in it.'

"He set out at once to seek his former pupil, embraced him warmly, begged his forgiveness, and endeavoured as far as possible to excuse his own fault. His labours continued as before; but his face was more frequently thoughtful. He prayed more, grew more taciturn, and expressed himself less sharply about people: even the rough exterior of his character was modified to some extent. But a certain occurrence soon disturbed him more than ever. He had seen nothing for a long time of the comrade who had begged the portrait of him. He had already decided to hunt him up, when the latter suddenly made his appearance in his room. After a few words and questions on both sides, he said, 'Well, brother, it was not without cause that you wished to burn that portrait. Devil take it, there's something horrible about it! I don't believe in sorcerers; but, begging your pardon, there's an unclean spirit in it.'

"'How so?' asked my father.

"'Well, from the very moment I hung it up in my room I felt such depression--just as if I wanted to murder some one. I never knew in my life what sleeplessness was; but I suffered not from sleeplessness alone, but from such dreams!--I cannot tell whether they were dreams, or what; it was as if a demon were strangling one: and the old man appeared to me in my sleep. In short, I can't describe my state of mind. I had a sensation of fear, as if expecting something unpleasant. I felt as if I could not speak a cheerful or sincere word to any one: it was just as if a spy were sitting over me. But from the very hour that I gave that portrait to my nephew, who asked for it, I felt as if a stone had been rolled from my shoulders, and became cheerful, as you see me now. Well, brother, you painted the very Devil!'

"During this recital my father listened with unswerving attention, and finally inquired, 'And your nephew now has the portrait?'

"'My nephew, indeed! he could not stand it!' said the jolly fellow: 'do you know, the soul of that usurer has migrated into it; he jumps out of the frame, walks about the room; and what my nephew tells of him is simply incomprehensible. I should take him for a lunatic, if I had not undergone a part of it myself. He sold it to some collector of pictures; and he could not stand it either, and got rid of it to some one else.'

"This story produced a deep impression on my father. He grew seriously pensive, fell into hypochondria, and finally became fully convinced that his brush had served as a tool of the Devil; and that a portion of the usurer's vitality had actually passed into the portrait, and was now troubling people, inspiring diabolical excitement, beguiling painters from the true path, producing the fearful torments of envy, and so forth. Three catastrophes which occurred afterwards, three sudden deaths of wife, daughter, and infant son, he regarded as a divine punishment on him, and firmly resolved to withdraw from the world.

"As soon as I was nine years old, he placed me in an academy of painting, and, paying all his debts, retired to a lonely cloister, where he soon afterwards took the vows. There he amazed every one by the strictness of his life, and his untiring observance of all the monastic rules. The prior of the monastery, hearing of his skill in painting, ordered him to paint the principal picture in the church. But the humble brother said plainly that he was unworthy to touch a brush, that his was contaminated, that with toil and great sacrifice must he first purify his spirit in order to render himself fit to undertake such a task. He increased the rigours of monastic life for himself as much as possible. At last, even they became insufficient, and he retired, with the approval of the prior, into the desert, in order to be quite alone. There he constructed himself a cell from branches of trees, ate only uncooked roots, dragged about a stone from place to place, stood in one spot with his hands lifted to heaven, from the rising until the going down of the sun, reciting prayers without cessation. In this manner did he for several years exhaust his body, invigorating it, at the same time, with the strength of fervent prayer.

"At length, one day he returned to the cloister, and said firmly to the prior, 'Now I am ready. If God wills, I will finish my task.' The subject he selected was the Birth of Christ. A whole year he sat over it, without leaving his cell, barely sustaining himself with coarse food, and praying incessantly. At the end of the year the picture was ready. It was a really wonderful work. Neither prior nor brethren knew much about painting; but all were struck with the marvellous holiness of the figures. The expression of reverent humility and gentleness in the face of the Holy Mother, as she bent over the Child; the deep intelligence in the eyes of the Holy Child, as though he saw something afar; the triumphant silence of the Magi, amazed by the Divine Miracle, as they bowed at his feet: and finally, the indescribable peace which emanated from the whole picture--all this was presented with such strength and beauty, that the impression it made was magical. All the brethren threw themselves on their knees before it; and the prior, deeply affected, exclaimed, 'No, it is impossible for any artist, with the assistance only of earthly art, to produce such a picture: a holy, divine power has guided thy brush, and the blessing of Heaven rested upon thy labour!'

"By that time I had completed my education at the academy, received the gold medal, and with it the joyful hope of a journey to Italy--the fairest dream of a twenty-year-old artist. It only remained for me to take leave of my father, from whom I had been separated for twelve years. I confess that even his image had long faded from my memory. I had heard somewhat of his grim saintliness, and rather expected to meet a hermit of rough exterior, a stranger to everything in the world, except his cell and his prayers, worn out, tried up, by eternal fasting and penance. But how great was my surprise when a handsome old man stood before me! No traces of exhaustion were visible on his countenance: it beamed with the light of a heavenly joy. His beard, white as snow, and his thin, almost transparent hair of the same silvery hue, fell picturesquely upon his breast, and upon the folds of his black gown, even to the rope with which his poor monastic garb was girded. But most surprising to me of all was to hear from his mouth such words and thoughts about art as, I confess, I long shall bear in mind, and I sincerely wish that all my comrades would do the same.

"'I expected you, my son,' he said, when I approached for his blessing. 'The path awaits you in which your life is henceforth to flow. Your path is pure--desert it not. You have talent: talent is the most priceless of God's gifts--destroy it not. Search out, subject all things to your brush; but in all see that you find the hidden soul, and most of all, strive to attain to the grand secret of creation. Blessed is the elect one who masters that! There is for him no mean object in nature. In lowly themes the artist creator is as great as in great ones: in the despicable there is nothing for him to despise, for it passes through the purifying fire of his mind. An intimation of God's heavenly paradise is contained for the artist in art, and by that alone is it higher than all else. But by as much as triumphant rest is grander than every earthly emotion, by so much is the lofty creation of art higher than everything else on earth. Sacrifice everything to it, and love it with passion--not with the passion breathing with earthly desire, but a peaceful, heavenly passion. It cannot plant discord in the spirit, but ascends, like a resounding prayer, eternally to God. But there are moments, dark moments--' He paused, and I observed that his bright face darkened, as though some cloud crossed it for a moment. 'There is one incident of my life,' he said. 'Up to this moment, I cannot understand what that terrible being was of whom I painted a likeness. It was certainly some diabolical apparition. I know that the world denies the existence of the Devil, and therefore I will not speak of him. I will only say that I painted him with repugnance: I felt no liking for my work, even at the time. I tried to force myself, and, stifling every emotion in a hard-hearted way, to be true to nature. I have been informed that this portrait is passing from hand to hand, and sowing unpleasant impressions, inspiring artists with feelings of envy, of dark hatred towards their brethren, with malicious thirst for persecution and oppression. May the Almighty preserve you from such passions! There is nothing more terrible.'

"He blessed and embraced me. Never in my life was I so grandly moved. Reverently, rather than with the feeling of a son, I leaned upon his breast, and kissed his scattered silver locks.

"Tears shone in his eyes. 'Fulfil my one request, my son,' said he, at the moment of parting. 'You may chance to see the portrait I have mentioned somewhere. You will know it at once by the strange eyes, and their peculiar expression. Destroy it at any cost.'

"Judge for yourselves whether I could refuse to promise, with an oath, to fulfil this request. In the space of fifteen years I had never succeeded in meeting with anything which in any way corresponded to the description given me by my father, until now, all of a sudden, at an auction--"

The artist did not finish his sentence, but turned his eyes to the wall in order to glance once more at the portrait. The entire throng of auditors made the same movement, seeking the wonderful portrait with their eyes. But, to their extreme amazement, it was no longer on the wall. An indistinct murmur and exclamation ran through the crowd, and then was heard distinctly the word, "stolen." Some one had succeeded in carrying it off, taking advantage of the fact that the attention of the spectators was distracted by the story. And those present long remained in a state of surprise, not knowing whether they had really seen those remarkable eyes, or whether it was simply a dream which had floated for an instant before their eyesight, strained with long gazing at old pictures.

THE CALASH

The town of B-- had become very lively since a cavalry regiment had taken up its quarters in it. Up to that date it had been mortally wearisome there. When you happened to pass through the town and glanced at its little mud houses with their incredibly gloomy aspect, the pen refuses to express what you felt. You suffered a terrible uneasiness as if you had just lost all your money at play, or had committed some terrible blunder in company. The plaster covering the houses, soaked by the rain, had fallen away in many places from their walls, which from white had become streaked and spotted, whilst old reeds served to thatch them.

Following a custom very common in the towns of South Russia, the chief of police has long since had all the trees in the gardens cut down to improve the view. One never meets anything in the town, unless it is a cock crossing the road, full of dust and soft as a pillow. At the slightest rain this dust is turned into mud, and then all the streets are filled with pigs.

Displaying to all their grave faces, they utter such grunts that travellers only think of pressing their horses to get away from them as soon as possible. Sometimes some country gentleman of the neighbourhood, the owner of a dozen serfs, passes in a vehicle which is a kind of compromise between a carriage and a cart, surrounded by sacks of flour, and whipping up his bay mare with her colt trotting by her side. The aspect of the marketplace is mournful enough. The tailor's house sticks out very stupidly, not squarely to the front but sideways. Facing it is a brick house with two windows, unfinished for fifteen years past, and further on a large wooden market-stall standing by itself and painted mud-colour. This stall, which was to serve as a model, was built by the chief of police in the time of his youth, before he got into the habit of falling asleep directly after dinner, and of drinking a kind of decoction of dried goose-berries every evening. All around the rest of the market-place are nothing but palings. But in the centre are some little sheds where a packet of round cakes, a stout woman in a red dress, a bar of soap, some pounds of bitter almonds, some lead, some cotton, and two shopmen playing at "svaika," a game resembling quoits, are always to be seen.

But on the arrival of the cavalry regiment everything changed. The streets became more lively and wore quite another aspect. Often from their little houses the inhabitants would see a tall and well-made officer with a plumed hat pass by, on his way to the quarters of one of his comrades to discuss the chances of promotion or the qualities of a new tobacco, or perhaps to risk at play his carriage, which might indeed be called the carriage of all the regiment, since it belonged in turn to every one of them. To-day it was the major who drove out in it, to-morrow it was seen in the lieutenant's coach-house, and a week later the major's servant was again greasing its wheels. The long hedges separating the houses were suddenly covered with soldiers' caps exposed to the sun, grey frieze cloaks hung in the doorways, and moustaches harsh and bristling as clothes brushes were to be met with in all the streets. These moustaches showed themselves everywhere, but above all at the market, over the shoulders of the women of the place who flocked there from all sides to make their purchases. The officers lent great animation to society at B--.

Society consisted up till then of the judge who was living with a deacon's wife, and of the chief of police, a very sensible man, but one who slept all day long from dinner till evening, and from evening till dinner-time.

This general liveliness was still further increased when the town of B-- became the residence of the general commanding the brigade to which the regiment belonged. Many gentlemen of the neighbourhood, whose very existence no one had even suspected, began to come into the town with the intention of calling on the officers, or, perhaps, of playing bank, a game concerning which they had up till then only a very confused notion, occupied as they were with their crops and the commissions of their wives and their hare-hunting. I am very sorry that I cannot recollect for what reason the general made up his mind one fine day to give a grand dinner. The preparations were overwhelming. The clatter of knives in the kitchen was heard as far as the town gates. The whole of the market was laid under contributions, so much so that the judge and the deacon's wife found themselves obliged that day to be satisfied with hasty puddings and cakes of flour. The little courtyard of the house occupied by the general was crowded with vehicles. The company only consisted of men, officers and gentlemen of the neighbourhood.

Amongst these latter was above all conspicuous Pythagoras Pythagoravitch Tchertokoutski, one of the leading aristocrats of the district of B--, the most fiery orator at the nobiliary elections and the owner of a very elegant turn-out. He had served in a cavalry regiment and had even passed for one of its most accomplished officers, having constantly shown himself at all the balls and parties wherever his regiment was quartered. Information respecting him may be asked of all the young ladies in the districts of Tamboff and Simbirsk. He would very probably have further extended his reputation in other districts if he had not been obliged to leave the service in consequence of one of those affairs which are spoken of as "a very unpleasant business." Had he given or received a blow? I cannot say with certainty, but what is indisputable is that he was asked to send in his resignation. However, this accident had no unpleasant effect upon the esteem in which he had been held up till then.

Tchertokoutski always wore a coat of a military cut, spurs and moustache, in order not to have it supposed that he had served in the infantry, a branch of the service upon which he lavished the most contemptuous expressions. He frequented the numerous fairs to which flock the whole of the population of Southern Russia, consisting of nursemaids, tall girls, and burly gentlemen who go there in vehicles of such strange aspect that no one has ever seen their match even in a dream. He instinctively guessed the spot in which a regiment of cavalry was to be found and never failed to introduce himself to the officers. On perceiving them he bounded gracefully from his light phaeton and soon made acquaintance with them. At the last election he had given to the whole of the nobility a grand dinner during which he declared that if he were elected marshal he would put all gentlemen on the best possible footing. He usually behaved after the fashion of a great noble. He had married a rather pretty lady with a dowry of two hundred serfs and some thousands of rubles. This money was at once employed in the purchase of six fine horses, some gilt bronze locks, and a tame monkey. He further engaged a French cook. The two hundred peasants of the lady, as well as two hundred more belonging to the gentleman, were mortgaged to the bank. In a word, he was a regular nobleman. Besides himself, several other gentlemen were amongst the general's guests, but it is not worth while speaking of them. The officers of the regiment, amongst whom were the colonel and the fat major, formed the majority of those present. The general himself was rather stout; a good officer, nevertheless, according to his subordinates. He had a rather deep bass voice.

The dinner was magnificent; there were sturgeons, sterlets, bustards, asparagus, quail, partridges, mushrooms. The flavour of all these dishes supplied an irrefutable proof of the sobriety of the cook during the twenty-four hours preceding the dinner. Four soldiers, who had been given him as assistants, had not ceased working all night, knife in hand, at the composition of ragouts and jellies. The immense quantity of long-necked bottles, mingled with shorter ones, holding claret and madeira; the fine summer day, the wide-open windows, the plates piled up with ice on the table, the crumpled shirt-fronts of the gentlemen in plain clothes, and a brisk and noisy conversation, now dominated by the general's voice, and now besprinkled with champagne, were all in perfect harmony. The guests rose from the table with a pleasant feeling of repletion, and, after having lit their pipes, all stepped out, coffee-cups in hand, on to the verandah.

"We can see her now," said the general. "Here, my dear fellow," added he, addressing his aide-de-camp, an active well-made young officer, "have the bay mare brought here. You shall see for yourselves, gentlemen."

At these words the general took a long pull at his pipe.

"She is not quite recovered yet; there is not a decent stable in this cursed little place. But she is not bad looking--" puff--puff, the general here let out the smoke which he had kept in his mouth till then--"the little mare."

"It is long since your excellency--" puff--puff--puff--"condescended to buy her?" asked Tchertokoutski.

Puff--puff--puff--puff. "Not very long, I had her from the breeding establishment two years ago."

"And did your excellency condescend to take her ready broken, or to have her broken in here yourself?"

Puff--puff--puff--puff. "Here."

As he spoke the general disappeared behind a cloud of smoke.

At that moment a soldier jumped out of the stable. The trampling of a horse's hoofs was heard, and another soldier with immense moustaches, and wearing a long white tunic, appeared, leading by the bridle the terrified and quivering mare, which, suddenly rearing, lifted him off his feet.

"Come, come, Agrafena Ivanovna," said he, leading her towards the verandah.

The mare's name was Agrafena Ivanovna. Strong and bold as a Southern beauty, she suddenly became motionless.

The general began to look at her with evident satisfaction, and left off smoking. The colonel himself went down the steps and patted her neck. The major ran his hand down her legs, and all the other officers clicked their tongues at her.

Tchertokoutski left the verandah to take up a position beside the mare. The soldier who held her bridle drew himself up and stared fixedly at the guests.

"She is very fine, very fine," said Tchertokoutski, "a very well-shaped beast. Will your excellency allow me to ask whether she is a good goer?"

"She goes well, but that idiot of a doctor, deuce take him, has given her some balls which have made her sneeze for the last two days."

"She is a fine beast, a very fine beast. Has your excellency a turn-out to match the horse?"

"Turn-out! but she's a saddle horse."

"I know. I put the question, your excellency, to know if you have an equipage worthy of your other horses?"

"No, I have not much in the way of equipages; I must admit that, for some time past, I have been wanting to buy a calash, such as they build now-a-days. I have written about it to my brother who is now at St. Petersburg, but I do not know whether he will be able to send me one."

"It seems to me, your excellency," remarked the colonel, "that there are no better calashes than those of Vienna."

"You are right." Puff--puff--puff.

"I have an excellent calash, your excellency, a real Viennese calash," said Tchertokoutski.

"That in which you came?"

"Oh no, I make use of that for ordinary service, but the other is something extraordinary. It is as light as a feather, and if you sit in it, it seems as if your nurse was rocking you in a cradle."

"It is very comfortable then?"

"Extremely comfortable; the cushions, the springs, and everything else are perfect."

"Ah! that is good."

"And what a quantity of things can be packed away in it. I have never seen anything like it, your excellency. When I was still in the service there was room enough in the body to stow away ten bottles of rum, twenty pounds of tobacco, six uniforms, and two pipes, the longest pipes imaginable, your excellency; and in the pockets inside you could stow away a whole bullock."

"That is very good."

"It cost four thousand rubles, your excellency."

"It ought to be good at that price. Did you buy it yourself?"

"No, your excellency, I had it by chance. It was bought by one of my oldest friends, a fine fellow with whom you would be very well pleased.

We are very intimate. What is mine is his, and what is his is mine. I won it of him at cards. Would your excellency have the kindness to honour me at dinner to-morrow? You could see my calash."

"I don't know what to say. Alone I could not--but if you would allow me to come with these officers--"

"I beg of them to come too. I shall esteem it a great honour, gentlemen, to have the pleasure of seeing you at my house."

The colonel, the major, and the other officers thanked Tchertokoutski.

"I am of opinion myself, your excellency, that if one buys anything it should be good; it is not worth the trouble of getting, if it turns out bad. If you do me the honour of calling on me to-morrow, I will show you some improvements I have introduced on my estate."

The general looked at him, and puffed out a fresh cloud of smoke.

Tchertokoutski was charmed with his notion of inviting the officers, and mentally ordered in advance all manner of dishes for their entertainment. He smiled at these gentlemen, who on their part appeared to increase their show of attention towards him, as was noticeable from the expression of their eyes and the little half-nods they bestowed upon him. His bearing assumed a certain ease, and his voice expressed his great satisfaction.

"Your excellency will make the acquaintance of the mistress of the house."

"That will be most agreeable to me," said the general, twirling his moustache.

Tchertokoutski was firmly resolved to return home at once in order to make all necessary preparations in good time. He had already taken his hat, but a strange fatality caused him to remain for some time at the general's. The card tables had been set out, and all the company, separating into groups of four, scattered itself about the room. Lights were brought in. Tchertokoutski did not know whether he ought to sit down to whist. But as the officers invited him, he thought that the rules of good breeding obliged him to accept. He sat down. I do not know how a glass of punch found itself at his elbow, but he drank it off without thinking. After playing two rubbers, he found another glass close to his hand which he drank off in the same way, though not without remarking:

"It is really time for me to go, gentlemen."

He began to play a fresh rubber. However, the conversation which was going on in every corner of the room took an especial turn. Those who were playing whist were quiet enough, but the others talked a great deal. A captain had taken up his position on a sofa, and leaning against a cushion, pipe in mouth, he captivated the attention of a circle of guests gathered about him by his eloquent narrative of amorous adventures. A very stout gentleman whose arms were so short that they looked like two potatoes hanging by his sides, listened to him with a very satisfied expression, and from time to time exerted himself to pull his tobacco-pouch out of his coat-tail pocket. A somewhat brisk discussion on cavalry drill had arisen in another corner, and Tchertokoutski, who had twice already played a knave for a king, mingled in the conversation by calling out from his place: "In what year?" or "What regiment?" without noticing that very often his question had no application whatever. At length, a few minutes before supper, play came to an end. Tchertokoutski could remember that he had won a great deal, but he did not take up his winnings, and after rising stood for some time in the position of a man who has no handkerchief in his pocket.

They sat down to supper. As might be expected, wine was not lacking, and Tchertokoutski kept involuntarily filling his glass with it, for he was surrounded with bottles. A lengthy conversation took place at table, but the guests carried it on after a strange fashion. A colonel, who had served in 1812, described a battle which had never taken place; and besides, no one ever could make out why he took a cork and stuck it into a pie. They began to break-up at three in the morning. The coachmen were obliged to take several of them in their arms like bundles; and Tchertokoutski himself, despite his aristocratic pride, bowed so low to the company, that he took home two thistles in his moustache.

The coachman who drove him home found every one asleep. He routed out, after some trouble, the valet, who, after having ushered his master through the hall, handed him over to a maid-servant. Tchertokoutski followed her as well as he could to the best room, and stretched himself beside his pretty young wife, who was sleeping in a night-gown as white as snow. The shock of her husband falling on the bed awoke her--she stretched out her arms, opened her eyes, closed them quickly, and then opened them again quite wide, with a half-vexed air. Seeing that her husband did not pay the slightest attention to her, she turned over on the other side, rested her fresh and rosy cheek on her hand, and went to sleep again.

It was late--that is, according to country customs--when the lady awoke again. Her husband was snoring more loudly than ever. She recollected that he had come home at four o'clock, and not wishing to awaken him, got up alone, and put on her slippers, which her husband had had sent for her from St. Petersburg, and a white dressing-gown which fell about her like the waters of a fountain. Then she passed into her dressing-room, and after washing in water as fresh as herself, went to her toilet table. She looked at herself twice in the glass, and thought she looked very pretty that morning. This circumstance, a very insignificant one apparently, caused her to stay two hours longer than usual before her glass. She dressed herself very tastefully and went into the garden.

The weather was splendid: it was one of the finest days of the summer. The sun, which had almost reached the meridian, shed its most ardent rays; but a pleasant coolness reigned under the leafy arcades; and the flowers, warmed by the sun, exhaled their sweetest perfume. The pretty mistress of the house had quite forgotten that it was noon at least, and that her husband was still asleep. Already she heard the snores of two coachmen and a groom, who were taking their siesta in the stable, after having dined copiously. But she was still sitting in a bower from which the deserted high road could be seen, when all at once her attention was caught by a light cloud of dust rising in the distance. After looking at it for some moments, she ended by making out several vehicles, closely following one another. First came a light calash, with two places, in which was the general, wearing his large and glittering epaulettes, with the colonel. This was followed by another with four places, containing the captain, the aide-de-camp and two lieutenants. Further on, came the celebrated regimental vehicle, the present owner of which was the major, and behind that another in which were packed five officers, one on his comrade's knees, the procession being closed by three more on three fine bays.

"Are they coming here?" thought the mistress of the house. "Good heavens, yes! they are leaving the main road."

She gave a cry, clasped her hands, and ran straight across the flower-beds to her bedroom, where her husband was still sleeping soundly.

"Get up! get up! get up at once," she cried, pulling him by the arm.

"What--what's the matter?" murmured Tchertokoutski, stretching his limbs without opening his eyes.

"Get up, get up. Visitors have come, do you hear? visitors."

"Visitors, what visitors?" After saying these words he uttered a little plaintive grunt like that of a sucking calf: "M-m-m. Let me kiss you."

"My dear, get up at once, for heaven's sake. The general has come with all his officers. Ah! goodness, you have got a thistle in your moustache."

"The general! Has he come already? But why the deuce did not they wake me? And the dinner, is the dinner ready?"

"What dinner?"

"But haven't I ordered a dinner?"

"A dinner! You got home at four o'clock in the morning and you did not answer a single word to all my questions. I did not wake you, since you had so little sleep."

Tchertokoutski, his eyes staring out of his head, remained motionless for some moments as though a thunderbolt had struck him. All at once he jumped out of bed in his shirt.

"Idiot that I am," he exclaimed, clasping his hand to his forehead; "I had invited them to dinner. What is to be done? are they far off?"

"They will be here in a moment."

"My dear, hide yourself. Ho there, somebody. Hi there, you girl. Come here, you fool; what are you afraid of? The officers are coming here; tell them I am not at home, that I went out early this morning, that I am not coming back. Do you understand? Go and repeat it to all the servants. Be off, quick."

Having uttered these words, he hurriedly slipped on his dressing-gown, and ran off to shut himself up in the coach-house, which he thought the safest hiding-place. But he fancied that he might be noticed in the corner in which he had taken refuge.

"This will be better," said he to himself, letting down the steps of the nearest vehicle, which happened to be the calash. He jumped inside, closed the door, and, as a further precaution, covered himself with the leather apron. There he remained, wrapped in his dressing-gown, in a doubled-up position.

During this time the equipages had drawn up before the porch. The general got out of his carriage and shook himself, followed by the colonel, arranging the feathers in his hat. After him came the stout major, his sabre under his arm, and the slim lieutenants, whilst the mounted officers also alighted.

"The master is not at home," said a servant appearing at the top of a flight of steps.

"What! not at home; but he is coming home for dinner, is he not?"

"No, he is not; he has gone out for the day and will not be back till this time to-morrow."

"Bless me," said the general; "but what the deuce--"

"What a joke," said the colonel laughing.

"No, no, such things are inconceivable," said the general angrily. "If he could not receive us, why did he invite us?"

"I cannot understand, your excellency, how it is possible to act in such a manner," observed a young officer.

"What?" said the general, who always made an officer under the rank of captain repeat his remarks twice over.

"I wondered, your excellency, how any one could do such a thing."

"Quite so; if anything has happened he ought to have let us know."

"There is nothing to be done, your excellency, we had better go back home," said the colonel.

"Certainly, there is nothing to be done. However, we can see the calash without him; probably he has not taken it with him. Come here, my man."

"What does your excellency want?"

"Show us your master's new calash."

"Have the kindness to step this way to the coach-house."

The general entered the coach-house followed by his officers.

"Let me pull it a little forward, your excellency," said the servant, "it is rather dark here."

"That will do."

The general and his officers walked around the calash, carefully inspecting the wheels and springs.

"There is nothing remarkable about it," said the general; "it is a very ordinary calash."

"Nothing to look at," added the colonel; "there is absolutely nothing good about it."

"It seems to me, your excellency, that it is not worth four thousand rubles," remarked a young officer.

"What?"

"I said, your excellency, that I do not think that it is worth four thousand rubles."

"Four thousand! It is not worth two. Perhaps, however, the inside is well fitted. Unbutton the apron."

And Tchertokoutski appeared before the officers' eyes, clad in his dressing-gown and doubled up in a singular fashion.

"Hullo, there you are," said the astonished general.

Then he covered Tchertokoutski up again and went off with his officers.

###

\

Made in United States
North Haven, CT
03 June 2023

37318844R00143